# Frederick Douglass

# The Narrative and Selected Writings

Modern Library
College Editions

ADVISOR

Donald McQuade
*Queens College, The City University of New York*

# Frederick Douglass
# The Narrative and Selected Writings

Edited, with an Introduction, by

MICHAEL MEYER
*University of Connecticut*

The Modern Library
New York
DISTRIBUTED BY McGRAW-HILL, INC.

First Edition
10 11 12 13 14 15 BAH BAH 9 9 8 7 6 5 4



**Library of Congress Cataloging in Publication Data**

Douglass, Frederick, 1817?-1895
The narrative and selected writings.

(Modern Library college edition)
Bibliography: p.
1. Douglass, Frederick, 1817?-1895. 2. Afro-Americans—History—Sources. 3. Afro-Americans—Biography. 4. Abolitionists—United States—Biography. I. Meyer, Michael, 1945- II. Title. III. Series.
E449.D7455 1983 973.8'092'4 [B] 82-25897
ISBN 0-07-554375-3

Cover design by Sara Eisenman

Manufactured in the United States of America

# *Contents*

SELECTED WRITINGS

# *Introduction*

Frederick Douglass (1818–1895) enjoyed a long, productive life as an abolitionist, orator, writer, newspaper publisher, politician, and high government official, ending his career as United States minister resident and consul general to Haiti. When he died on February 20, 1895, he was praised in the *Chicago Tribune* as "the most illustrious representative of the negro race in the United States," a sentiment widely shared, for example, by the *New York Tribune*, which described him as "the representative man of his race in America by virtue of self-help." However, Douglass would not have become one of America's principal spokesmen for human rights during the nineteenth century had he not also been a thief. Born into slavery on a plantation on the Eastern Shore of Maryland, Douglass escaped from his master in 1838 and headed north. Within three years, he was lecturing as an agent for the Massachusetts Anti-Slavery Society, standing before audiences as "a thief and robber," because "this head, these limbs, this body," as he put it, were "stolen from my *master*!" The irony of Douglass' self-possession was that his example pointed so clearly to the absurdity of any person's having the legal or moral right to enslave another human being. Freedom and independence were Douglass' lifelong concerns, and he insisted throughout his career that a country founded upon the principles of the Declaration of Independence had better be concerned with them too.

The remarkable course of Douglass' life could hardly have been predicted from his childhood. Descriptions of

Douglass' early life are included in his three autobiographies (*Narrative of the Life of Frederick Douglass*, 1845; *My Bondage and My Freedom*, 1855; and *Life and Times of Frederick Douglass*, 1881), but the accounts are necessarily fragmentary. His slave mother, he noted years later, had many children but no family. He saw her only infrequently, and she died by the time he was eight years old. He never knew his father, though it was "whispered that my master was my father," nor did he have accurate knowledge of his age. (He calculated that he was born in 1817, but recent evidence indicates that he was born in February of 1818.) Slavery, Douglass reflected in *My Bondage and My Freedom*, "left me without an intelligible beginning in the world."

Slavery also left him without any formal education. While still a young boy, Douglass was sent from Colonel Edward Lloyd's plantation on the Eastern Shore to the Hugh Auld family in Baltimore, where he enjoyed privileges and opportunities denied plantation slaves. Baltimore's urban setting provided a rich environment that helped to develop Douglass' natural intellectual abilities and exposed him to a variety of people and ideas. Mrs. Sophia Auld treated Douglass kindly, teaching him the alphabet and the rudiments of reading. But when Hugh Auld found out, he forbade this unlawful instruction, reminding his wife that "Learning would *spoil* the best nigger in the world," because "there would be no keeping him. It would forever unfit him to be a slave." So Douglass learned a valuable lesson: If reading and writing were dangerous—if knowing more than just what the master wanted him to know were antithetical to being a slave—then education would be an essential means for Douglass to find a path from slavery to freedom. Determined to steal the knowledge he was forbidden, Douglass carried a Webster's pocket spelling book everywhere and learned from the school lessons of his white playmates on the streets of Baltimore.

Once he could read on his own, Douglass began to see that there were alternatives to the physical deprivations, injustices, and dehumanizing effects of slavery. He was no longer bound only to his master's world. Newspapers and books gave him a more independent perspective on human experience than the circumscribed view available to slaves. At about the age of thirteen, he bought *The Columbian Orator*, a book widely used in the schools. It contained powerful speeches denouncing oppression, including a dialogue between a master and his slave in which the slave successfully argues against the master's claims to enslave him. Equipped with such arguments, Douglass increasingly saw slavery—no matter how benevolently arranged—as little better than a crime. Moreover, he felt the intense anguish of having a free mind trapped in a slave's body. Auld had been right: Douglass had been rendered unfit to be a slave by his reading. Finally, he read an article in the columns of the *Baltimore American*, where he learned about organized efforts to abolish slavery. Douglass now had the desire to be free, the arguments to justify his freedom, and a movement that gave him hope.

But at the age of fifteen he had to leave the relatively liberal and free atmosphere of Baltimore, where city slaves were sometimes hired out to merchants (their earnings being paid to their masters) and could hope that their wages might be used to buy their freedom. Because of deaths and changes in Hugh Auld's family, Douglass was sent back to the Eastern Shore to work on Thomas Auld's plantation. From there, because he was suspected of being too spirited for a plantation slave, Douglass was sent for a year to work as a field hand for Edward Covey, who had a local reputation for breaking young blacks into submission. Within three days of his arrival at Covey's farm, Douglass was severely flogged for upsetting an oxcart, and for the next six months he was whipped every week for one kind of minor infraction or another. For a time, Covey succeeded in breaking Douglass' spirit. The severe discipline and hard work exhausted his desire for reading and thinking and he was made to feel more like an animal than a human being:

> I was broken in body, soul and spirit. My natural elasticity was crushed, my intellect languished, the disposition to read departed, the cheerful spark that lingered about my eye died; the dark night of slavery closed in upon me; and behold a man transformed into a brute!

This passage from the *Narrative* makes it clear that Douglass' determination and self-education were not enough to withstand the "soul-killing" effects of slavery. There was another crucial step to be taken if he were to continue on his path to freedom. That step was resistance. Halfway into his year with Covey, Douglass let it be known that he would no longer be whipped.

By the age of sixteen, Douglass had grown into a large, strong field hand. There was no question that he could beat Covey in a fair fight, but as a slave he had to submit to a whipping whenever Covey decided to inflict one. One day Douglass, not knowing what generated his resolution, decided he would resist a beating, and he held Covey at bay for nearly two hours. The battle was the "turning-point" in Douglass' life as a slave, because his resistance, as he explains in the *Narrative*, "rekindled the few expiring embers of freedom, and revived within me a sense of my own manhood." If he were to be a man rather than a slave, he would have to resist; he would bide his time waiting for the chance to escape, but he would not submit as he had before: "I did not hesitate to let it be known of me, that the white man who expected to succeed in whipping, must also succeed in killing me." As for Covey, Douglass was puzzled and surprised that he did not take revenge; the only explanation Douglass could supply was that Covey wanted to protect his reputation as an effective overseer and slave breaker.

Douglass approached adulthood knowing that for a slave to be educated laws had to be broken and that if he were going to be a man he had to resist being brutalized. He also stole what he needed from his masters when he did not have enough to eat. But he felt no moral culpability for any of this, because he reasoned that slaveholding was a far greater crime than any its victims could commit. As moral as resistance was for Douglass, he also knew that it was not possible to sustain: he could be sold into the Deep South, where conditions were even worse, or be turned over to another slave breaker who, unlike Covey, was not afraid to punish him publicly or to kill him. The only course left for Douglass was to escape to the North.

After two years working on farms on the Eastern Shore (and one unsuccessful escape attempt), Douglass was sent back to Baltimore to work for Hugh Auld as a caulker in the shipyards. There, he once again had some freedom of movement; he joined the East Baltimore Mental Improvement Society, where he met many free blacks, including Anna Murray, who worked as a maid in the city. Their friendship developed into love, and they were engaged by September 3, 1838. It was on that day that Douglass borrowed a free black seaman's papers and, disguised as a sailor, boarded a train bound for New York. Though nearly discovered several times, Douglass arrived safely the next day on free soil. Anna Murray joined him in New York, and they were married on September 15. They settled in New Bedford, Massachusetts, where there were fewer slave catchers hunting fugitives from the South than in New York.

In New Bedford he changed his name from Bailey—his mother's name—to Douglass (he had long before dropped his two middle names, Augustus Washington), so that he would be more difficult to find. He began his life in New Bedford with a new name, a new wife, and a new sense of life's possibilities. Within a few years he had become deeply involved in antislavery activities in Massachusetts. His speeches impressed such abolitionist leaders as William Lloyd Garrison and Wendell Phillips, as well as the many audiences he addressed in New England, New York, and the Midwest.

Slavery and racial discrimination blighted the American landscape for Douglass. He refused to accept the legitimacy of a system that demanded blacks contribute to the economy with their labor while denying them the democratic rights and privileges available to whites. Douglass' characteristic passionate conviction that slavery must end can be heard in a Fourth of July oration delivered at Rochester, New York, in 1852. Douglass celebrated the principles of the founding fathers, but then went on to contrast the "immeasurable distance" between the conditions of whites and blacks in the United States. The following excerpt suggests the power of Douglass' rhetoric, an effect that is especially apparent when the passage is read aloud:

> What to the American slave is your Fourth of July? I answer, a day that reveals to him, more than all other days in the year, the gross injustice and cruelty to which he is the constant victim. To him, your celebration is a sham, your boasted liberty, an unholy license; your national greatness, swelling vanity; your sounds of rejoicing are empty and heartless; your denunciations of tyrants, brass-fronted impudence; your shout of liberty and equality, hollow mockery; your prayers and hymns, your sermons and thanksgivings, with all your religious parade and solemnity, are to him mere bombast and fraud, deception, impiety, and hypocrisy—a thin veil to cover up crimes which would disgrace a nation of savages.

Douglass committed himself in his lectures and writings to the task of making whites aware of the injustice blacks endured behind that veil. He set out to rouse the nation's conscience and startle the complacent by describing his own life in slavery, a life that he consciously used not simply as an example of one person's odyssey from bondage to freedom but as a validation of his insistence that blacks are the equals of whites.

Douglass' oratorical abilities made him one of the most popular speakers to appear before antislavery meetings. Former slaves frequently stood on platforms to tell their stories and to refute the often heard proslavery arguments that blacks were inherently inferior to whites, but none matched Douglass' power as a speaker. His personal appeal, coupled with his firsthand accounts of his experiences as a slave, effectively laid bare the injustices of slavery. His mostly white audiences were confronted with an articulate, intelligent, handsome man who gave the lie to the shuffling, dark stereotypes propagated by proslavery advocates, who argued the system was beneficent and protective. His contemporaries consistently described him as graceful, distinguished, imposing, strong, manly, confident, and modest. There was nothing apologetic or tentative about Douglass. He knew that he was an attractive personality, and he used that advantage to establish the dignity of all black people. Douglass worked his audiences with the controlled inflections of his rich and powerful voice; his carefully spoken words were reinforced with a variety of facial expressions and gestures to convey amusement, anger, sorrow, outrage, or humility. He charmed his audiences with his style. His speeches, sometimes as long as two hours, were well-received performances, balanced by humor, satire, mimicry, story-telling, and sentimentality.

Douglass' forceful presentations were criticized by some Northern whites, however, as reckless and impudent attacks on American culture. Northerners were no more accustomed to being criticized by a black than

Southerners. Douglass would have been easier to accept, no doubt, if he had seemed less certain of his cause and more willing to sound like a slave rather than a master. Indeed, one abolitionist friend even suggested to him that it would be prudent to use "a little of the plantation speech" rather than "seem too learned." He was also advised to limit his talks to his own experiences in slavery and not speak out on complex issues that were being debated by various factions within the abolitionist movement. Douglass rejected these limitations and refused to avoid issues by simply reciting his personal history. If he were going to be used as a symbol, *he* would decide what his meaning would be, not those who would cast him merely as a victim.

Douglass had to struggle anew to preserve his integrity when it was threatened by the sometimes paternalistic advice of his abolitionist friends. This struggle was more subtle but no less troublesome than the problems he faced with the hostile audiences who jeered him and occasionally attacked him with everything from rotten tomatoes to their fists. Despite these challenges, Douglass continued to impress large audiences with his repudiation of slavery and all who were complicit in it. He relentlessly condemned corruption wherever he found it, in the North or the South, in the church or the state. He forthrightly denounced the Constitution as a proslavery document. In lecture after lecture, he described the dehumanizing effects of slavery on blacks and its corrupting influence on whites.

Ironically, the more successful he became as a lecturer in the early 1840s, the more his audiences seemed to doubt that so eloquent a speaker could actually have been a slave. He was under considerable pressure to disclose the details of his past that previously he had withheld to avoid being pursued by fugitive-slave hunters. During the winter of 1844, Douglass committed himself to revealing the specifics of his identity when he began writing the story of his life as a slave. In a letter that would eventually be published with the *Narrative*, Wendell Phillips urged Douglass to burn his manuscript so as not to risk being recaptured, but Douglass, never shy about taking risks, refused. The Boston Anti-Slavery Society published his autobiography in May 1845.

Although *Narrative of the Life of Frederick Douglass, an American Slave, Written by Himself* was one of a number of popular slave narratives published during the nineteenth century, Douglass' story became one of the most widely read, and it is regarded today as a classic of its genre. In the *Narrative* Douglass fleshes out the anecdotes he used as an abolitionist lecturer. Many of the incidents he describes are characteristic ingredients of the slave autobiographies of the time. His opening chapter vividly illustrates and emphasizes the disintegration of family life. In the story of Aunt Hester's beating, the sexual abuse of slaves is presented as the master's prerogative, against which black women and men could only rage powerless. Overworked, underfed, denied education and human dignity, Douglass is beaten and some slaves are even murdered for the slightest infractions. Despite these and other hardships, Douglass emerges with the will and strength to escape to the North, where he dedicates himself to helping those who remain in chains. This pattern of endurance, heroism, and dedication to abolitionism was clearly not Douglass' alone, but the *Narrative* is distinguished from many other slave autobiographies by his skillful use of language and experiences designed to control his reader's feelings and attitudes about the world he left behind.

Judging from the sales of the *Narrative*, Douglass' readers recognized the book's quality, and it quickly became an important propaganda tool in the abolitionists' attempts to discredit slavery. Almost any American writer contemporary to Douglass—including Ralph Waldo Emerson, Henry David Thoreau, Walt Whitman, Nathaniel Hawthorne and Herman Melville—would have envied the impressive sales of the book; the first edition of five thousand copies was sold within months and additional printings followed, not only in America but in England, Ireland, and France. This brief volume moved readers as much as Douglass' speeches stirred his audiences.

Margaret Fuller, the prominent American critic whose *Woman in the Nineteenth Century* was published in the same year, reviewed the *Narrative* for the *New York Tribune* in June of 1845. She anticipated the response of most readers when she noted that "as a narrative, we have never read one more simple, true, coherent, and warm with genuine feeling." Fuller also identified the social significance and political value of Douglass' story by characterizing it as "an excellent piece of writing and on that score to be prized as a specimen of the powers of the Black Race, which Prejudice persists in disputing." Unlike a number of slave narratives written or edited by whites (for example, *The Slave: or Memoirs of Archy Moore* [1836], actually written by Richard Hildreth, a white abolitionist), Douglass' was, as he insisted on the title page of the book, "written by himself." What helped to make the book successful was the power of his writing and authentic details that rendered his abolitionist message all the more effective.

The *Narrative* does, however, include some overwritten exhortatory passages that echo the melodramatic flourishes so typical of nineteenth-century abolitionists. For example, when Douglass describes his master's shabby treatment of his "poor old grandmother," he reverts to the platform rhetoric that moved his audiences, but which strikes modern readers as emotionally extravagant:

> The hearth is desolate . . . the devoted mother of twelve children is left all alone, in yonder little hut, before a few dim embers. She stands—she sits—she staggers—she falls—she groans—she dies—and there are none of her children or grandchildren present, to wipe from her wrinkled brow the cold sweat of death, or to place beneath the sod her fallen remains. Will not a righteous God visit for these things?

The quality of this writing is informed more by sermons and sentimental romances than by Douglass' best instincts for allowing details to speak for themselves—and for using irony to expose hypocrisy, as when he observes that "it is almost an unpardonable offence to teach slaves to read in this Christian country." But Douglass more typically avoids heavy-handedness in the *Narrative* and mostly succeeds in writing clear, straightforward prose that presents his experiences without special pleading or emotional excesses.

Fuller, in her review of the *Narrative*, made a useful contrast between the "over-emphatic style" of "violent invective and denunciation" that characterized William Lloyd Garrison's preface and Douglass' "just and temperate" tone. A comparison of the first few paragraphs of Garrison's preface and the opening paragraphs of Douglass' first chapter makes clear the distinction between Garrison's emotional exclamations and Douglass' understated, quiet tone. When Douglass writes that he did not know when he was born, his account is restrained but no less effective for resisting an emotional outburst. Instead, he challenges his readers to think about what it means to have such an uncertain past: "I do not remember to have ever met a slave who could tell of his birthday. They seldom come nearer to it than planting-time, harvest-time, cherry-time, spring-time, or fall-time." The reader is made to feel Douglass' bewilderment and unhappiness over being forced to live outside normal, human time. Douglass' strategy is to focus on the victims of slavery rather than to inveigh indignantly against the masters. This allows him to emphasize the barbarousness of the slave system and to avoid personal attacks on the individuals in his life who had been agents of that peculiar institution. The result is that his own experiences seem to be presented objectively and are, therefore, more convincing.

Readers of the *Narrative* are invited to see how a slave is transformed into a man, but there are few glimpses of the man himself. Douglass presents a series of detailed, disturbing images of slavery in the South, but he does not reveal himself personally except for the facts that constitute his early history and his yearnings for freedom. Perhaps the best example of this is the brief, impersonal account of his marriage to Anna Murray. Douglass never mentions the woman to whom he was engaged until the final chapter of the book; there is nothing about when and how they met or the problems and frustrations they must have endured in Baltimore. This omission helps to identify Douglass' primary purpose in writing the *Narrative*. He could have presented his life as a remarkable story of romance and adventure filled with love for Anna Murray and hatred for his oppressors; instead he emphasizes his reformist role as a runaway slave in his effort to convince white readers that abolitionism is the only logical, decent response to slavery. He gives his readers a representative black man struggling for his identity, not an intimate portrait of his private, inner life.

Although Douglass revealed little about his personal life in the *Narrative*, that little was enough to place himself in danger of being recaptured. In August 1845, he prudently decided to go to Great Britain, where he delivered a series of antislavery and reform lectures. There he was eagerly listened to and accepted. As a black man he did not have to worry about being served in restaurants or hotels. The irony of finding more tolerance and freedom in the hierarchical British society than in the American democracy he left behind became a theme of many of his speeches. His two-year tour was enormously successful and was reported not only in American abolitionist publications such as the *Liberator* and *National Anti-Slavery Standard*, but also in major newspapers in New York, Boston, and elsewhere. When he returned to the United States in the spring of 1847, he was firmly established as an important voice in American abolitionism. He also returned home a free man: several British friends raised a little more than seven hundred dollars to purchase his freedom from the Auld family in Baltimore. Some abolitionists objected to Douglass' buying his freedom, because the purchase seemed to suggest that Auld had a right to be compensated, but Douglass defended his friends' action as a practical measure that allowed him to move freely in the North without the fear of being seized and returned to the South.

In December 1847, Douglass published the first issue of his abolitionist weekly, the *North Star*, in Rochester, New York. Garrison and others had urged him not to divert himself from his lectures by adding a new publication to the many black newspapers that had already failed. Douglass, however, asserted his independence once again and chose to publish his own voice rather than simply be a spokesman for white abolitionists: "We shall try to have a mind of our own," he wrote in the first issue, "harmonizing with all as far as we can, and differing from any and all where we must." In the *North Star* Douglass made it clear that his concerns went beyond the emancipation of slaves. He discussed a variety of issues affecting the general welfare of black people in the North and South alike: education, employment, segregation, emigration, and racism, among others.

Douglass published his newspaper despite continual financial difficulties and heavy commitments to lecturing that kept him away from his desk. Eventually the *North Star* was merged with the *Liberty Party Paper* in 1851 and renamed *Frederick Douglass' Paper*; this survived until 1860, when high costs and dwindling subscriptions made its weekly publication prohibitive. Meanwhile, in 1858, Douglass had begun a monthly publication for circulation abroad known as *Douglass' Monthly*; this was also distributed in the United States until 1863, when it too folded. Although these papers also included reviews, poems, and serialized novels, they were primarily devoted to reporting on abolitionist speeches and activities and contained little news of general interest.

Douglass' newspaper writing provided him with an opportunity to think and develop independently. He subsequently assessed the period from the late 1840s to 1860 as the time when he was most likely to have produced memorable or significant writing and speeches. His editorials and printed speeches reflected his views on a wide range of subjects, including the Union, the Constitution, voting, religion, political parties, the rights of women, the responsibilities of blacks, colonization, land reform, Northern prejudice, the Fugitive Slave Law, presidential elections, war, Harriet Beecher Stowe, and John Brown. The selected writings in this volume focus primarily on these years, when Douglass was most active in the abolitionist cause.

Douglass' earliest antislavery activities and beliefs had been strongly influenced by the strategies and principles of the Garrisonian abolitionists who had helped him get started in Massachusetts. By the late 1840s, however, Douglass was forming his own views, and he began to question Garrison's repudiation of the Constitution and rejection of political action as a means to end slavery. In 1851 Douglass made public his differences with Garrison. While Garrison had burned the Constitution for being a proslavery document, Douglass now interpreted it as prohibiting slavery, and he wanted to use it to guarantee blacks their freedom. Like other abolitionists who felt the need to go beyond moral suasion, Douglass saw the necessity of using the political process as a tool for ending slavery. If the vote could be extended to all adults, then slavery could be abolished under the Constitution, and there would be no reason to dissolve the Union as Garrison had urged. Douglass opposed disunion because he believed that once the North separated from the South, the slaves would be abandoned. Garrison perceived Douglass' support for political action and the Constitution as a betrayal of both himself and the abolitionist movement. He accused Douglass of opportunism and compromise, a charge that resulted in bitter accusations on both sides. Douglass would not be shaken in his determination to effect change, however, even if it meant working with politicians and party platforms that were not always compatible with his principles.

It was also during the 1850s that Douglass moved beyond Garrison's philosophy of nonresistance and advocated the moral right of slaves to overthrow their oppressors. As a Garrisonian, Douglass had once said that "nothing but God's truth and love can cleanse the land. We must change the moral sentiment." Echoing pacifist principles, Douglass had declared in 1847 that when he was a slave he had been "a man of war" and "had dreams, horrid dreams of freedom through a sea of blood," but after joining Garrison's antislavery movement, he placed his trust in the power of love. Unfortunately, it had become bitterly apparent in the 1850s that the power of love had not been successful in putting an end to slavery, and Douglass came to see pacifism as an ineffective strategy. Moreover, Douglass had not forgotten how after his battle with Covey he had had a revived sense of his "own manhood." If blacks responded only passively to their enslavement, then they were likely to remain slaves. If they resisted, there was at least the possibility of human dignity. This did not mean that Douglass supported desperate, suicidal uprisings (in *My Bondage and My Freedom* he wrote that he never saw "much use in fighting unless there is a reasonable probability of whipping somebody"), but it did indicate that he saw the value of using force when necessary.

Late in 1847 Douglass met the radical abolitionist, John Brown, who had a lasting impact on his thinking. Douglass acknowledged that "while I continued to write and speak against slavery, I became all the same less hopeful of its peaceful abolition. My utterances became more and more tinged by the color of this man's strong impressions." Douglass' writings and lectures increasingly condoned the use of violence. One interesting example is Douglass' fictional treatment of a slave named Madison Washington who led a mutiny on board the slave ship *Creole* in 1841. In *The Heroic Slave* (1853), Douglass creates a hero who, after endless hardships, resists slavery and leads others to freedom. Though there is some killing during the mutiny, Douglass has his hero declare: "I am not a murderer. God is my witness that Liberty, not *malice*, is the motive. . . . We have struck for our freedom, and if a true man's heart be in you, you will honor us for the deed." Similarly, though Douglass could not support Brown's ill-planned raid at Harpers Ferry in 1859 because he thought it doomed to failure, he honored the man and the deed because Brown had struck for freedom.

As a firm advocate of human rights, Douglass was also

an early supporter of women's rights. Nineteenth-century advocates of women's rights frequently compared the limited status and oppression of women to that of blacks. Both were discriminated against in education, employment, and legal matters. Given the significant number of women active in abolitionist societies, it was particularly appropriate that Douglass supported their efforts for equality. The motto on the masthead of the *North Star* read "Right is of no sex—Truth is of no color." In 1848, Douglass attended the Seneca Falls Convention, which began the women's rights movement in the United States, and supported the list of demands drawn up at the meeting. Douglass was instrumental in gaining support at the convention for the most controversial demand—the right of women to vote, an idea that was ridiculed and rejected by most of his contemporaries. Douglass remained committed to women's rights throughout his life. Indeed, the last meeting he attended was the National Council of Women in Washington, D.C., on the morning of the day he died. Though a coincidence, this simple fact underscores Douglass' abiding commitment to further the cause of freedom.

In the midst of his antislavery activities in 1855, Douglass published an expanded and more detailed account of his life in *My Bondage and My Freedom*, which also reflected some of the changes in his outlook since 1845. Nearly four times longer than the *Narrative*, it describes his two-year tour of Great Britain as well as "various incidents" since his return to the United States, including the establishment of the *North Star* and his falling out with Garrison. In addition to the few pages he devotes to their differences, their estrangement can be seen in Douglass' deletion of Garrison's preface in favor of an introduction by a black abolitionist. Douglass also deleted the original appendix to the *Narrative*, in which he had sought to make it clear that he was criticizing the distorted and self-serving religion of slaveholders, not Christianity in general. In its place Douglass put excerpts from his writings and speeches. Instead of ending with a slightly nervous apology, the book concludes with more of Douglass' own forthright views.

In 1881 Douglass published his third autobiography, *Life and Times of Frederick Douglass*. Again, he tells of his early years as a slave in Maryland, but the story is less detailed than in *My Bondage and My Freedom* to leave space for an account of the years from 1855 to 1881. Among the more recent experiences he describes are his helping fugitive slaves to escape along the Underground Railroad, his relationships with John Brown, Harriet Beecher Stowe, and President Lincoln, his work on behalf of emancipation during the Civil War, his efforts to recruit black soldiers for the Union Army, his campaign to secure the civil rights of blacks after the war, and his role in the Republican party. In 1892, Douglass published an expanded version of his 1881 autobiography, adding the events of his life as a public official that led to his appointment by President Harrison in 1889 as minister resident and consul general to Haiti. The final version of the third autobiography is 752 pages long.

Of Douglass' three autobiographies, the *Narrative* is the most satisfying because it is the most direct and focused. It is a graphic account of one man's struggle to raise himself out of a system that was calculated to destroy a sense of personal identity and worth. As he labors to discover and assert his own true nature—his humanity and his manhood—his readers discover the horrendous corruption of slavery. The *Narrative* moves swiftly and surely toward the establishment of the narrator's identity and liberation.

Douglass' writing in *My Bondage and My Freedom* and the *Life and Times of Frederick Douglass* is less successful. The style is often looser and less controlled than that of the *Narrative*. There is not the directness, simplicity, and energy that characterizes the 1845 text. Compare, for example, these accounts of the significance of his climactic battle with Covey:

> This battle with Mr. Covey was the turning-point in my career as a slave. It rekindled the few expiring embers of freedom, and revived within me a sense of my own manhood. It recalled the departed self-confidence, and inspired me again with a determination to be free. (1845)

> Well, my dear reader, this battle with Mr. Covey,—undignified as it was, and as I fear my narration of it is—was the turning-point in my "*life as a slave.*" It rekindled in my breast the smouldering embers of liberty; it brought up my Baltimore dreams, and revived a sense of my own manhood. I was a changed being after that fight. I was *nothing* before; I was A MAN NOW. It recalled to life my crushed self-respect and my self-confidence, and inspired me with a renewed determination to be A FREEMAN. A man, without force, is without the essential dignity of humanity. Human nature is so constituted, that it cannot *honor* a helpless man, although it can *pity* him; and even this it cannot do long, if the signs of power do not arise. (1855)

In the second version Douglass' description is inflated. He self-consciously lectures the reader with a redundant account of how he revives his manhood and then abstracts further significance about how resistance is a sign of dignity and humanity. Douglass seems to have his reader more in mind than his story; his didactic intention undercuts the drama of the moment.

Also, since, in the final third of *My Bondage and My Freedom,* the focus is no longer on his struggle to gain his freedom, Douglass' account of his lectures in Great Britain and his return to the United States is disjointed and abrupt. Many readers become impatient with the rapid and seemingly random movement from anecdote to anecdote. The only continuity to the story is Douglass' moving through a variety of challenges in which he remains a model of black potential. There is no drama or suspense, and little human interest.

In *Life and Times of Frederick Douglass*, there is an even stronger sense that Douglass wants to present his life as a symbol of black success that offers nearly as many lessons as Benjamin Franklin's *Autobiography*, which also chronicled a life of personal achievement and public success. In the introduction to the 1881 edition by the prominent Judge George L. Ruffin, Douglass is described as a man who "stands upon a pedestal," whose life is "the story of the rise and progress of our most celebrated colored man." Ironically, the book sold poorly in all its editions because interest in slavery diminished during the last two decades of the nineteenth century, as blacks were losing rather than gaining ground. As blacks lost power, so too did Douglass' voice.

Still, Douglass never faltered in his determination to address and expose the problems facing blacks in the thirty years after the Civil War. In his final autobiography, he describes the failures of Reconstruction, the Supreme Court's ruling striking down the Civil Rights Act of 1875, and the persistent, corrosive racial discrimination that permeated American life. However, because Douglass does not present these events with the intense personal commitment that characterized his earlier writing, the conflicts seem less compelling. He tends to document rather than dramatize the issues by including them amid numerous excerpts from speeches and letters. In *The Journey Back: Issues in Black Literature and Criticism*, Houston Baker has described this final autobiography as a work that "is public, rooted in the language of its time, and considerably less existential in tone than the 1845 *Narrative*. What we have is a verbose and somewhat hackneyed story of a life, written by a man of achievement."

Although most readers will probably agree that the literary qualities of the *Narrative* are superior to those of Douglass' later autobiographies, *My Bondage and My Freedom* and the *Life and Times* are important books. They provide valuable glimpses of how Douglass perceived and shaped his own life into a model that he hoped blacks would emulate. As a prominent spokesman and leader of his people, he ceaselessly sought to improve their condition both before and after the Emancipation Proclamation. Moreover, these later autobiographies offer an important historical record of people, events, and conflicts related to slavery, the most significant social, political, and moral issue in nineteenth-century America. The abolitionist movement, the Civil War, Reconstruction, industrialization, and the post-Reconstruction reversals for blacks are critical milestones in his life, writings, and times. Douglass provides a black perspective that is not available in white histories. He lets his reader know what it meant and how it felt to be black in the nineteenth century. In the *Life and Times* he explains that that is one of the central purposes of his writings:

> The time is at hand when the last American slave and the last American slaveholder will disappear behind the curtain which separates the living from the dead and when neither master nor slave will be left to tell the story of their respective relations or what happened to either in those relations. My part has been to tell the story of the slave. The story of the master never wanted for narrators.

It is fitting that Douglass is best remembered for the *Narrative* rather than the extraordinary personal achievements he records in his later autobiographies. For what he ultimately provides his readers is not simply a model for success that is held out as a possibility for blacks who work hard and discipline themselves. The truer lesson is to be found in his struggle to create an identity for himself in the *Narrative*. His heroic effort to establish a simple human identity is more important than the public man that he created.

Though Douglass wrote the *Narrative* early in his life, it commands a central place in his writings. The insistence upon justice and decency that informs the *Narrative* can be found in nearly all of his writings. Douglass' struggle for freedom and autonomy—the principal theme of his life's work—resulted in a classic slave narrative that continues to move readers. But Douglass should be read for more than just the *Narrative*. His other writings, including his later autobiographies and many speeches, offer perceptions of nineteenth-century American life and race relations that were largely neglected until they were rediscovered by the civil-rights movement of the 1960s. The historical perspectives Douglass provides are significant because they help to complete the record. Equally important are the insights his writings present to readers today, when human rights often remain a goal rather than an achievement. Douglass might be pursued with considerably more effect in the twentieth century than in his own.

Michael Meyer
Storrs, Connecticut
November 1982

# *Suggested Readings*

Bontemps, Arna. *Free at Last: The Life of Frederick Douglass.* New York: Dodd, Mead, 1971.

Chestnutt, Charles W. *Frederick Douglass.* Boston: Small, Maynard, 1899.

Douglass, Frederick. *The Life and Writings of Frederick Douglass.* Edited by Philip S. Foner. 5 vols. New York: International Publishers, 1950–1975. Combines biography with addresses, letters, and essays; the most complete collection of his writings to date.

———. *The Frederick Douglass Papers: Series One: Speeches, Debates, and Interviews. Volume I: 1841–46.* Edited by John W. Blassingame *et al.* New Haven: Yale University Press, 1979. Subsequent volumes are planned which, when complete, will be the standard edition.

———. *Frederick Douglass on Women's Rights.* Edited by Philip S. Foner. Westport, Conn.: Greenwood Press, 1976.

Foner, Philip S. *Frederick Douglass.* New York: Citadel, 1964. This collects in one volume the biographical chapters of the first four volumes of Foner's *The Life and Writings of Frederick Douglass.*

Huggins, Nathan Irvin. *Slave and Citizen: The Life of Frederick Douglass.* Boston: Little, Brown, 1980. See pp. 182–86 for a discussion of useful books related to Douglass' life and times.

Inge, Thomas, *et al.*, eds. *Black American Writers: Bibliographical Essays.* London: MacMillan, 1978. Vol. I. See pp. 58–72 for a valuable listing and discussion of the writings, reprints, biographies, critical studies, and historical backgrounds.

Preston, Dickson J. *Young Frederick Douglass: The Maryland Years.* Baltimore: Johns Hopkins University Press, 1980.

Quarles, Benjamin. *Frederick Douglass.* Washington, D.C.: Associated Publishers, 1948. This biography remains standard to date.

Walker, Peter F. *Moral Choices: Memory, Desire, and Imagination in Nineteenth-Century American Abolition*. Baton Rouge: Louisiana State University Press, 1978. See pp. 209–261 for a discussion of how Douglass shaped his life in his autobiographies.

Washington, Booker T. *Frederick Douglass*. Philadelphia: Jacobs, 1907.

# *A Note on the Texts*

The text for the *Narrative of the Life of Frederick Douglass* is from the first edition (Boston: Boston Anti-Slavery Society, 1845). The excerpts from *My Bondage and My Freedom* are also from the first edition (New York: Miller, Orton & Mulligan, 1855). The excerpts from *Life and Times of Frederick Douglass*, first published in 1881, are from the revised and enlarged edition (Boston: DeWolfe, Fiske & Co., 1892). The source of each text for the selected writings following Douglass' autobiographies is indicated at the end of each selection. Bracketed titles have been supplied by the editor.

*Autobiographies*

# NARRATIVE

## OF THE

# LIFE

## OF

# FREDERICK DOUGLASS

## AN

# AMERICAN SLAVE

## WRITTEN BY HIMSELF

Published in 1845, the *Narrative* tells the story of Douglass' life from his early childhood in Maryland to his escape north in 1838, just months before he turned twenty-one. He describes in vivid detail his journey from slavehood to manhood. The events Douglass relates are both autobiographical and polemical, for his purpose is to offer his experiences as a demonstration of the inherent evils of slavery.

# *Preface*

In the month of August, 1841, I attended an anti-slavery convention in Nantucket, at which it was my happiness to become acquainted with FREDERICK DOUGLASS, the writer of the following Narrative. He was a stranger to nearly every member of that body; but, having recently made his escape from the southern prison-house of bondage, and feeling his curiosity excited to ascertain the principles and measures of the abolitionists,—of whom he had heard a somewhat vague description while he was a slave,—he was induced to give his attendance, on the occasion alluded to, though at that time a resident in New Bedford.

Fortunate, most fortunate occurrence!—fortunate for the millions of his manacled brethren, yet panting for deliverance from their awful thraldom!—fortunate for the cause of negro emancipation, and of universal liberty!—fortunate for the land of his birth, which he has already done so much to save and bless!—fortunate for a large circle of friends and acquaintances, whose sympathy and affection he has strongly secured by the many sufferings he has endured, by his virtuous traits of character, by his ever-abiding remembrance of those who are in bonds, as being bound with them!—fortunate for the multitudes, in various parts of our republic, whose minds he has enlightened on the subject of slavery, and who have been melted to tears by his pathos, or roused to virtuous indignation by his stirring eloquence against the enslavers of men!—fortunate for himself, as it at once brought him into the field of public usefulness, "gave the world assurance of a MAN," quickened the slumbering energies of his soul, and consecrated him to the great work of breaking the rod of the oppressor, and letting the oppressed go free!

I shall never forget his first speech at the convention—the extraordinary emotion it excited in my own mind—the powerful impression it created upon a crowded auditory, completely taken by surprise—the applause which followed from the beginning to the end of his felicitous remarks. I think I never hated slavery so intensely as at that moment; certainly, my perception of the enormous outrage which is inflicted by it, on the godlike nature of its victims, was rendered far more clear than ever. There stood one, in physical proportion and stature commanding and exact—in intellect richly endowed—in natural eloquence a prodigy—in soul manifestly "created but a little lower than the angels"—yet a slave, ay, a fugitive slave,—trembling for his safety, hardly daring to believe that on the American soil, a single white person could be found who would befriend him at all hazards, for the love of God and humanity! Capable of high attainments as an intellectual and moral being—needing nothing but a comparatively small amount of cultivation to make him an ornament to society and a blessing to his race—by the law of the land, by the voice of the people, by the terms of the slave code, he was only a piece of property, a beast of burden, a chattel personal, nevertheless!

A beloved friend from New Bedford prevailed on Mr. DOUGLASS to address the convention. He came forward to the platform with a hesitancy and embarrassment, necessarily the attendants of a sensitive mind in such a novel position. After apologizing for his ignorance, and reminding the audience that slavery was a poor school for the human intellect and heart, he proceeded to narrate some of the facts in his own history as a slave, and in the course of his speech gave utterance to many noble thoughts and thrilling reflections. As soon as he had taken his seat, filled with hope and admiration, I rose, and declared that PATRICK HENRY, of revolutionary fame, never made a speech more eloquent in the cause of liberty, than the one we had just listened to from the lips of that hunted fugitive. So I believed at that time—such is my belief now. I reminded the audience of the peril which surrounded this self-emancipated young man at the North,—even in Massachusetts, on the soil of the Pilgrim Fathers, among the descendants of revolutionary sires; and I appealed to them, whether they would ever allow him to be carried back into slavery,—law or no law, constitution or no constitution. The response was unanimous and in thunder-tones—"NO!" "Will you succor and protect him as a brother-man—a resident of the old Bay State?" "YES!" shouted the whole mass, with an energy so startling, that the ruthless tyrants south of Mason and Dixon's line might almost have heard the mighty burst of feeling, and recognized it as the pledge of an invincible determination, on the part of those who gave it, never to betray him that wanders, but to hide the outcast, and firmly to abide the consequences.

It was at once deeply impressed upon my mind, that, if Mr. DOUGLASS could be persuaded to consecrate his time and talents to the promotion of the anti-slavery enterprise, a powerful impetus would be given to it, and a stunning blow at the same time inflicted on northern prejudice against a colored complexion. I therefore endeavored to instil hope and courage into his mind, in order that he might dare to engage in a vocation so anomalous and responsible for a person in his situation; and I was seconded in this effort by warm-hearted friends, especially by the late General Agent of the Massachusetts Anti-Slavery Society, Mr. JOHN A. COLLINS, whose judgment in this instance entirely coincided with my own. At first, he could give no encouragement;

with unfeigned diffidence, he expressed his conviction that he was not adequate to the performance of so great a task; the path marked out was wholly an untrodden one; he was sincerely apprehensive that he should do more harm than good. After much deliberation, however, he consented to make a trial; and ever since that period, he has acted as a lecturing agent, under the auspices either of the American or the Massachusetts Anti-Slavery Society. In labors he has been most abundant; and his success in combating prejudice, in gaining proselytes, in agitating the public mind, has far surpassed the most sanguine expectations that were raised at the commencement of his brilliant career. He has borne himself with gentleness and meekness, yet with true manliness of character. As a public speaker, he excels in pathos, wit, comparison, imitation, strength of reasoning, and fluency of language. There is in him that union of head and heart, which is indispensable to an enlightenment of the heads and a winning of the hearts of others. May his strength continue to be equal to his day! May he continue to "grow in grace, and in the knowledge of God," that he may be increasingly serviceable in the cause of bleeding humanity, whether at home or abroad!

It is certainly a very remarkable fact, that one of the most efficient advocates of the slave population, now before the public, is a fugitive slave, in the person of FREDERICK DOUGLASS; and that the free colored population of the United States are as ably represented by one of their own number, in the person of CHARLES LENOX REMOND, whose eloquent appeals have extorted the highest applause of multitudes on both sides of the Atlantic. Let the calumniators of the colored race despise themselves for their baseness and illiberality of spirit, and henceforth cease to talk of the natural inferiority of those who require nothing but time and opportunity to attain to the highest point of human excellence.

It may, perhaps, be fairly questioned, whether any other portion of the population of the earth could have endured the privations, sufferings and horrors of slavery, without having become more degraded in the scale of humanity than the slaves of African descent. Nothing has been left undone to cripple their intellects, darken their minds, debase their moral nature, obliterate all traces of their relationship to mankind; and yet how wonderfully they have sustained the mighty load of a most frightful bondage, under which they have been groaning for centuries! To illustrate the effect of slavery on the white man,—to show that he has no powers of endurance, in such a condition, superior to those of his black brothers,—DANIEL O'CONNELL, the distinguished advocate of universal emancipation, and the mightiest champion of prostrate but not conquered Ireland, relates the following anecdote in a speech delivered by him in the Conciliation Hall, Dublin, before the Loyal National Repeal Association, March 31, 1845. "No matter," said Mr. O'CONNELL, "under what specious term it may disguise itself, slavery is still hideous. *It has a natural, an inevitable tendency to brutalize every noble faculty of man.* An American sailor, who was cast away on the shore of Africa, where he was kept in slavery for three years, was, at the expiration of that period, found to be imbruted and stultified—he had lost all reasoning power; and having forgotten his native language, could only utter some savage gibberish between Arabic and English, which nobody could understand, and which even he himself found difficulty in pronouncing. So much for the humanizing influence of THE DOMESTIC INSTITUTION!" Admitting this to have been an extraordinary case of mental deterioration, it proves at least that the white slave can sink as low in the scale of humanity as the black one.

Mr. DOUGLASS has very properly chosen to write his own Narrative, in his own style, and according to the best of his ability, rather than to employ some one else. It is, therefore, entirely his own production; and, considering how long and dark was the career he had to run as a slave,—how few have been his opportunities to improve his mind since he broke his iron fetters,—it is, in my judgment, highly creditable to his head and heart. He who can peruse it without a tearful eye, a heaving breast, an afflicted spirit,—without being filled with an unutterable abhorrence of slavery and all its abettors, and animated with a determination to seek the immediate overthrow of that execrable system,—without trembling for the fate of this country in the hands of a righteous God, who is ever on the side of the oppressed, and whose arm is not shortened that it cannot save,—must have a flinty heart, and be qualified to act the part of a trafficker "in slaves and the souls of men." I am confident that it is essentially true in all its statements; that nothing has been set down in malice, nothing exaggerated, nothing drawn from the imagination; that it comes short of the reality, rather than overstates a single fact in regard to SLAVERY AS IT IS. The experience of FREDERICK DOUGLASS, as a slave, was not a peculiar one; his lot was not especially a hard one; his case may be regarded as a very fair specimen of the treatment of slaves in Maryland, in which State it is conceded that they are better fed and less cruelly treated than in Georgia, Alabama, or Louisiana. Many have suffered incomparably more, while very few on the plantations have suffered less, than himself. Yet how deplorable was his situation! what terrible chastisements were inflicted upon his person! what still more shocking outrages were perpetrated upon his mind! with all his noble powers and sublime aspirations, how like a brute was he treated, even by those professing to have the same mind in them that was in Christ Jesus! to what dreadful liabilities was he continually subjected! how destitute of friendly counsel and aid, even in his greatest extremities! how heavy was the midnight of woe which shrouded in blackness the last ray of hope, and filled the future with terror and gloom! what longings after freedom took possession of his breast, and how his misery augmented, in proportion as he grew reflective and intelligent,—thus demonstrating that a happy slave is an extinct man! how he thought, reasoned, felt, under the lash of the driver, with the chains upon his limbs! what perils he encountered in his endeavors to escape from his horrible doom! and how signal have been his deliverance and preservation in the midst of a nation of pitiless enemies!

This Narrative contains many affecting incidents, many passages of great eloquence and power; but I think the most thrilling one of them all is the description DOUGLASS gives of his feelings, as he stood soliloquizing respecting his fate, and the chances of his one day being a freeman, on the banks of the Chesapeake Bay—viewing the receding vessels as they flew with their white wings before the breeze, and apostrophizing them as animated by the living spirit of freedom. Who can read that passage, and be insensible to its pathos and sublimity? Compressed into it is a whole Alexandrian library of thought, feeling, and sentiment—all that can, all that need be urged, in the form of expostulation, entreaty, rebuke, against that crime of crimes,—making man the property of his fellow-man! O, how accursed is that system, which entombs the godlike mind of man, defaces the divine image, reduces those who by creation were crowned with glory and honor to a level with four-footed beasts, and exalts the dealer in human flesh above all that is called God! Why should its existence be prolonged one hour? Is it not evil, only evil, and that continually? What does its presence imply but the absence of all fear of God, all regard for man, on the part of the people of the United States? Heaven speed its eternal overthrow!

So profoundly ignorant of the nature of slavery are many persons, that they are stubbornly incredulous whenever they read or listen to any recital of the cruelties which are daily inflicted on its victims. They do not deny that the slaves are held as property; but that terrible fact seems to convey to their minds no idea of injustice, exposure to outrage, or savage barbarity. Tell them of cruel scourgings, of mutilations and brandings, of scenes of pollution and blood, of the banishment of all light and knowledge, and they affect to be greatly indignant at such enormous exaggerations, such wholesale misstatements, such abominable libels on the character of the southern planters! As if all these direful outrages were not the natural results of slavery! As if it were less cruel to reduce a human being to the condition of a thing, than to give him a severe flagellation, or to deprive him of necessary food and clothing! As if whips, chains, thumb-screws, paddles, bloodhounds, overseers, drivers, patrols, were not all indispensable to keep the slaves down, and to give protection to their ruthless oppressors! As if, when the marriage institution is abolished, concubinage, adultery, and incest, must not necessarily abound; when all the rights of humanity are annihilated, any barrier remains to protect the victim from the fury of the spoiler; when absolute power is assumed over life and liberty, it will not be wielded with destructive sway! Skeptics of this character abound in society. In some few instances, their incredulity arises from a want of reflection; but, generally, it indicates a hatred of the light, a desire to shield slavery from the assaults of its foes, a contempt of the colored race, whether bond or free. Such will try to discredit the shocking tales of slaveholding cruelty which are recorded in this truthful Narrative; but they will labor in vain. Mr. DOUGLASS has frankly disclosed the place of his birth, the names of those who claimed ownership in his body and soul, and the names also of those who committed the crimes which he has alleged against them. His statements, therefore, may easily be disproved, if they are untrue.

In the course of his Narrative, he relates two instances of murderous cruelty,—in one of which a planter deliberately shot a slave belonging to a neighboring plantation, who had unintentionally gotten within his lordly domain in quest of fish; and in the other, an overseer blew out the brains of a slave who had fled to a stream of water to escape a bloody scourging. Mr. DOUGLASS states that in neither of these instances was any thing done by way of legal arrest or judicial investigation. The Baltimore American, of March 17, 1845, relates a similar case of atrocity, perpetrated with similar impunity—as follows:—"*Shooting a Slave.*—We learn, upon the authority of a letter from Charles county, Maryland, received by a gentleman of this city, that a young man named Matthews, a nephew of General Matthews, and whose father, it is believed, holds an office at Washington, killed one of the slaves upon his father's farm by shooting him. The letter states that young Matthews had been left in charge of the farm; that he gave an order to the servant, which was disobeyed, when he proceeded to the house, *obtained a gun, and, returning, shot the servant.* He immediately, the letter continues, fled to his father's residence, where he still remains unmolested."—Let it never be forgotten, that no slaveholder or overseer can be convicted of any outrage perpetrated on the person of a slave, however diabolical it may be, on the testimony of colored witnesses, whether bond or free. By the slave code, they are adjudged to be as incompetent to testify against a white man, as though they were indeed a part of the brute creation. Hence, there is no legal protection in fact, whatever there may be in form, for the slave population; and any amount of cruelty may be inflicted on them with impunity. Is it possible for the human mind to conceive of a more horrible state of society?

The effect of a religious profession on the conduct of southern masters is vividly described in the following Narrative, and shown to be any thing but salutary. In the nature of the case, it must be in the highest degree pernicious. The testimony of Mr. DOUGLASS, on this point, is sustained by a cloud of witnesses, whose veracity is unimpeachable. "A slaveholder's profession of Christianity is a palpable imposture. He is a felon of the highest grade. He is a man-stealer. It is of no importance what you put in the other scale."

Reader! are you with the man-stealers in sympathy and purpose, or on the side of their down-trodden victims? If with the former, then are you the foe of God and man. If with the latter, what are you prepared to do and dare in their behalf? Be faithful, be vigilant, be untiring in your efforts to break every yoke, and let the oppressed go free. Come what may—cost what it may—inscribe on the banner which you unfurl to the breeze, as your religious and political motto—"NO COMPROMISE WITH SLAVERY! NO UNION WITH SLAVEHOLDERS!"

WM. LLOYD GARRISON.

BOSTON, *May* 1, 1845.

## LETTER

### *From Wendell Phillips, Esq.*

BOSTON, *April* 22, 1845.

MY DEAR FRIEND:

You remember the old fable of "The Man and the Lion," where the lion complained that he should not be so misrepresented "when the lions wrote history."

I am glad the time has come when the "lions write history." We have been left long enough to gather the character of slavery from the involuntary evidence of the masters. One might, indeed, rest sufficiently satisfied with what, it is evident, must be, in general, the results of such a relation, without seeking farther to find whether they have followed in every instance. Indeed, those who stare at the half-peck of corn a week, and love to count the lashes on the slave's back, are seldom the "stuff" out of which reformers and abolitionists are to be made. I remember that, in 1838, many were waiting for the results of the West India experiment, before they could come into our ranks. Those "results" have come long ago; but, alas! few of that number have come with them, as converts. A man must be disposed to judge of emancipation by other tests than whether it has increased the produce of sugar,—and to hate slavery for other reasons than because it starves men and whips women,—before he is ready to lay the first stone of his anti-slavery life.

I was glad to learn, in your story, how early the most neglected of God's children waken to a sense of their rights, and of the injustice done them. Experience is a keen teacher; and long before you had mastered your A B C, or knew where the "white sails" of the Chesapeake were bound, you began, I see, to gauge the wretchedness of the slave, not by his hunger and want, not by his lashes and toil, but by the cruel and blighting death which gathers over his soul.

In connection with this, there is one circumstance which makes your recollections peculiarly valuable, and renders your early insight the more remarkable. You come from that part of the country where we are told slavery appears with its fairest features. Let us hear, then, what it is at its best estate—gaze on its bright side, if it has one; and then imagination may task her powers to add dark lines to the picture, as she travels southward to that (for the colored man) Valley of the Shadow of Death, where the Mississippi sweeps along.

Again, we have known you long, and can put the most entire confidence in your truth, candor, and sincerity. Every one who has heard you speak has felt, and, I am confident, every one who reads your book will feel, persuaded that you give them a fair specimen of the whole truth. No one-sided portrait,—no wholesale complaints,—but strict justice done, whenever individual kindliness has neutralized, for a moment, the deadly system with which it was strangely allied. You have been with us, too, some years, and can fairly compare the twilight of rights, which your race enjoy at the North, with that "noon of night" under which they labor south of Mason and Dixon's line. Tell us whether, after all, the half-free colored man of Massachusetts is worse off than the pampered slave of the rice swamps!

In reading your life, no one can say that we have unfairly picked out some rare specimens of cruelty. We know that the bitter drops, which even you have drained from the cup, are no incidental aggravations, no individual ills, but such as must mingle always and necessarily in the lot of every slave. They are the essential ingredients, not the occasional results, of the system.

After all, I shall read your book with trembling for

you. Some years ago, when you were beginning to tell me your real name and birthplace, you may remember I stopped you, and preferred to remain ignorant of all. With the exception of a vague description, so I continued, till the other day, when you read me your memoirs. I hardly knew, at the time, whether to thank you or not for the sight of them, when I reflected that it was still dangerous, in Massachusetts, for honest men to tell their names! They say the fathers, in 1776, signed the Declaration of Independence with the halter about their necks. You, too, publish your declaration of freedom with danger compassing you around. In all the broad lands which the Constitution of the United States overshadows, there is no single spot,—however narrow or desolate,—where a fugitive slave can plant himself and say, "I am safe." The whole armory of Northern Law has no shield for you. I am free to say that, in your place, I should throw the MS. into the fire.

You, perhaps, may tell your story in safety, endeared as you are to so many warm hearts by rare gifts, and a still rarer devotion of them to the service of others. But it will be owing only to your labors, and the fearless efforts of those who, trampling the laws and Constitution of the country under their feet, are determined that they will "hide the outcast," and that their hearths shall be, spite of the law, an asylum for the oppressed, if, some time or other, the humblest may stand in our streets, and bear witness in safety against the cruelties of which he has been the victim.

Yet it is sad to think, that these very throbbing hearts which welcome your story, and form your best safeguard in telling it, are all beating contrary to the "statute in such case made and provided." Go on, my dear friend, till you, and those who, like you, have been saved, so as by fire, from the dark prison-house, shall stereotype these free, illegal pulses into statutes; and

New England, cutting loose from a blood-stained Union, shall glory in being the house of refuge for the oppressed;—till we no longer merely "*hide* the outcast," or make a merit of standing idly by while he is hunted in our midst; but, consecrating anew the soil of the Pilgrims as an asylum for the oppressed, proclaim our *welcome* to the slave so loudly, that the tones shall reach every hut in the Carolinas, and make the broken-hearted bondman leap up at the thought of old Massachusetts.

God speed the day!
Till then, and ever,
Yours truly,
WENDELL PHILLIPS.

FREDERICK DOUGLASS.

## CHAPTER I

I was born in Tuckahoe, near Hillsborough, and about twelve miles from Easton, in Talbot county, Maryland. I have no accurate knowledge of my age, never having seen any authentic record containing it. By far the larger part of the slaves know as little of their age as horses know of theirs, and it is the wish of most masters within my knowledge to keep their slaves thus ignorant. I do not remember to have ever met a slave who could tell of his birthday. They seldom come nearer to it than planting-time, harvest-time, cherry-time, spring-time, or fall-time. A want of information concerning my own was a source of unhappiness to me even during childhood. The white children could tell their ages. I could not tell why I ought to be deprived of the same privilege. I was not allowed to make any inquiries of my master concerning it. He deemed all such inquiries on the part of a slave improper and impertinent, and evidence of a restless spirit. The nearest estimate I can give makes me now between twenty-seven and twenty-eight years of age. I come to this, from hearing my master say, some time during 1835, I was about seventeen years old.

My mother was named Harriet Bailey. She was the daughter of Isaac and Betsey Bailey, both colored, and quite dark. My mother was of a darker complexion than either my grandmother or grandfather.

My father was a white man. He was admitted to be such by all I ever heard speak of my parentage. The opinion was also whispered that my master was my father; but of the correctness of this opinion, I know nothing; the means of knowing was withheld from me. My mother and I were separated when I was but an infant—before I knew her as my mother. It is a common custom, in the part of Maryland from which I ran away, to part children from their mothers at a very early age. Frequently, before the child has reached its twelfth month, its mother is taken from it, and hired out on some farm a considerable distance off, and the child is placed under the care of an old woman, too old for field labor. For what this separation is done, I do not know, unless it be to hinder the development of the child's affection toward its mother, and to blunt and destroy the natural affection of the mother for the child. This is the inevitable result.

I never saw my mother, to know her as such, more than four or five times in my life; and each of these times was very short in duration, and at night. She was hired by a Mr. Stewart, who lived about twelve miles from my home. She made her journeys to see me in the night, travelling the whole distance on foot, after the performance of her day's work. She was a field hand, and a whipping is the penalty of not being in the field at sunrise, unless a slave has special permission from his or her master to the contrary—a permission which they seldom get, and one that gives to him that gives it the proud name of being a kind master. I do not recollect of ever seeing my mother by the light of day. She was with me in the night. She would lie down with me, and get me to sleep, but long before I waked she was gone. Very little communication ever took place between us. Death soon ended what little we could have while she lived, and with it her hardships and suffering. She died when I was about seven years old, on one of my master's farms, near Lee's Mill. I was not allowed to be present during her illness, at her death, or burial. She was gone long before I knew any thing about it. Never having enjoyed, to any considerable extent, her soothing presence, her tender and watchful care, I received the tidings of her death with much the same emotions I should have probably felt at the death of a stranger.

Called thus suddenly away, she left me without the slightest intimation of who my father was. The whisper that my master was my father, may or may not be true; and, true or false, it is of but little consequence to my purpose whilst the fact remains, in all its glaring odiousness, that slaveholders have ordained, and by law established, that the children of slave women shall in all cases follow the condition of their mothers; and this is done too obviously to administer to their own lusts, and make a gratification of their wicked desires profitable as well as pleasurable; for by this cunning arrangement, the slaveholder, in cases not a few, sustains to his slaves the double relation of master and father.

I know of such cases; and it is worthy of remark that such slaves invariably suffer greater hardships, and have more to contend with, than others. They are, in the first place, a constant offence to their mistress. She is ever disposed to find fault with them; they can seldom do any thing to please her; she is never better pleased than when she sees them under the lash, especially when she suspects her husband of showing to his mulatto children favors which he withholds from his black slaves. The master is frequently compelled to sell this class of his slaves, out of deference to the feelings of his white wife; and, cruel as the deed may strike any one to be, for a man to sell his own children to human flesh-mongers, it is often the dictate of humanity for him to do so; for, unless he does this, he must not only whip them himself, but must stand by and see one white son tie up his brother, of but few shades darker complexion than himself, and ply the gory lash to his naked back; and if he lisp one word of disapproval, it is set down to his parental partiality, and only makes a bad matter worse, both for himself and the slave whom he would protect and defend.

Every year brings with it multitudes of this class of

slaves. It was doubtless in consequence of a knowledge of this fact, that one great statesman of the south predicted the downfall of slavery by the inevitable laws of population. Whether this prophecy is ever fulfilled or not, it is nevertheless plain that a very different-looking class of people are springing up at the south, and are now held in slavery, from those originally brought to this country from Africa; and if their increase will do no other good, it will do away the force of the argument, that God cursed Ham, and therefore American slavery is right. If the lineal descendants of Ham are alone to be scripturally enslaved, it is certain that slavery at the south must soon become unscriptural; for thousands are ushered into the world, annually, who, like myself, owe their existence to white fathers, and those fathers most frequently their own masters.

I have had two masters. My first master's name was Anthony. I do not remember his first name. He was generally called Captain Anthony—a title which, I presume, he acquired by sailing a craft on the Chesapeake Bay. He was not considered a rich slaveholder. He owned two or three farms, and about thirty slaves. His farms and slaves were under the care of an overseer. The overseer's name was Plummer. Mr. Plummer was a miserable drunkard, a profane swearer, and a savage monster. He always went armed with a cowskin and a heavy cudgel. I have known him to cut and slash the women's heads so horribly, that even master would be enraged at his cruelty, and would threaten to whip him if he did not mind himself. Master, however, was not a humane slaveholder. It required extraordinary barbarity on the part of an overseer to affect him. He was a cruel man, hardened by a long life of slaveholding. He would at times seem to take great pleasure in whipping a slave. I have often been awakened at the dawn of day by the most heart-rending shrieks of an own aunt of mine, whom he used to tie up to a joist, and whip upon her naked back till she was literally covered with blood. No words, no tears, no prayers, from his gory victim, seemed to move his iron heart from its bloody purpose. The louder she screamed, the harder he whipped; and where the blood ran fastest, there he whipped longest. He would whip her to make her scream, and whip her to make her hush; and not until overcome by fatigue, would he cease to swing the blood-clotted cowskin. I remember the first time I ever witnessed this horrible exhibition. I was quite a child, but I well remember it. I never shall forget it whilst I remember any thing. It was the first of a long series of such outrages, of which I was doomed to be a witness and a participant. It struck me with awful force. It was the blood-stained gate, the entrance to the hell of slavery, through which I was about to pass. It was a most terrible spectacle. I wish I could commit to paper the feelings with which I beheld it.

This occurrence took place very soon after I went to live with my old master, and under the following circumstances. Aunt Hester went out one night,—where or for what I do not know,—and happened to be absent when my master desired her presence. He had ordered her not to go out evenings, and warned her that she must never let him catch her in company with a young man, who was paying attention to her belonging to Colonel Lloyd. The young man's name was Ned Roberts, generally called Lloyd's Ned. Why master was so careful of her, may be safely left to conjecture. She was a woman of noble form, and of graceful proportions, having very few equals, and fewer superiors, in personal appearance, among the colored or white women of our neighborhood.

Aunt Hester had not only disobeyed his orders in going out, but had been found in company with Lloyd's

Ned; which circumstance, I found, from what he said while whipping her, was the chief offence. Had he been a man of pure morals himself, he might have been thought interested in protecting the innocence of my aunt; but those who knew him will not suspect him of any such virtue. Before he commenced whipping Aunt Hester, he took her into the kitchen, and stripped her from neck to waist, leaving her neck, shoulders, and back, entirely naked. He then told her to cross her hands, calling her at the same time a d—d b—h. After crossing her hands, he tied them with a strong rope, and led her to a stool under a large hook in the joist, put in for the purpose. He made her get upon the stool, and tied her hands to the hook. She now stood fair for his infernal purpose. Her arms were stretched up at their full length, so that she stood upon the ends of her toes. He then said to her, "Now, you d—d b—h, I'll learn you how to disobey my orders!" and after rolling up his sleeves, he commenced to lay on the heavy cowskin, and soon the warm, red blood (amid heart-rending shrieks from her, and horrid oaths from him) came dripping to the floor. I was so terrified and horror-stricken at the sight, that I hid myself in a closet, and dared not venture out till long after the bloody transaction was over. I expected it would be my turn next. It was all new to me. I had never seen any thing like it before. I had always lived with my grandmother on the outskirts of the plantation, where she was put to raise the children of the younger women. I had therefore been, until now, out of the way of the bloody scenes that often occurred on the plantation.

## CHAPTER II

My master's family consisted of two sons, Andrew and Richard; one daughter, Lucretia, and her husband, Captain Thomas Auld. They lived in one house, upon the home plantation of Colonel Edward Lloyd. My master was Colonel Lloyd's clerk and superintendent. He was what might be called the overseer of the overseers. I spent two years of childhood on this plantation in my old master's family. It was here that I witnessed the bloody transaction recorded in the first chapter; and as I received my first impressions of slavery on this plantation, I will give some description of it, and of slavery as it there existed. The plantation is about twelve miles north of Easton, in Talbot county, and is situated on the border of Miles River. The principal products raised upon it were tobacco, corn, and wheat. These were raised in great abundance; so that, with the products of this and the other farms belonging to him, he was able to keep in almost constant employment a large sloop, in carrying them to market at Baltimore. This sloop was named Sally Lloyd, in honor of one of the colonel's daughters. My master's son-in-law, Captain Auld, was master of the vessel; she was otherwise manned by the colonel's own slaves. Their names were Peter, Isaac, Rich, and Jake. These were esteemed very highly by the other slaves, and looked upon as the privileged ones of the plantation; for it was no small affair, in the eyes of the slaves, to be allowed to see Baltimore.

Colonel Lloyd kept from three to four hundred slaves on his home plantation, and owned a large number more on the neighboring farms belonging to him. The names of the farms nearest to the home plantation were Wye Town and New Design. "Wye Town" was under the overseership of a man named Noah Willis. New Design was under the overseership of a Mr. Townsend. The overseers of these, and all the rest of the farms, numbering over twenty, received advice and direction from the managers of the home plantation. This was the great business place. It was the seat of government for the whole twenty farms. All disputes among the overseers were settled here. If a slave was convicted of any high misdemeanor, became unmanageable, or evinced a determination to run away, he was brought immediately here, severely whipped, put on board the sloop, carried to Baltimore, and sold to Austin Woolfolk, or some other slave-trader, as a warning to the slaves remaining.

Here, too, the slaves of all the other farms received their monthly allowance of food, and their yearly clothing. The men and women slaves received, as their monthly allowance of food, eight pounds of pork, or its equivalent in fish, and one bushel of corn meal. Their yearly clothing consisted of two coarse linen shirts, one pair of linen trousers, like the shirts, one jacket, one pair of trousers for winter, made of coarse negro cloth, one pair of stockings, and one pair of shoes; the whole of which could not have cost more than seven dollars. The allowance of the slave children was given to their mothers, or the old women having the care of them. The children unable to work in the field had neither shoes, stockings, jackets, nor trousers, given to them; their clothing consisted of two coarse linen shirts per year. When these failed them, they went naked until the next allowance-day. Children from seven to ten years old, of both sexes, almost naked, might be seen at all seasons of the year.

There were no beds given the slaves, unless one coarse blanket be considered such, and none but the men and women had these. This, however, is not considered a very great privation. They find less difficulty from the want of beds, than from the want of time to sleep; for when their day's work in the field is done, the most of them having their washing, mending, and cooking to do, and having few or none of the ordinary facilities for doing either of these, very many of their sleeping hours are consumed in preparing for the field the coming day; and when this is done, old and young, male and female, married and single, drop down side by side, on one common bed,—the cold, damp floor,—each covering himself or herself with their miserable blankets; and here they sleep till they are summoned to the field by the driver's horn. At the sound of this, all must rise, and be off to the field. There must be no halting; every one must be at his or her post; and woe betides them who hear not this morning summons to the field; for if they are not awakened by the sense of hearing, they are by the sense of feeling: no age nor sex finds any favor. Mr. Severe, the overseer, used to stand by the door of the quarter, armed with a large hickory stick and heavy cowskin, ready to whip any one who was so unfortunate as not to hear, or, from any other cause, was prevented from being ready to start for the field at the sound of the horn.

Mr. Severe was rightly named: he was a cruel man. I have seen him whip a woman, causing the blood to run half an hour at the time; and this, too, in the midst of her crying children, pleading for their mother's release. He seemed to take pleasure in manifesting his fiendish barbarity. Added to his cruelty, he was a profane swearer. It was enough to chill the blood and stiffen the hair of an ordinary man to hear him talk. Scarce a sentence escaped him but that was commenced or concluded by some horrid oath. The field was the place to witness his cruelty and profanity. His presence made it both the field of blood and of blasphemy. From the rising till the going down of the sun, he was cursing, raving, cutting, and slashing among the slaves of the field, in the most frightful manner. His career was short. He died very soon after I went to Colonel Lloyd's; and he died as he lived, uttering, with his dying groans, bitter curses and horrid oaths. His death was regarded by the slaves as the result of a merciful providence.

Mr. Severe's place was filled by a Mr. Hopkins. He was a very different man. He was less cruel, less profane, and made less noise, than Mr. Severe. His course was characterized by no extraordinary demonstrations of cruelty. He whipped, but seemed to take no pleasure in it. He was called by the slaves a good overseer.

The home plantation of Colonel Lloyd wore the appearance of a country village. All the mechanical operations for all the farms were performed here. The shoemaking and mending, the blacksmithing, cartwrighting, coopering, weaving, and grain-grinding, were all performed by the slaves on the home plantation. The whole place wore a business-like aspect very unlike the neighboring farms. The number of houses, too, conspired to give it advantage over the neighboring farms. It was called by the slaves the *Great House Farm.* Few privileges were esteemed higher, by the slaves of the out-farms, than that of being selected to do errands at the Great House Farm. It was associated in their minds with greatness. A representative could not be prouder of his election to a seat in the American Congress, than a slave on one of the out-farms would be of his election to do errands at the Great House Farm. They regarded it as evidence of great confidence reposed in them by their overseers; and it was on this account, as well as a constant desire to be out of the field from under the driver's lash, that they esteemed it a high privilege, one worth careful living for. He was called the smartest and most trusty fellow, who had this honor conferred upon him the most frequently. The competitors for this office sought as diligently to please their overseers, as the office-seekers in the political parties seek to please and deceive the people. The same traits of character might be seen in Colonel Lloyd's slaves, as are seen in the slaves of the political parties.

The slaves selected to go to the Great House Farm, for the monthly allowance for themselves and their fellow-slaves, were peculiarly enthusiastic. While on their way, they would make the dense old woods, for miles around, reverberate with their wild songs, revealing at once the highest joy and the deepest sadness. They would compose and sing as they went along, consulting neither time nor tune. The thought that came up, came out—if not in the word, in the sound;—and as frequently in the one as in the other. They would sometimes sing the most pathetic sentiment in the most rapturous tone, and the most rapturous sentiment in the most pathetic tone. Into all of their songs they would manage to weave something of the Great House Farm. Especially would they do this, when leaving home. They would then sing most exultingly the following words:—

"I am going away to the Great House Farm!
Oh, yea! O, yea! O!"

This they would sing, as a chorus, to words which to many would seem unmeaning jargon, but which, nevertheless, were full of meaning to themselves. I have sometimes thought that the mere hearing of those songs would do more to impress some minds with the horrible character of slavery, than the reading of whole volumes of philosophy on the subject could do.

I did not, when a slave, understand the deep meaning of those rude and apparently incoherent songs. I was myself within the circle; so that I neither saw nor heard as those without might see and hear. They told a tale of woe which was then altogether beyond my feeble comprehension; they were tones loud, long, and deep; they breathed the prayer and complaint of souls boiling over with the bitterest anguish. Every tone was a testimony against slavery, and a prayer to God for deliverance from chains. The hearing of those wild notes always depressed my spirit, and filled me with ineffable sadness. I have frequently found myself in tears while hearing them. The mere recurrence to those songs, even now, afflicts me; and while I am writing these lines, an expression of feeling has already found its way down my cheek. To those songs I trace my first glimmering conception of the dehumanizing character of slavery. I can never get rid of that conception. Those songs still follow me, to deepen my hatred of slavery, and quicken my sympathies for my brethren in bonds. If any one wishes to be impressed with the soul-killing effects of slavery, let him go to Colonel Lloyd's plantation, and, on allowance-day, place himself in the deep pine woods, and there let him, in silence, analyze the sounds that shall pass through the chambers of his soul,—and if he is not thus impressed, it will only be because "there is no flesh in his obdurate heart."

I have often been utterly astonished, since I came to the north, to find persons who could speak of the singing, among slaves, as evidence of their contentment and happiness. It is impossible to conceive of a greater mistake. Slaves sing most when they are most unhappy. The songs of the slave represent the sorrows of his heart; and he is relieved by them, only as an aching heart is relieved by its tears. At least, such is my experience. I have often sung to drown my sorrow, but seldom to express my happiness. Crying for joy, and singing for joy, were alike uncommon to me while in the jaws of slavery. The singing of a man cast away upon a desolate island might be as appropriately considered as evidence of contentment and happiness, as the singing of a slave; the songs of the one and of the other are prompted by the same emotion.

## CHAPTER III

Colonel Lloyd kept a large and finely cultivated garden, which afforded almost constant employment for four men, besides the chief gardener, (Mr. M'Durmond.) This garden was probably the greatest attraction of the place. During the summer months, people came from far and near—from Baltimore, Easton, and Annapolis—to see it. It abounded in fruits of almost every description, from the hardy apple of the north to the delicate orange of the south. This garden was not the least source of trouble on the plantation. Its excellent fruit was quite a temptation to the hungry swarms of boys, as well as the older slaves, belonging to the colonel, few of whom had the virtue or the vice to resist it. Scarcely a day passed, during the summer, but that some slave had to take the lash for stealing fruit. The colonel had to resort to all kinds of stratagems to keep his slaves out of the garden. The last and most successful one was that of tarring his fence all around; after which, if a slave was caught with any tar upon his person, it was deemed sufficient proof that he had either been into the garden, or had tried to get in. In either case, he was severely whipped by the chief gardener. This plan worked well; the slaves became as fearful of tar as of the lash. They seemed to realize the impossibility of touching *tar* without being defiled.

The colonel also kept a splendid riding equipage. His stable and carriage-house presented the appearance of some of our large city livery establishments. His horses were of the finest form and noblest blood. His carriage-house contained three splendid coaches, three or four gigs, besides dearborns and barouches of the most fashionable style.

This establishment was under the care of two slaves—

old Barney and young Barney—father and son. To attend to this establishment was their sole work. But it was by no means an easy employment; for in nothing was Colonel Lloyd more particular than in the management of his horses. The slightest inattention to these was unpardonable, and was visited upon those, under whose care they were placed, with the severest punishment; no excuse could shield them, if the colonel only suspected any want of attention to his horses—a supposition which he frequently indulged, and one which, of course, made the office of old and young Barney a very trying one. They never knew whey they were safe from punishment. They were frequently whipped when least deserving, and escaped whipping when most deserving it. Every thing depended upon the looks of the horses, and the state of Colonel Lloyd's own mind when his horses were brought to him for use. If a horse did not move fast enough, or hold his head high enough, it was owing to some fault of his keepers. It was painful to stand near the stable-door and hear the various complaints against the keepers when a horse was taken out for use. "This horse has not had proper attention. He has not been sufficiently rubbed and curried, or he has not been properly fed; his food was too wet or too dry; he got it too soon or too late; he was too hot or too cold; he had too much hay, and not enough of grain; or he had too much grain, and not enough of hay; instead of old Barney's attending to the horse, he had very improperly left it to his son." To all these complaints, no matter how unjust, the slave must answer never a word. Colonel Lloyd could not brook any contradiction from a slave. When he spoke, a slave must stand, listen, and tremble; and such was literally the case. I have seen Colonel Lloyd make old Barney, a man between fifty and sixty years of age, uncover his bald head, kneel down upon the cold, damp ground, and receive upon his naked and toil-worn shoulders more than thirty lashes at the time. Colonel Lloyd had three sons—Edward, Murray, and Daniel,—and three sons-in-law, Mr. Winder, Mr. Nicholson, and Mr. Lowndes. All of these lived at the Great House Farm, and enjoyed the luxury of whipping the servants when they pleased, from old Barney down to William Wilkes, the coach-driver. I have seen Winder make one of the house-servants stand off from him a suitable distance to be touched with the end of his whip, and at every stroke raise great ridges upon his back.

To describe the wealth of Colonel Lloyd would be almost equal to describing the riches of Job. He kept from ten to fifteen house-servants. He was said to own a thousand slaves, and I think this estimate quite within the truth. Colonel Lloyd owned so many that he did not know them when he saw them; nor did all the slaves of the out-farms know him. It is reported of him, that, while riding along the road one day, he met a colored man, and addressed him in the usual manner of speaking to colored people on the public highways of the south: "Well, boy, whom do you belong to?" "To Colonel Lloyd," replied the slave. "Well, does the colonel treat you well?" "No, sir," was the ready reply. "What, does he work you too hard?" "Yes, sir." "Well, don't he give you enough to eat?" "Yes, sir, he gives me enough, such as it is."

The colonel, after ascertaining where the slave belonged, rode on; the man also went on about his business, not dreaming that he had been conversing with his master. He thought, said, and heard nothing more of the matter, until two or three weeks afterwards. The poor man was then informed by his overseer that, for having found fault with his master, he was now to be sold to a Georgia trader. He was immediately chained and handcuffed; and thus, without a moment's warning, he was snatched away, and forever sundered, from his family and friends, by a hand more unrelenting than death. This is the penalty of telling the truth, of telling the simple truth, in answer to a series of plain questions.

It is partly in consequence of such facts, that slaves, when inquired of as to their condition and the character of their masters, almost universally say they are contented, and that their masters are kind. The slaveholders have been known to send in spies among their slaves, to ascertain their views and feelings in regard to their condition. The frequency of this has had the effect to establish among the slaves the maxim, that a still tongue makes a wise head. They suppress the truth rather than take the consequences of telling it, and in so doing prove themselves a part of the human family. If they have any thing to say of their masters, it is generally in their masters' favor, especially when speaking to an untried man. I have been frequently asked, when a slave, if I had a kind master, and do not remember ever to have given a negative answer; nor did I, in pursuing this course, consider myself as uttering what was absolutely false; for I always measured the kindness of my master by the standard of kindness set up among slaveholders around us. Moreover, slaves are like other people, and imbibe prejudices quite common to others. They think their own better than that of others. Many, under the influence of this prejudice, think their own masters are better than the masters of other slaves; and this, too, in some cases, when the very reverse is true. Indeed, it is not uncommon for slaves even to fall out and quarrel among themselves about the relative goodness of their masters, each contending for the superior goodness of his own over that of the others. At the very same time, they mutually execrate their masters when viewed separately. It was so on our plantation. When Colonel Lloyd's slaves met the slaves of Jacob Jepson, they seldom parted without a quarrel about their masters;

Colonel Lloyd's slaves contending that he was the richest, and Mr. Jepson's slaves that he was the smartest, and most of a man. Colonel Lloyd's slaves would boast his ability to buy and sell Jacob Jepson. Mr. Jepson's slaves would boast his ability to whip Colonel Lloyd. These quarrels would almost always end in a fight between the parties, and those that whipped were supposed to have gained the point of issue. They seemed to think that the greatness of their masters was transferable to themselves. It was considered as being bad enough to be a slave; but to be a poor man's slave was deemed a disgrace indeed!

## CHAPTER IV

Mr. Hopkins remained but a short time in the office of overseer. Why his career was so short, I do not know, but suppose he lacked the necessary severity to suit Colonel Lloyd. Mr. Hopkins was succeeded by Mr. Austin Gore, a man possessing, in an eminent degree, all those traits of character indispensable to what is called a first-rate overseer. Mr. Gore had served Colonel Lloyd, in the capacity of overseer, upon one of the out-farms, and had shown himself worthy of the high station of overseer upon the home or Great House Farm.

Mr. Gore was proud, ambitious, and persevering. He was artful, cruel, and obdurate. He was just the man for such a place, and it was just the place for such a man. It afforded scope for the full exercise of all his powers, and he seemed to be perfectly at home in it. He was one of those who could torture the slightest look, word, or gesture, on the part of the slave, into impudence, and would treat it accordingly. There must be no answering back to him; no explanation was allowed a slave, showing himself to have been wrongfully accused. Mr. Gore acted fully up to the maxim laid down by slaveholders,—"It is better that a dozen slaves suffer under the lash, than that the overseer should be convicted, in the presence of the slaves, of having been at fault." No matter how innocent a slave might be—it availed him nothing, when accused by Mr. Gore of any misdemeanor. To be accused was to be convicted, and to be convicted was to be punished; the one always following the other with immutable certainty. To escape punishment was to escape accusation; and few slaves had the fortune to do either, under the overseership of Mr. Gore. He was just proud enough to demand the most debasing homage of the slave, and quite servile enough to crouch, himself, at the feet of the master. He was ambitious enough to be contented with nothing short of the highest rank of overseers, and persevering enough to reach the height of his ambition. He was cruel enough to inflict the severest punishment, artful enough to descend to the lowest trickery, and obdurate enough to be insensible to the voice of reproving conscience. He was, of all the overseers, the most dreaded by the slaves. His presence was painful; his eye flashed confusion; and seldom was his sharp, shrill voice heard, without producing horror and trembling in their ranks.

Mr. Gore was a grave man, and, though a young man, he indulged in no jokes, said no funny words, seldom smiled. His words were in perfect keeping with his looks, and his looks were in perfect keeping with his words. Overseers will sometimes indulge in a witty word, even with the slaves; not so with Mr. Gore. He spoke but to command, and commanded but to be obeyed; he dealt sparingly with his words, and bountifully with his whip, never using the former where the latter would answer as well. When he whipped, he seemed to do so from a sense of duty, and feared no consequences. He did nothing reluctantly, no matter how disagreeable; always at his post, never inconsistent. He never promised but to fulfil. He was, in a word, a man of the most inflexible firmness and stone-like coolness.

His savage barbarity was equalled only by the consummate coolness with which he committed the grossest and most savage deeds upon the slaves under his charge. Mr. Gore once undertook to whip one of Colonel Lloyd's slaves, by the name of Demby. He had given Demby but few stripes, when, to get rid of the scourging, he ran and plunged himself into a creek, and stood there at the depth of his shoulders, refusing to come out. Mr. Gore told him that he would give him three calls, and that, if he did not come out at the third call, he would shoot him. The first call was given. Demby made no response, but stood his ground. The second and third calls were given with the same result. Mr. Gore then, without consultation or deliberation with any one, not even giving Demby an additional call, raised his musket to his face, taking deadly aim at his standing victim, and in an instant poor Demby was no more. His mangled body sank out of sight, and blood and brains marked the water where he had stood.

A thrill of horror flashed through every soul upon the plantation, excepting Mr. Gore. He alone seemed cool and collected. He was asked by Colonel Lloyd and my old master, why he resorted to this extraordinary expedient. His reply was, (as well as I can remember,) that Demby had become unmanageable. He was setting a dangerous example to the other slaves,—one which, if suffered to pass without some such demonstration on his part, would finally lead to the total subversion of all rule and order upon the plantation. He argued that if one slave refused to be corrected, and escaped with his life, the other slaves would soon copy the example; the result of which would be, the freedom of the slaves, and the enslavement of the whites. Mr. Gore's defence was satisfactory. He was continued in his station as overseer upon the home plantation. His fame as an overseer went abroad. His horrid crime was not even submitted to judicial investigation. It was committed in the presence of slaves, and they of course could neither institute a suit, nor testify against him; and thus the guilty perpetrator of one of the bloodiest and most foul murders goes unwhipped of justice, and uncensured by the community in which he lives. Mr. Gore lived in St. Michael's, Talbot county, Maryland, when I left there; and if he is still alive, he very probably lives there now; and if so, he is now, as he was then, as highly esteemed and as much respected as though his guilty soul had not been stained with his brother's blood.

I speak advisedly when I say this,—that killing a slave, or any colored person, in Talbot county, Maryland, is not treated as a crime, either by the courts or the community. Mr. Thomas Lanman, of St. Michael's, killed two slaves, one of whom he killed with a hatchet, by knocking his brains out. He used to boast of the commission of the awful and bloody deed. I have heard him do so laughingly, saying, among other things, that he was the only benefactor of his country in the company, and that when others would do as much as he had done, we should be relieved of "the d—d niggers."

The wife of Mr. Giles Hicks, living but a short distance from where I used to live, murdered my wife's cousin, a young girl between fifteen and sixteen years of age, mangling her person in the most horrible manner, breaking her nose and breastbone with a stick, so that the poor girl expired in a few hours afterward. She was immediately buried, but had not been in her untimely grave but a few hours before she was taken up and examined by the coroner, who decided that she had come to her death by severe beating. The offence for which this girl was thus murdered was this:—She had been set that night to mind Mrs. Hicks's baby and during the night she fell asleep, and the baby cried. She, having lost her rest for several nights previous, did not hear the crying. They were both in the room with Mrs. Hicks. Mrs. Hicks, finding the girl slow to move, jumped from her bed, seized an oak stick of wood by the fireplace, and with it broke the girl's nose and breastbone, and thus ended her life. I will not say that this most horrid murder produced no sensation in the community. It did produce sensation, but not enough to bring the murderess to punishment. There was a warrant issued for her arrest, but it was never served. Thus she escaped not only punishment, but even the pain of being arraigned before a court for her horrid crime.

Whilst I am detailing bloody deeds which took place during my stay on Colonel Lloyd's plantation, I will briefly narrate another, which occurred about the same time as the murder of Demby by Mr. Gore.

Colonel Lloyd's slaves were in the habit of spending a part of their nights and Sundays in fishing for oysters, and in this way made up the deficiency of their scanty allowance. An old man belonging to Colonel Lloyd, while thus engaged, happened to get beyond the limits of Colonel Lloyd's, and on the premises of Mr. Beal Bondly. At this trespass, Mr. Bondly took offence, and with his musket came down to the shore, and blew its deadly contents into the poor old man.

Mr. Bondly came over to see Colonel Lloyd the next day, whether to pay him for his property, or to justify himself in what he had done, I know not. At any rate, this whole fiendish transaction was soon hushed up. There was very little said about it at all, and nothing done. It was a common saying, even among little white boys, that it was worth a half-cent to kill a "nigger," and a half-cent to bury one.

## CHAPTER V

As to my own treatment while I lived on Colonel Lloyd's plantation, it was very similar to that of the other slave children. I was not old enough to work in the field, and there being little else than field work to do, I had a great deal of leisure time. The most I had to do was to drive up the cows at evening, keep the fowls out of the garden, keep the front yard clean, and run of errands for my old master's daughter, Mrs. Lucretia Auld. The most of my leisure time I spent in helping Master Daniel Lloyd in finding his birds, after he had shot them. My connection with Master Daniel was of some advantage to me. He became quite attached to me, and was a sort of protector of me. He would not allow the older boys to impose upon me, and would divide his cakes with me.

I was seldom whipped by my old master, and suffered little from any thing else than hunger and cold. I suffered much from hunger, but much more from cold. In hottest summer and coldest winter, I was kept almost naked—no shoes, no stockings, no jacket, no trousers, nothing on but a coarse tow linen shirt, reaching only to my knees. I had no bed. I must have perished with cold, but that, the coldest nights, I used to steal a bag which was used for carrying corn to the mill. I would crawl into this bag, and there sleep on the cold, damp, clay floor, with my head in and feet out. My feet have been so cracked with the frost, that the pen with which I am writing might be laid in the gashes.

We were not regularly allowanced. Our food was coarse corn meal boiled. This was called *mush.* It was put into a large wooden tray or trough, and set down upon the ground. The children were then called, like so many pigs, and like so many pigs they would come and devour the mush; some with oyster-shells, others with pieces of shingle, some with naked hands, and none with spoons. He that ate fastest got most; he that was strongest secured the best place; and few left the trough satisfied.

I was probably between seven and eight years old when I left Colonel Lloyd's plantation. I left it with joy. I shall never forget the ecstasy with which I received the intelligence that my old master (Anthony) had determined to let me go to Baltimore, to live with Mr. Hugh Auld, brother to my old master's son-in-law, Captain Thomas Auld. I received this information about three days before my departure. They were three of the happiest days I ever enjoyed. I spent the most part of all these three days in the creek, washing off the plantation scurf, and preparing myself for my departure.

The pride of appearance which this would indicate was not my own. I spent the time in washing, not so much because I wished to, but because Mrs. Lucretia had told me I must get all the dead skin off my feet and knees before I could go to Baltimore; for the people in Baltimore were very cleanly, and would laugh at me if I looked dirty. Besides, she was going to give me a pair of trousers, which I should not put on unless I got all the dirt off me. The thought of owning a pair of trousers was great indeed! It was almost a sufficient motive, not only to make me take off what would be called by pig-drovers the mange, but the skin itself. I went at it in good earnest, working for the first time with the hope of reward.

The ties that ordinarily bind children to their homes were all suspended in my case. I found no severe trial in my departure. My home was charmless; it was not home to me; on parting from it, I could not feel that I was leaving any thing which I could have enjoyed by staying. My mother was dead, my grandmother lived far off, so that I seldom saw her. I had two sisters and one brother, that lived in the same house with me; but the early separation of us from our mother had well nigh blotted the fact of our relationship from our memories. I looked for home elsewhere, and was confident of finding none which I should relish less than the one which I was leaving. If, however, I found in my new home hardship, hunger, whipping, and nakedness, I had the consolation that I should not have escaped any one of them by staying. Having already had more than a taste of them in the house of my old master, and having endured them there, I very naturally inferred my ability to endure them elsewhere, and especially at Baltimore; for I had something of the feeling about Baltimore that is expressed in the proverb, that "being hanged in England is preferable to dying a natural death in Ireland." I had the strongest desire to see Baltimore. Cousin Tom, though not fluent in speech, had inspired me with that desire by his eloquent description of the place. I could never point out any thing at the Great House, no matter how beautiful or powerful, but that he had seen something at Baltimore far exceeding, both in beauty and strength, the object which I pointed out to him. Even the Great House itself, with all its pictures, was far inferior to many buildings in Baltimore. So strong was my desire, that I thought a gratification of it would fully compensate for whatever loss of comforts I should sustain by the exchange. I left without a regret, and with the highest hopes of future happiness.

We sailed out of Miles River for Baltimore on a Saturday morning. I remember only the day of the week, for at that time I had no knowledge of the days of the month, nor the months of the year. On setting sail, I walked aft, and gave to Colonel Lloyd's plantation what I hoped would be the last look. I then placed myself in the bows of the sloop, and there spent the remainder of the day in looking ahead, interesting myself in what was in the distance rather than in things near by or behind.

In the afternoon of that day, we reached Annapolis, the capital of the State. We stopped but a few moments, so that I had no time to go on shore. It was the first large town that I had ever seen, and though it would look small compared with some of our New England factory villages, I thought it a wonderful place for its size—more imposing even than the Great House Farm!

We arrived at Baltimore early on Sunday morning, landing at Smith's Wharf, not far from Bowley's Wharf. We had on board the sloop a large flock of sheep; and after aiding in driving them to the slaughter-house of Mr. Curtis on Louden Slater's Hill, I was conducted by Rich, one of the hands belonging on board of the sloop, to my new home in Alliciana Street, near Mr. Gardner's ship-yard, on Fells Point.

Mr. and Mrs. Auld were both at home, and met me at the door with their little son Thomas, to take care of whom I had been given. And here I saw what I had never seen before; it was a white face beaming with the most kindly emotions; it was the face of my new mistress, Sophia Auld. I wish I could describe the rapture that flashed through my soul as I beheld it. It was a new and strange sight to me, brightening up my pathway with the light of happiness. Little Thomas was told, there was his Freddy,—and I was told to take care of little Thomas; and thus I entered upon the duties of my new home with the most cheering prospect ahead.

I look upon my departure from Colonel Lloyd's plantation as one of the most interesting events of my life. It is possible, and even quite probable, that but for the mere circumstance of being removed from that plantation to Baltimore, I should have to-day, instead of being here seated by my own table, in the enjoyment of freedom and the happiness of home, writing this Narrative, been confined in the galling chains of slavery. Going to live at Baltimore laid the foundation, and opened the gateway, to all my subsequent prosperity. I have ever regarded it as the plain manifestation of that kind providence which has ever since attended me, and marked my life with so many favors. I regarded the selection of myself as being somewhat remarkable. There were a number of slave children that might have been sent from the plantation to Baltimore. There were those younger, those older, and those of the same age. I was chosen from among them all, and was the first, last, and only choice.

I may be deemed superstitious, and even egotistical, in regarding this event as a special interposition of divine Providence in my favor. But I should be false to the earliest sentiments of my soul, if I suppressed the opinion. I prefer to be true to myself, even at the hazard of incurring the ridicule of others, rather than to be false, and incur my own abhorrence. From my earliest recollection, I date the entertainment of a deep conviction that slavery would not always be able to hold me within its foul embrace; and in the darkest hours of my career in slavery, this living word of faith and spirit of hope departed not from me, but remained like ministering angels to cheer me through the gloom. This good spirit was from God, and to him I offer thanksgiving and praise.

## CHAPTER VI

My new mistress proved to be all she appeared when I first met her at the door,—a woman of the kindest heart and finest feelings. She had never had a slave under her control previously to myself, and prior to her marriage she had been dependent upon her own industry for a living. She was by trade a weaver; and by constant application to her business, she had been in a good degree preserved from the blighting and dehumanizing effects of slavery. I was utterly astonished at her goodness. I scarcely knew how to behave towards her. She was entirely unlike any other white woman I had ever seen. I could not approach her as I was accustomed to approach other white ladies. My early instruction was all out of place. The crouching servility, usually so acceptable a quality in a slave, did not answer when manifested toward her. Her favor was not gained by it; she seemed to be disturbed by it. She did not deem it impudent or unmannerly for a slave to look her in the face. The meanest slave was put fully at ease in her presence, and none left without feeling better for having seen her. Her face was made of heavenly smiles, and her voice of tranquil music.

But, alas! this kind heart had but a short time to remain such. The fatal poison of irresponsible power was already in her hands, and soon commenced its infernal work. That cheerful eye, under the influence of slavery, soon became red with rage; that voice, made all of sweet accord, changed to one of harsh and horrid discord; and that angelic face gave place to that of a demon.

Very soon after I went to live with Mr. and Mrs. Auld, she very kindly commenced to teach me the A, B, C. After I had learned this, she assisted me in learning to spell words of three or four letters. Just at this point of my progress, Mr. Auld found out what was going on, and at once forbade Mrs. Auld to instruct me further, telling her, among other things, that it was unlawful, as well as unsafe, to teach a slave to read. To use his own words, further, he said, "If you give a nigger an inch, he will take an ell. A nigger should know nothing but to obey his master—to do as he is told to do. Learning would *spoil* the best nigger in the world. Now," said he, "if you teach that nigger (speaking of myself) how to read, there would be no keeping him. It would forever unfit him to be a slave. He would at once become unmanageable, and of no value to his master. As to himself, it could do him no good, but a great deal of harm. It would make him discontented and unhappy." These words sank deep into my heart, stirred up sentiments within that lay slumbering, and called into existence an entirely new train of thought. It was a new and special revelation, explaining dark and mysterious things, with which my youthful understanding had struggled, but struggled in vain. I now understood what had been to me a most perplexing difficulty—to wit, the white man's power to enslave the black man. It was a grand achievement, and I prized it highly. From that moment, I understood the pathway from slavery to freedom. It was just what I wanted, and I got it at a time when I the least expected it. Whilst I was saddened by the thought of losing the aid of my kind mistress, I was gladdened by the invaluable instruction which, by the merest accident, I had gained from my master. Though conscious of the difficulty of learning without a teacher, I set out with high hope, and a fixed purpose, at whatever cost of trouble, to learn how to read. The very decided manner with which he spoke, and strove to impress his wife with the evil consequences of giving me instruction, served to convince me that he was deeply sensible of the truths he was uttering. It gave me the best assurance that I might rely with the utmost confidence on the results which, he said, would flow from teaching me to read. What he most dreaded, that I most desired. What he most loved, that I most hated. That which to him was a great evil, to be carefully shunned, was to me a great good, to be diligently sought; and the argument which he so warmly urged, against my learning to read, only served to inspire me with a desire and determination to learn. In learning to read, I owe almost as much to the bitter opposition of my master, as to the kindly aid of my mistress. I acknowledge the benefit of both.

I had resided but a short time in Baltimore before I observed a marked difference, in the treatment of slaves, from that which I had witnessed in the country. A city slave is almost a freeman, compared with a slave on the plantation. He is much better fed and clothed, and enjoys privileges altogether unknown to the slave on the plantation. There is a vestige of decency, a sense of shame, that does much to curb and check those outbreaks of atrocious cruelty so commonly enacted upon the plantation. He is a desperate slaveholder, who will shock the humanity of his nonslaveholding neighbors with the cries of his lacerated slave. Few are willing to incur the odium attaching to the reputation of being a cruel master; and above all things, they would not be known as not giving a slave enough to eat. Every city slaveholder is anxious to have it known of him, that he feeds his slaves well; and it is due to them to say, that most of them do give their slaves enough to eat. There are, however, some painful exceptions to this rule. Directly opposite to us, on Philpot Street, lived Mr. Thomas Hamilton. He owned two slaves. Their names were Henrietta and Mary. Henrietta was about twenty-two years of age, Mary was about fourteen; and of all the mangled and emaciated creatures I ever looked upon, these two were the most so. His heart must be harder than stone, that could look upon these unmoved. The head, neck, and shoulders of Mary were literally cut to pieces. I have frequently felt her head, and found it nearly covered with festering sores, caused by the lash of her cruel mistress. I do not know that her master ever whipped her, but I have been an eye-witness to the cruelty of Mrs. Hamilton. I used to be in Mr. Hamilton's house nearly every day. Mrs. Hamilton used to sit in a large chair in the middle of the room, with a heavy cowskin always by her side, and scarce an hour passed during the day but was marked by the blood of one of these slaves. The girls seldom passed her without her saying, "Move faster, you *black gip!*" at the same time giving them a blow with the cowskin over the head or shoulders, often drawing the blood. She would then say, "Take that, you *black gip!*"—continuing, "If you don't move faster, I'll move you!" Added to the cruel lashings to which these slaves were subjected, they were kept nearly half-starved. They seldom knew what it was to eat a full meal. I have seen Mary contending with the pigs for the offal thrown into the street. So much was Mary kicked and cut to pieces, that she was oftener called "*pecked*" than by her name.

# CHAPTER VII

I lived in Master Hugh's family about seven years. During this time, I succeeded in learning to read and write. In accomplishing this, I was compelled to resort to various stratagems. I had no regular teacher. My mistress, who had kindly commenced to instruct me, had, in compliance with the advice and direction of her husband, not only ceased to instruct, but had set her face against my being instructed by any one else. It is due, however, to my mistress to say of her, that she did not adopt this course of treatment immediately. She at first lacked the depravity indispensable to shutting me up in mental darkness. It was at least necessary for her to have some training in the exercise of irresponsible power, to make her equal to the task of treating me as though I were a brute.

My mistress was, as I have said, a kind and tender-hearted woman; and in the simplicity of her soul she commenced, when I first went to live with her, to treat me as she supposed one human being ought to treat another. In entering upon the duties of a slaveholder, she did not seem to perceive that I sustained to her the relation of a mere chattel, and that for her to treat me as a human being was not only wrong, but dangerously so. Slavery proved as injurious to her as it did to me. When I went there, she was a pious, warm, and tender-hearted woman. There was no sorrow or suffering for which she had not a tear. She had bread for the hungry, clothes for the naked, and comfort for every mourner that came within her reach. Slavery soon proved its ability to divest her of these heavenly qualities. Under its influence, the tender heart became stone, and the lamblike disposition gave way to one of tiger-like fierceness. The first step in her downward course was in her ceasing to instruct me.

She now commenced to practise her husband's precepts. She finally became even more violent in her opposition than her husband himself. She was not satisfied with simply doing as well as he had commanded; she seemed anxious to do better. Nothing seemed to make her more angry than to see me with a newspaper. She seemed to think that here lay the danger. I have had her rush at me with a face made all up of fury, and snatch from me a newspaper, in a manner that fully revealed her apprehension. She was an apt woman; and a little experience soon demonstrated, to her satisfaction, that education and slavery were incompatible with each other.

From this time I was most narrowly watched. If I was in a separate room any considerable length of time, I was sure to be suspected of having a book, and was at once called to give an account of myself. All this, however, was too late. The first step had been taken. Mistress, in teaching me the alphabet, had given me the *inch,* and no precaution could prevent me from taking the *ell.*

The plan which I adopted, and the one by which I was most successful, was that of making friends of all the little white boys whom I met in the street. As many of these as I could, I converted into teachers. With their kindly aid, obtained at different times and in different places, I finally succeeded in learning to read. When I was sent of errands, I always took my book with me, and by going one part of my errand quickly, I found time to get a lesson before my return. I used also to carry bread with me, enough of which was always in the house, and to which I was always welcome; for I was much better off in this regard than many of the poor white children in our neighborhood. This bread I used to bestow upon the hungry little urchins, who, in return, would give me that more valuable bread of knowledge. I am strongly tempted to give the names of two or three of those little boys, as a testimonial of the gratitude and affection I bear them; but prudence forbids;—not that it would injure me, but it might embarrass them; for it is almost an unpardonable offence to teach slaves to read in this Christian country. It is enough to say of the dear little fellows, that they lived on Philpot Street, very near Durgin and Bailey's ship-yard. I used to talk this matter of slavery over with them. I would sometimes say to them, I wished I could be as free as they would be when they got to be men. "You will be free as soon as you are twenty-one, *but I am a slave for life!* Have not I as good a right to be free as you have?" These words used to trouble them; they would express for me the liveliest sympathy, and console me with the hope that something would occur by which I might be free.

I was now about twelve years old, and the thought of being *a slave for life* began to bear heavily upon my heart. Just about this time, I got hold of a book entitled "The Columbian Orator." Every opportunity I got, I used to read this book. Among much of other interesting matter, I found in it a dialogue between a master and his slave. The slave was represented as having run away from his master three times. The dialogue represented the conversation which took place between them, when the slave was retaken the third time. In this dialogue, the whole argument in behalf of slavey was brought forward by the master, all of which was disposed of by the slave. The slave was made to say some very smart as well as impressive things in reply to his master—things which had the desired though unexpected effect; for the conversation resulted in the voluntary emancipation of the slave on the part of the master.

In the same book, I met with one of Sheridan's mighty speeches on and in behalf of Catholic emancipation. These were choice documents to me. I read them over and over again with unabated interest. They gave tongue to interesting thoughts of my own soul, which had frequently flashed through my mind, and died away for want of utterance. The moral which I gained from the dialogue was the power of truth over the conscience of even a slaveholder. What I got from Sheridan was a bold denunciation of slavery, and a powerful vindication of human rights. The reading of these documents enabled me to utter my thoughts, and to meet the arguments brought forward to sustain slavery; but while they relieved me of one difficulty, they brought on another even more painful than the one of which I was relieved. The more I read, the more I was led to abhor and detest my enslavers. I could regard them in no other light than a band of successful robbers, who had left their homes, and gone to Africa, and stolen us from our homes, and in a strange land reduced us to slavery. I loathed them as being the meanest as well as the most wicked of men. As I read and contemplated the subject, behold! that very discontentment which Master Hugh had predicted would follow my learning to read had already come, to torment and sting my soul to unutterable anguish. As I writhed under it, I would at times feel that learning to read had been a curse rather than a blessing. It had given me a view of my wretched condition, without the remedy. It opened my eyes to the horrible pit, but to no ladder upon which to get out. In moments of agony, I envied my fellow-slaves for their stupidity. I have often wished myself a beast. I preferred the condition of the meanest reptile to my own. Any thing, no matter what, to get rid of thinking! It was this everlasting thinking of my condition that tormented me. There was no getting rid of it. It was pressed upon me by every object within sight or hearing, animate or inanimate. The silver trump of freedom had roused my soul to eternal wakefulness. Freedom now appeared, to disappear no more forever. It was heard in every sound, and seen in every thing. It was ever present to torment me with a sense of my wretched condition. I saw nothing without seeing it, I heard nothing without hearing it, and felt nothing without feeling it. It looked from every star, it smiled in every calm, breathed in every wind, and moved in every storm.

I often found myself regretting my own existence, and wishing myself dead; and but for the hope of being free, I have no doubt but that I should have killed myself, or done something for which I should have been killed. While in this state of mind, I was eager to hear any one speak of slavery. I was a ready listener. Every little while, I could hear something about the abolitionists. It was some time before I found what the word meant. It was always used in such connections as to make it an interesting word to me. If a slave ran away and succeeded in getting clear, or if a slave killed his master, set fire to a barn, or did any thing very wrong in the mind of a slaveholder, it was spoken of as the fruit of *abolition.* Hearing the word in this connection very often, I set about learning what it meant. The dictionary afforded me little or no help. I found it was "the act of abolishing;" but then I did not know what was to be abolished. Here I was perplexed. I did not dare to ask any one about its meaning, for I was satisfied that it was something they wanted me to know very little about. After a patient waiting, I got one of our city papers, containing an account of the number of petitions from the north, praying for the abolition of slavery in the District of Columbia, and of the slave trade between the States. From this time I understood the words *abolition* and *abolitionist*, and always drew near when that word was spoken, expecting to hear something of importance to myself and fellow-slaves. The light broke in upon me by degrees. I went one day down on the wharf of Mr. Waters; and seeing two Irishmen unloading a scow of stone, I went, unasked, and helped them. When we had finished, one of them came to me and asked me if I were a slave. I told him I was. He asked, "Are ye a slave for life?" I told him that I was. The good Irishman seemed to be deeply affected by the statement. He said to the other that it was a pity so fine a little fellow as myself should be a slave for life. He said it was a shame to hold me. They both advised me to run away to the north; that I should find friends there, and that I should be free. I pretended not to be interested in what they said, and treated them as if I did not understand them; for I feared they might be treacherous. White men have been known to encourage slaves to escape, and then, to get the reward, catch them and return them to their masters. I was afraid that these seemingly good men might use me so; but I nevertheless remembered their advice, and from that time I resolved to run away. I looked forward to a time at which it would be safe for me to escape. I was too young to think of doing so immediately; besides, I wished to learn how to write, as I might have occasion to write my own pass. I consoled myself with the hope that I should one day find a good chance. Meanwhile, I would learn to write.

The idea as to how I might learn to write was suggested to me by being in Durgin and Bailey's ship-yard, and frequently seeing the ship carpenters, after hewing, and getting a piece of timber ready for use, write on the timber the name of that part of the ship for which it was intended. When a piece of timber was intended for the larboard side, it would be marked thus—"L." When a piece was for the starboard side, it would be marked thus—"S." A piece for the larboard side forward, would be marked thus—"L.F." When a piece was for starboard side forward, it would be marked thus—"S.F." For larboard aft, it would be marked thus—"L.A." For starboard aft, it would be marked thus—"S.A." I soon learned the names of these letters, and for what they were intended when placed upon a piece of timber in the ship-yard. I immediately commenced copying them, and in a short time was able to make the four letters named. After that, when I met with any boy who I knew could write, I would tell him I could write as well as he. The next word would be, "I don't believe you. Let me see you try it." I would then make the letters which I had been so fortunate as to learn, and ask him to beat that. In this way I got a good many lessons in writing, which it is quite possible I should never have gotten in any other way. During this time, my copy-book was the board fence, brick wall, and pavement; my pen and ink was a lump of chalk. With these, I learned mainly how to write. I then commenced and continued copying the Italics in Webster's Spelling Book, until I could make them all without looking on the book. By this time, my little Master Thomas had gone to school, and learned how to write, and had written over a number of copy-books. These had been brought home, and shown to some of our near neighbors, and then laid aside. My mistress used to go to class meeting at the Wilk Street meeting-house every Monday afternoon, and leave me to take care of the house. When left thus, I used to spend the time in writing in the spaces left in Master Thomas's copy-book, copying what he had written. I continued to do this until I could write a hand very similar to that of Master Thomas. Thus, after a long, tedious effort for years, I finally succeeded in learning how to write.

## CHAPTER VIII

In a very short time after I went to live at Baltimore, my old master's youngest son Richard died; and in about three years and six months after his death, my old master, Captain Anthony, died, leaving only his son, Andrew, and daughter, Lucretia, to share his estate. He died while on a visit to see his daughter at Hillsborough. Cut off thus unexpectedly, he left no will as to the disposal of his property. It was therefore necessary to have a valuation of the property, that it might be equally divided between Mrs. Lucretia and Master Andrew. I was immediately sent for, to be valued with the other property. Here again my feelings rose up in detestation of slavery. I had now a new conception of my degraded condition. Prior to this, I had become, if not insensible to my lot, at least partly so. I left Baltimore with a young heart overborne with sadness, and a soul full of apprehension. I took passage with Captain Rowe, in the schooner Wild Cat, and, after a sail of about twenty-four hours, I found myself near the place of my birth. I had now been absent from it almost, if not quite, five years. I, however, remembered the place very well. I was only about five years old when I left it, to go and live with my old master on Colonel Lloyd's plantation; so that I was now between ten and eleven years old.

We were all ranked together at the valuation. Men and women, old and young, married and single, were ranked with horses, sheep, and swine. There were horses and men, cattle and women, pigs and children, all holding the same rank in the scale of being, and were all subjected to the same narrow examination. Silvery-headed age and sprightly youth, maids and matrons, had to undergo the same indelicate inspection. At this moment, I saw more clearly than ever the brutalizing effects of slavery upon both slave and slaveholder.

After the valuation, then came the division. I have no language to express the high excitement and deep anxiety which were felt among us poor slaves during this time. Our fate for life was now to be decided. We had no more voice in that decision than the brutes among whom we were ranked. A single word from the white men was enough—against all our wishes, prayers, and entreaties—to sunder forever the dearest friends, dearest kindred, and strongest ties known to human beings. In addition to the pain of separation, there was the horrid dread of falling into the hands of Master Andrew. He was known to us all as being a most cruel wretch,—a common drunkard, who had, by his reckless mismanagement and profligate dissipation, already wasted a large portion of his father's property. We all felt that we might as well be sold at once to the Georgia traders, as to pass into his hands; for we knew that that would be our inevitable condition,—a condition held by us all in the utmost horror and dread.

I suffered more anxiety than most of my fellow-slaves. I had known what it was to be kindly treated; they had known nothing of the kind. They had seen little or nothing of the world. They were in very deed men and women of sorrow, and acquainted with grief. Their backs had been made familiar with the bloody lash, so that they had become callous; mine was yet tender; for while at Baltimore I got few whippings, and few slaves could boast of a kinder master and mistress than myself; and the thought of passing out of their hands into those of Master Andrew—a man who, but a few days before, to give me a sample of his bloody disposition, took my little brother by the throat, threw him on the ground, and with the heel of his boot stamped upon his head till the blood gushed from his nose and ears—was well calculated to make me anxious as to my fate. After he had committed this savage outrage upon my brother, he turned to me, and said that was the way he meant to serve me one of these days,—meaning, I suppose, when I came into his possession.

Thanks to a kind Providence, I fell to the portion of Mrs. Lucretia, and was sent immediately back to Baltimore, to live again in the family of Master Hugh. Their joy at my return equalled their sorrow at my departure. It was a glad day to me. I had escaped a worse than lion's jaws. I was absent from Baltimore, for the purpose of valuation and division, just about one month, and it seemed to have been six.

Very soon after my return to Baltimore, my mistress, Lucretia, died, leaving her husband and one child, Amanda; and in a very short time after her death, Master Andrew died. Now all the property of my old master, slaves included, was in the hands of strangers,—strangers who had had nothing to do with accumulating it. Not a slave was left free. All remained slaves, from the youngest to the oldest. If any one thing in my experience, more than another, served to deepen my conviction of the infernal character of slavery, and to fill me with unutterable loathing of slaveholders, it was their base ingratitude to my poor old grandmother. She had served my old master faithfully from youth to old age. She had been the source of all his wealth; she had peopled his plantation with slaves; she had become a great grandmother in his service. She had rocked him in infancy, attended him in childhood, served him through life, and at his death wiped from his icy brow the cold death-sweat, and closed his eyes forever. She was nevertheless left a slave—a slave for life—a slave in the hands of strangers; and in their hands she saw her children, her grandchildren, and her great-grandchildren, divided, like so many sheep, without being gratified with the small privilege of a single word, as to their or her own destiny. And, to cap the climax of their base ingratitude and fiendish barbarity, my grandmother, who was now very old, having outlived my old master and all his children, having seen the beginning and end of all of them, and her present owners finding she was of but little value, her frame already racked with the pains of old age, and complete helplessness fast stealing over her once active limbs, they took her to the woods, built her a little hut, put up a little mud-chimney, and then made her welcome to the privilege of supporting herself there in perfect loneliness; thus virtually turning her out to die! If my poor old grandmother now lives, she lives to suffer in utter loneliness; she lives to remember and mourn over the loss of children, the loss of grandchildren, and the loss of great-grandchildren. They are, in the language of the slave's poet, Whittier,—

> "Gone, gone, sold and gone
> To the rice swamp dank and lone,
> Where the slave-whip ceaseless swings,
> Where the noisome insect stings,
> Where the fever-demon strews
> Poison with the falling dews,
> Where the sickly sunbeams glare
> Through the hot and misty air:—
>   Gone, gone, sold and gone
>   To the rice swamp dank and lone,
>   From Virginia hills and waters—
>   Woe is me, my stolen daughters!"

The hearth is desolate. The children, the unconscious children, who once sang and danced in her presence, are gone. She gropes her way, in the darkness of age, for a drink of water. Instead of the voices of her children, she hears by day the moans of the dove, and by night the screams of the hideous owl. All is gloom. The grave is at the door. And now, when weighed down by the pains and aches of old age, when the head inclines to the feet, when the beginning and ending of human existence meet, and helpless infancy and painful old age combine together—at this time, this most needful time, the time for the exercise of that tenderness and affection which children only can exercise towards a declining parent—my poor old grandmother, the devoted mother of twelve children, is left all alone, in yonder little hut, before a few dim embers. She stands—she sits—she staggers—she falls—she groans—she dies—and there are none of her children or grandchildren present, to wipe from her wrinkled brow the cold sweat of death, or to place beneath the sod her fallen remains. Will not a righteous God visit for these things?

In about two years after the death of Mrs. Lucretia, Master Thomas married his second wife. Her name was Rowena Hamilton. She was the eldest daughter of Mr. William Hamilton. Master now lived in St. Michael's. Not long after his marriage, a misunderstanding took place between himself and Master Hugh; and as a means of punishing his brother, he took me from him to live with himself at St. Michael's. Here I underwent another most painful separation. It, however, was not so severe as the one I dreaded at the division of property; for, during this interval, a great change had taken place in Master Hugh and his once kind and affectionate wife. The influence of brandy upon him, and of slavery upon her, had effected a disastrous change in the characters of both; so that, as far as they were concerned, I thought I had little to lose by the change. But it was not to them that I was attached. It was to those little Baltimore boys that I felt the strongest attachment. I had received many good lessons from them, and was still receiving them, and the thought of leaving them was painful indeed. I was leaving, too, without the hope of ever being allowed to return. Master Thomas had said he would never let me return again. The barrier betwixt himself and brother he considered impassable.

I then had to regret that I did not at least make the attempt to carry out my resolution to run away; for the chances of success are tenfold greater from the city than from the country.

I sailed from Baltimore for St. Michael's in the sloop Amanda, Captain Edward Dodson. On my passage, I paid particular attention to the direction which the steamboats took to go to Philadelphia. I found, instead of going down, on reaching North Point they went up the bay, in a northeasterly direction. I deemed this knowledge of the utmost importance. My determination to run away was again revived. I resolved to wait only so long as the offering of a favorable opportunity. When that came, I was determined to be off.

## CHAPTER IX

I have now reached a period of my life when I can give dates. I left Baltimore, and went to live with Master Thomas Auld, at St. Michael's, in March, 1832. It was now more than seven years since I lived with him in the family of my old master, on Colonel Lloyd's plantation. We of course were now almost entire strangers to each other. He was to me a new master, and I to him a new slave. I was ignorant of his temper and disposition; he was equally so of mine. A very short time, however, brought us into full acquaintance with each other. I was made acquainted with his wife not less than with himself. They were well matched, being equally mean and cruel. I was now, for the first time during a space of more than seven years, made to feel the painful gnawings of hunger—a something which I had not experienced before since I left Colonel Lloyd's plantation. It went hard enough with me then, when I could look back to no period at which I had enjoyed a sufficiency. It was tenfold harder after living in Master Hugh's family, where I had always had enough to eat, and of that which was good. I have said Master Thomas was a mean man. He was so. Not to give a slave enough to eat, is regarded as the most aggravated development of meanness even among slaveholders. The rule is, no matter how coarse the food, only let there be enough of it. This is the theory; and in the part of Maryland from which I came, it is the general practice,—though there are many exceptions. Master Thomas gave us enough of neither coarse nor fine food. There were four slaves of us in the kitchen—my sister Eliza, my aunt Priscilla, Henny, and myself; and we were allowed less than a half of a bushel of corn-meal per week, and very little else, either in the shape of meat or vegetables. It was not enough for us to subsist upon. We were therefore reduced to the wretched necessity of living at the expense of our neighbors. This we did by begging and stealing, whichever came handy in the time of need, the one being considered as legitimate as the other. A great many times have we poor creatures been nearly perishing with hunger, when food in abundance lay mouldering in the safe and smoke-house, and our pious mistress was aware of the fact; and yet that mistress and her husband would kneel every morning, and pray that God would bless them in basket and store!

Bad as all slaveholders are, we seldom meet one destitute of every element of character commanding respect. My master was one of this rare sort. I do not know of one single noble act ever performed by him. The leading trait in his character was meanness; and if there were any other element in his nature, it was made subject to this. He was mean; and, like most other mean men, he lacked the ability to conceal his meanness. Captain Auld was not born a slaveholder. He had been a poor man, master only of a Bay craft. He came into possession of all his slaves by marriage; and of all men, adopted slaveholders are the worst. He was cruel, but cowardly. He commanded without firmness. In the enforcement of his rules, he was at times rigid, and at times lax. At times, he spoke to his slaves with the firmness of Napoleon and the fury of a demon; at other times, he might well be mistaken for an inquirer who had lost his way. He did nothing of himself. He might have passed for a lion, but for his ears. In all things noble which he attempted, his own meanness shone most conspicuous. His airs, words, and actions, were the airs, words, and actions of born slaveholders, and, being assumed, were awkward enough. He was not even a good imitator. He possessed all the disposition to deceive, but wanted the power. Having no resources within himself, he was compelled to be the copyist of many, and being such, he was forever the victim of inconsistency; and of consequence he was an object of contempt, and was held as such even by his slaves. The luxury of having slaves of his own to wait upon him was something new and unprepared for. He was a slaveholder without the ability to hold slaves. He found himself incapable of managing his slaves either by force, fear, or fraud. We seldom called him "master;" we generally called him "Captain Auld," and were hardly disposed to title him at all. I doubt not that our conduct had much to do with making him appear awkward, and of consequence fretful. Our want of reverence for him must have perplexed him greatly. He wished to have us call him master, but lacked the firmness necessary to command us to do so. His wife used to insist upon our calling him so, but to no purpose. In August, 1832, my master attended a Methodist camp-meeting held in the Bay-side, Talbot county, and there experienced religion. I indulged a faint hope that his conversion would lead him to emancipate his slaves, and that, if he did not do this, it would, at any rate, make him more kind and humane. I was disappointed in both these respects. It neither made him to be humane to his slaves, nor to emancipate them. If it had any effect on his character, it made him more cruel and hateful in all his ways; for I believe him to have been a much worse man after his conversion than before. Prior to his conversion, he relied upon his own depravity to shield and sustain him in his savage barbarity; but after his conversion, he found religious sanction and support for his slaveholding cruelty. He made the greatest pretensions to piety. His house was the house of prayer. He prayed morning, noon, and night. He very soon distinguished himself among his brethren, and was soon made a class-leader and exhorter. His activity in revivals was great, and he proved himself an instrument in the hands of the church in converting many souls. His house was the preachers' home. They used to take great pleasure in coming there to put up; for while he starved us, he stuffed them. We have had three or four preachers there at a time. The names of those who used to come most frequently while I lived there, were Mr. Storks, Mr. Ewery, Mr. Humphry, and Mr. Hickey. I have also seen Mr. George Cookman at our house. We slaves loved Mr. Cookman. We believed him to be a good man. We thought him instrumental in getting Mr. Samuel Harrison, a very rich slaveholder, to emancipate his slaves; and by some means got the impression that he was laboring to effect the emancipation of all the slaves. When he was at our house, we were sure to be called in to prayers. When the others were there, we were sometimes called in and sometimes not. Mr. Cookman took more notice of us than either of the other ministers. He could not come among us without betraying his sympathy for us, and, stupid as we were, we had the sagacity to see it.

While I lived with my master in St. Michael's, there was a white young man, a Mr. Wilson, who proposed to keep a Sabbath school for the instruction of such slaves as might be disposed to learn to read the New Testament. We met but three times, when Mr. West and Mr. Fairbanks, both class-leaders, with many others, came upon us with sticks and other missiles, drove us off, and forbade us to meet again. Thus ended our little Sabbath school in the pious town of St. Michael's.

I have said my master found religious sanction for his cruelty. As an example, I will state one of many facts going to prove the charge. I have seen him tie up a lame young woman, and whip her with a heavy cowskin upon her naked shoulders, causing the warm red blood to drip; and, in justification of the bloody deed, he would quote this passage of Scripture—"He that knoweth his master's will, and doeth it not, shall be beaten with many stripes."

Master would keep this lacerated young woman tied up in this horrid situation four or five hours at a time. I have known him to tie her up early in the morning, and whip her before breakfast; leave her, go to his store, return at dinner, and whip her again, cutting her in the places already made raw with his cruel lash. The secret of master's cruelty toward "Henny" is found in the fact of her being almost helpless. When quite a child, she fell into the fire, and burned herself horribly. Her hands were so burnt that she never got the use of them. She could do very little but bear heavy burdens. She was to master a bill of expense; and as he was a mean man, she was a constant offence to him. He seemed desirous of getting the poor girl out of existence. He gave her away once to his sister; but, being a poor gift, she was not disposed to keep her. Finally, my benevolent master, to use his own words, "set her adrift to take care of herself." Here was a recently-converted man, holding on upon the mother, and at the same time turning out her helpless child, to starve and die! Master Thomas was one of the many pious slaveholders who hold slaves for the very charitable purpose of taking care of them.

My master and myself had quite a number of differences. He found me unsuitable to his purpose. My city life, he said, had had a very pernicious effect upon me. It had almost ruined me for every good purpose, and fitted me for every thing which was bad. One of my greatest faults was that of letting his horse run away, and go down to his father-in-law's farm, which was about five miles from St. Michael's. I would then have to go after it. My reason for this kind of carelessness, or carefulness, was, that I could always get something to eat when I went there. Master William Hamilton, my master's father-in-law, always gave his slaves enough to eat. I never left there hungry, no matter how great the need of my speedy return. Master Thomas at length said he would stand it no longer. I had lived with him nine months, during which time he had given me a number of severe whippings, all to no good purpose. He resolved to put me out, as he said, to be broken; and, for this purpose, he let me for one year to a man named Edward Covey. Mr. Covey was a poor man, a farm-renter. He rented the place upon which he lived, as also the hands with which he tilled it. Mr. Covey had acquired a very high reputation for breaking young slaves, and this reputation was of immense value to him. It enabled him to get his farm tilled with much less expense to himself than he could have had it done without such a reputation. Some slaveholders thought it not much loss to allow Mr. Covey to have their slaves one year, for the sake of the training to which they were subjected, without any other compensation. He could hire young help with great ease, in consequence of this reputation. Added to the natural good qualities of Mr. Covey, he was a professor of religion—a pious soul—a member and a class-leader in the Methodist church. All of this added weight to his reputation as a "nigger-breaker." I was aware of all the facts, having been made acquainted with them by a young man who had lived there. I nevertheless made the change gladly; for I was sure of getting enough to eat, which is not the smallest consideration to a hungry man.

## CHAPTER X

I left Master Thomas's house, and went to live with Mr. Covey, on the 1st of January, 1833. I was now, for the first time in my life, a field hand. In my new employment, I found myself even more awkward than a country boy appeared to be in a large city. I had been at my new home but one week before Mr. Covey gave me a very severe whipping, cutting my back causing the blood to run, and raising ridges on my flesh as large as my little finger. The details of this affair are as follows: Mr. Covey sent me, very early in the morning of one of our coldest days in the month of January, to the woods, to get a load of wood. He gave me a team of unbroken oxen. He told me which was the in-hand ox, and which the off-hand one. He then tied the end of a large rope around the horns of the in-hand ox, and gave me the other end of it, and told me, if the oxen started to run, that I must hold on upon the rope. I had never driven oxen before, and of course I was very awkward. I, however, succeeded in getting to the edge of the woods with little difficulty; but I had got a very few rods into the woods, when the oxen took fright, and started full tilt, carrying the cart against trees, and over stumps, in the most frightful manner. I expected every moment that my brains would be dashed out against the trees. After running thus for a considerable distance, they finally upset the cart, dashing it with great force against a tree, and threw themselves into a dense thicket. How I escaped death, I do not know. There I was, entirely alone, in a thick wood, in a place new to me. My cart was upset and shattered, my oxen were entangled among the young trees, and there was none to help me. After a long spell of effort, I succeeded in getting my cart righted, my oxen disentangled, and again yoked to the cart. I now proceeded with my team to the place where I had, the day before, been chopping wood, and loaded my cart pretty heavily, thinking in this way to tame my oxen. I then proceeded on my way home. I had now consumed one half of the day. I got out of the woods safely, and now felt out of danger. I stopped my oxen to open the woods gate; and just as I did so, before I could get hold of my ox-rope, the oxen again started, rushed through the gate, catching it between the wheel and the body of the cart, tearing it to pieces, and coming within a few inches of crushing me against the gate-post. Thus twice, in one short day, I escaped death by the merest chance. On my return, I told Mr. Covey what had happened, and how it happened. He ordered me to return to the woods again immediately. I did so, and he followed on after me. Just as I got into the woods, he came up and told me to stop my cart, and that he would teach me how to trifle away my time, and break gates. He then went to a large gum-tree, and with his axe cut three large switches, and, after trimming them up neatly with his pocket-knife, he ordered me to take off my clothes. I made him no answer, but stood with my clothes on. He repeated his order. I still made him no answer, nor did I move to strip myself. Upon this he rushed at me with the fierceness of a tiger, tore off my clothes, and lashed me till he had worn out his switches, cutting me so savagely as to leave the marks visible for a long time after. This whipping was the first of a number just like it, and for similar offences.

I lived with Mr. Covey one year. During the first six months, of that year, scarce a week passed without his whipping me. I was seldom free from a sore back. My awkwardness was almost always his excuse for whipping me. We were worked fully up to the point of endurance. Long before day we were up, our horses fed, and by the first approach of day we were off to the field with our hoes and ploughing teams. Mr. Covey gave us enough to eat, but scarce time to eat it. We were often less than five minutes taking our meals. We were often in the field from the first approach of day till its last lingering ray had left us; and at saving-fodder time, midnight often caught us in the field binding blades.

Covey would be out with us. The way he used to stand it, was this. He would spend the most of his afternoons in bed. He would then come out fresh in the evening, ready to urge us on with his words, example, and frequently with the whip. Mr. Covey was one of the few slaveholders who could and did work with his hands. He was a hard-working man. He knew by himself just what a man or a boy could do. There was no deceiving him. His work went on in his absence almost as well as in his presence; and he had the faculty of making us feel that he was ever present with us. This he did by surprising us. He seldom approached the spot where we were at work openly, if he could do it secretly. He always aimed at taking us by surprise. Such was his cunning, that we used to call him, among ourselves, "the snake." When we were at work in the cornfield, he would sometimes crawl on his hands and knees to avoid detection, and all at once he would rise nearly in our midst, and scream out, "Ha, ha! Come, come! Dash on, dash on!" This being his mode of attack, it was never safe to stop a single minute. His comings were like a thief in the night. He appeared to us as being ever at hand. He was under every tree, behind every stump, in every bush, and at every window, on the plantation. He would sometimes mount his horse, as if bound to St. Michael's, a distance of seven miles, and in half an hour afterwards you would see him coiled up in the corner of the wood-fence, watching every motion of the slaves. He would, for this purpose, leave his horse tied up in the woods. Again, he would sometimes walk up to us, and give us orders as though he was upon the point of starting on a long journey, turn his back upon us, and make as though he was going to the house to get ready; and, before he would get half way thither, he would turn short and crawl into a fence-corner, or behind some tree, and there watch us till the going down of the sun.

Mr. Covey's *forte* consisted in his power to deceive. His life was devoted to planning and perpetrating the grossest deceptions. Every thing he possessed in the shape of learning or religion, he made conform to his disposition to deceive. He seemed to think himself equal to deceiving the Almighty. He would make a short prayer in the morning, and a long prayer at night; and, strange as it may seem, few men would at times appear more devotional than he. The exercises of his family devotions were always commenced with singing; and, as he was a very poor singer himself, the duty of raising the hymn generally came upon me. He would read his hymn, and nod at me to commence. I would at times do so; at others, I would not. My non-compliance would almost always produce much confusion. To show himself independent of me, he would start and stagger through with his hymn in the most discordant manner. In this state of mind, he prayed with more than ordinary spirit. Poor man! such was his disposition, and success at deceiving, I do verily believe that he sometimes deceived himself into the solemn belief, that he was a sincere worshipper of the most high God; and this, too, at a time when he may be said to have been guilty of compelling his woman slave to commit the sin of adultery. The facts in the case are these: Mr. Covey was a poor man; he was just commencing in life; he was only able to buy one slave; and, shocking as is the fact, he bought her, as he said, for *a breeder.* This woman was named Caroline. Mr. Covey bought her from Mr. Thomas Lowe, about six miles from St. Michael's. She was a large, able-bodied woman, about twenty years old. She had already given birth to one child, which proved her to be just what he wanted. After buying her, he hired a married man of Mr. Samuel Harrison, to live with him one year; and him he used to fasten up with her every night! The result was, that, at the end of the year, the miserable woman gave birth to twins. At this result Mr. Covey seemed to be highly pleased, both with the man and the wretched woman. Such was his joy, and that of his wife, that nothing they could do for Caroline during her confinement was too good, or too hard, to be done. The children were regarded as being quite an addition to his wealth.

If at any one time of my life more than another, I was made to drink the bitterest dregs of slavery, that time was during the first six months of my stay with Mr. Covey. We were worked in all weathers. It was never too hot or too cold; it could never rain, blow hail, or snow, too hard for us to work in the field. Work, work, work, was scarcely more the order of the day than of the night. The longest days were too short for him, and the shortest nights too long for him. I was somewhat unmanageable when I first went there, but a few months of this discipline tamed me. Mr. Covey succeeded in breaking me. I was broken in body, soul, and spirit. My natural elasticity was crushed, my intellect languished, the disposition to read departed, the cheerful spark that lingered about my eye died; the dark night of slavery closed in upon me; and behold a man transformed into a brute!

Sunday was my only leisure time. I spent this in a sort of beast-like stupor, between sleep and wake, under some large tree. At times I would rise up, a flash of energetic freedom would dart through my soul, accompanied with a faint beam of hope, that flickered for a moment, and then vanished. I sank down again, mourning over my wretched condition. I was sometimes prompted to take my life, and that of Covey, but was prevented by a combination of hope and fear. My sufferings on this plantation seem now like a dream rather than a stern reality.

Our house stood within a few rods of the Chesapeake Bay, whose broad bosom was ever white with sails from every quarter of the habitable globe. Those beautiful vessels, robed in purest white, so delightful to the eye of freemen, were to me so many shrouded ghosts, to terrify and torment me with thoughts of my wretched condition. I have often, in the deep stillness of a summer's Sabbath, stood all alone upon the lofty banks of that noble bay, and traced, with saddened heart and tearful eye, the countless number of sails moving off to the mighty ocean. The sight of these always affected me powerfully. My thoughts would compel utterance; and there, with no audience but the Almighty, I would pour out my soul's complaint, in my rude way, with an apostrophe to the moving multitude of ships:—

"You are loosed from your moorings, and are free; I am fast in my chains, and am a slave! You move merrily before the gentle gale, and I sadly before the bloody whip! You are freedom's swift-winged angels, that fly round the world; I am confined in bands of iron! O that I were free! O, that I were on one of your gallant decks, and under your protecting wing! Alas! betwixt me and you, the turbid waters roll. Go on, go on. O that I could also go! Could I but swim! If I could fly! O, why was I born a man, of whom to make a brute! The glad ship is gone; she hides in the dim distance. I am left in the hottest hell of unending slavery. O God, save me! God, deliver me! Let me be free! Is there any God? Why am I a slave? I will run away. I will not stand it. Get caught, or get clear, I'll try it. I had as well die with ague as the fever. I have only one life to lose. I had as well be killed running as die standing. Only think of it; one hundred miles straight north, and I am free! Try it? Yes! God helping me, I will. It cannot be that I shall live and die a slave. I will take to the water. This very bay shall yet bear me into freedom. The steamboats steered in a north-east course from North Point. I will do the same; and when I get to the head of the bay, I will turn my canoe adrift, and walk straight through Delaware into Pennsylvania. When I get there, I shall not be required to have a pass; I can travel without being disturbed. Let but the first opportunity offer, and, come what will, I am off. Meanwhile, I will try to bear up under the yoke. I am not the only slave in the world. Why should I fret? I can bear as much as any of them. Besides, I am but a boy, and all boys are bound to some one. It may be that my misery in slavery will only increase my happiness when I get free. There is a better day coming."

Thus I used to think, and thus I used to speak to myself; goaded almost to madness at one moment, and at the next reconciling myself to my wretched lot.

I have already intimated that my condition was much worse, during the first six months of my stay at Mr. Covey's, than in the last six. The circumstances leading to the change in Mr. Covey's course toward me form an epoch in my humble history. You have seen how a man was made a slave; you shall see how a slave was made a man. On one of the hottest days of the month of August, 1833, Bill Smith, William Hughes, a slave named Eli, and myself, were engaged in fanning wheat. Hughes was clearing the fanned wheat from before the fan, Eli was turning, Smith was feeding, and I was carrying wheat to the fan. The work was simple, requiring strength rather than intellect; yet, to one entirely unused to such work, it came very hard. About three o'clock of that day, I broke down; my strength failed me; I was seized with a violent aching of the head, attended with extreme dizziness; I trembled in every limb. Finding what was coming, I nerved myself up, feeling it would never do to stop work. I stood as long as I could stagger to the hopper with grain. When I could stand no longer, I fell, and felt as if held down by an immense weight. The fan of course stopped; every one had his own work to do; and no one could do the work of the other, and have his own go on at the same time.

Mr. Covey was at the house, about one hundred yards from the treading-yard where we were fanning. On hearing the fan stop, he left immediately, and came to the spot where we were. He hastily inquired what the matter was. Bill answered that I was sick, and there was no one to bring wheat to the fan. I had by this time crawled away under the side of the post and rail-fence by which the yard was enclosed, hoping to find relief by getting out of the sun. He then asked where I was. He was told by one of the hands. He came to the spot, and, after looking at me awhile, asked me what was the matter. I told him as well as I could, for I scarce had strength to speak. He then gave me a savage kick in the side, and told me to get up. I tried to do so, but fell back in the attempt. He gave me another kick, and again told me to rise. I again tried, and succeeded in gaining my feet; but, stooping to get the tub with which I was feeding the fan, I again staggered and fell. While down in this situation, Mr. Covey took up the hickory slat with which Hughes had been striking off the half-bushel measure, and with it gave me a heavy blow upon the head, making a large wound, and the blood ran freely; and with this again told me to get up. I made no effort to comply, having now made up my mind to let him do his worst. In a short time after receiving this blow, my head grew better. Mr. Covey had now left me to my fate. At this moment I resolved, for the first time, to go to my master, enter a complaint, and ask his protection. In order to [do] this, I must that afternoon walk seven miles; and this, under the circumstances, was truly a severe undertaking. I was exceedingly feeble; made so as much by the kicks and blows which I received, as by the severe fit of sickness to which I had been subjected. I, however, watched my chance, while Covey was looking in an opposite direction, and started for St. Michael's. I succeeded in getting a considerable distance on my way to the woods, when Covey discovered me, and called after me to come back, threatening what he would do if I did not come. I disregarded both his calls and his threats, and made my way to the woods as fast as my feeble state would allow; and thinking I might be overhauled by him if I kept the road, I walked through the woods, keeping far enough from the road to avoid detection, and near enough to prevent losing my way I had not gone far before my little strength again failed me. I could go no farther. I fell down, and lay for a considerable time. The blood was yet oozing from the wound on my head. For a time I thought I should bleed to death; and think now that I should have done so, but that the blood so matted my hair as to stop the wound. After lying there about three quarters of an hour, I nerved myself up again, and started on my way, through bogs and briers, barefooted and bareheaded, tearing my feet sometimes at nearly every step; and after a journey of about seven miles, occupying some five hours to perform it, I arrived at master's store. I then presented an appearance enough to affect any but a heart of iron. From the crown of my head to my feet, I was covered with blood. My hair was all clotted with dust and blood; my shirt was stiff with blood. My legs and feet were torn in sundry places with briers and thorns, and were also covered with blood. I suppose I looked like a man who had escaped a den of wild beasts, and barely escaped them. In this state I appeared before my master, humbly entreating him to interpose his authority for my protection. I told him all the circumstances as well as I could, and it seemed, as I spoke, at times to affect him. He would then walk the floor, and seek to justify Covey by saying he expected I deserved it. He asked me what I wanted. I told him, to let me get a new home; that as sure as I lived with Mr. Covey again, I should live with but to die with him; that Covey would surely kill me; he was in a fair way for it. Master Thomas ridiculed the idea that there was any danger of Mr. Covey's killing me, and said that he knew Mr. Covey; that he was a good man, and that he could not think of taking me from him; that, should he do so, he would lose the whole year's wages; that I belonged to Mr. Covey for one year, and that I must go back to him, come what might; and that I must not trouble him with any more stories, or that he would himself *get hold of me.* After threatening me thus, he gave me a very large dose of salts, telling me that I might remain in St. Michael's that night, (it being quite late,) but that I must be off back to Mr. Covey's early in the morning; and that if I did not, he would *get hold of me,* which meant that he would whip me. I remained all night, and, according to his orders, I started off to Covey's in the morning, (Saturday morning,) wearied in body and broken in spirit. I got no supper that night, or breakfast that morning. I reached Covey's about nine o'clock; and just as I was getting over the fence that divided Mrs. Kemp's fields from ours, out ran Covey with his cowskin, to give me another whipping. Before he could reach me, I succeeded in getting to the cornfield; and as the corn was very high, it afforded me the means of hiding. He seemed very angry, and searched for me a long time. My behavior was altogether unaccountable. He finally gave up the chase, thinking, I suppose, that I must come home for something to eat; he would give himself no further trouble in looking for me. I spent that day mostly in the woods, having the alternative before me,—to go home and be whipped to death, or stay in the woods and be starved to death. That night, I fell in with Sandy Jenkins, a slave with whom I was somewhat acquainted. Sandy had a free wife who lived about four miles from Mr. Covey's; and it being Saturday, he was on his way to see her. I told him my circumstances, and he very kindly invited me to go home with him. I went home with him, and talked this whole matter over, and got his advice as to what course it was best for me to pursue. I found Sandy an old adviser. He told me, with great solemnity, I must go back to Covey; but that before I went, I must go with him into another part of the woods, where there was a certain *root,* which, if I would take some of it with me, carrying it *always on my right side,* would render it impossible for Mr. Covey, or any other white man, to whip me. He said he had carried it for years; and since he had done so, he had never received a blow, and never expected to while he carried it. I at first rejected the idea, that the simple carrying of a root in my pocket would have any such effect as he had said, and was not disposed to take it; but Sandy impressed the necessity with much earnestness, telling me it could do no harm, if it did no good. To please him, I at length took the root, and, according to his direction, carried it upon my right side. This was Sunday morning. I immediately started for home; and upon entering the yard gate, out came Mr. Covey on his way to meeting. He spoke to me very kindly, made me drive the pigs from a lot near by, and passed on towards the church. Now, this singular conduct of Mr. Covey really made me begin to think that there was something in the *root* which Sandy had given me; and had it been on any other day than Sunday, I could have attributed the conduct to no other cause than the influence of that root; and as it was, I was half inclined to think the *root* to be something more than I at first had taken it to be. All went well till Monday morning. On this morning, the virtue of the *root* was fully tested. Long before daylight, I was called to go and rub, curry, and feed, the horses. I obeyed, and was glad to obey. But whilst thus engaged, whilst in the act of throwing down some blades from the loft, Mr. Covey entered the stable with a long rope; and just as I was half out of the loft, he caught hold of my legs, and was about tying me. As soon as I found what he was up to, I gave a sudden spring, and as I did so, he holding to my legs, I was brought sprawling on the stable floor. Mr. Covey seemed now to think he had me, and could do what he pleased; but at this moment—from whence came the spirit I don't know—I resolved to fight; and, suiting my action to the resolution, I seized Covey hard by the throat; and as I did so, I rose. He held on to me, and I to him. My resistance was so entirely unexpected, that Covey seemed taken all aback. He trembled like a leaf. This gave me assurance, and I held him uneasy, causing the blood to run where I touched him with the ends of my fingers. Mr. Covey soon called out to Hughes for help. Hughes came, and, while Covey held me, attempted to tie my right hand. While he was in the act of doing so, I watched my chance, and gave him a heavy kick close under the ribs. This kick fairly sickened Hughes, so that he left me in the hands of Mr. Covey. This kick had the effect of not only weakening Hughes, but Covey also. When he saw Hughes bending over with pain, his courage quailed. He asked me if I meant to persist in my resistance. I told him I did, come what might; that he had used me like a brute for six months, and that I was determined to be used so no longer. With that, he strove to drag me to a stick that was lying just out of the stable door. He meant to knock me down. But just as he was leaning over to get the stick, I seized him with both hands by his collar, and brought him by a sudden snatch to the ground. By this time, Bill came. Covey called upon him for assistance. Bill wanted to know what he could do. Covey said, "Take hold of him, take hold of him!" Bill said his master hired him out to work, and not to help to whip me; so he left Covey and myself to fight our own battle out. We were at it for nearly two hours. Covey at length let me go, puffing and blowing at a great rate, saying that if I had not resisted, he would not have whipped me half so much. The truth was, that he had not whipped me at all. I considered him as getting entirely the worst end of the bargain; for he had drawn no blood from me, but I had from him. The whole six months afterwards, that I spent with Mr. Covey, he never laid the weight of his finger upon me in anger. He would occasionally say, he didn't want to get hold of me again. "No," thought I, "you need not; for you will come off worse than you did before."

This battle with Mr. Covey was the turning-point in my career as a slave. It rekindled the few expiring embers of freedom, and revived within me a sense of my own manhood. It recalled the departed self-confidence, and inspired me again with a determination to be free. The gratification afforded by the triumph was a full compensation for whatever else might follow, even death itself. He only can understand the deep satisfaction which I experienced, who has himself repelled by force the bloody arm of slavery. I felt as I never felt before. It was a glorious resurrection, from the tomb of slavery, to the heaven of freedom. My long-crushed spirit rose, cowardice departed, bold defiance took its place; and I now resolved that, however long I might remain a slave in form, the day had passed forever when I could be a slave in fact. I did not hesitate to let it be known of me, that the white man who expected to succeed in whipping, must also succeed in killing me

From this time I was never again what might be called fairly whipped, though I remained a slave four years afterwards. I had several fights, but was never whipped.

It was for a long time a matter of surprise to me why Mr. Covey did not immediately have me taken by the constable to the whipping-post, and there regularly whipped for the crime of raising my hand against a white man in defence of myself. And the only explanation I can now think of does not entirely satisfy me; but such as it is, I will give it. Mr. Covey enjoyed the most unbounded reputation for being a first-rate overseer and negro-breaker. It was of considerable importance to him. That reputation was at stake; and had he sent me—a boy about sixteen years old—to the public whipping-post, his reputation would have been lost; so, to save his reputation, he suffered me to go unpunished.

My term of actual service to Mr. Edward Covey ended on Christmas day, 1833. The days between Christmas and New Year's day are allowed as holidays; and, accordingly, we were not required to perform any labor, more than to feed and take care of the stock. This time we regarded as our own, by the grace of our masters; and we therefore used or abused it nearly as we pleased. Those of us who had families at a distance, were generally allowed to spend the whole six days in their society. This time, however, was spent in various ways. The staid, sober, thinking and industrious ones of our number would employ themselves in making corn-brooms, mats, horse-collars, and baskets; and another class of us would spend the time in hunting opossums, hares, and coons. But by far the larger part engaged in such sports and merriments as playing ball, wrestling, running foot-races, fiddling, dancing, and drinking whisky; and this latter mode of spending the time was by far the most agreeable to the feelings of our masters. A slave who would work during the holidays was considered by our masters as scarcely deserving them. He was regarded as one who rejected the favor of his master. It was deemed a disgrace not to get drunk at Christmas; and he was regarded as lazy indeed, who had not provided himself with the necessary means, during the year, to get whisky enough to last him through Christmas.

From what I know of the effect of these holidays upon the slave, I believe them to be among the most effective means in the hands of the slaveholder in keeping down the spirit of insurrection. Were the slaveholders at once to abandon this practice, I have not the slightest doubt it would lead to an immediate insurrection among the slaves. These holidays serve as conductors, or safety-valves, to carry off the rebellious spirit of enslaved humanity. But for these, the slave would be forced up to the wildest desperation; and woe betide the slaveholder, the day he ventures to remove or hinder the operation of those conductors! I warn him that, in such an event, a spirit will go forth in their midst, more to be dreaded than the most appalling earthquake.

The holidays are part and parcel of the gross fraud, wrong, and inhumanity of slavery. They are professedly a custom established by the benevolence of the slave-holders; but I undertake to say, it is the result of selfishness, and one of the grossest frauds committed upon the down-trodden slave. They do not give the slaves this time because they would not like to have their work during its continuance, but because they know it would be unsafe to deprive them of it. This will be seen by the fact, that the slaveholders like to have their slaves spend those days just in such a manner as to make them as glad of their ending as of their beginning. Their object seems to be, to disgust their slaves with freedom, by plunging them into the lowest depths of dissipation. For instance, the slaveholders not only like to see the slave drink of his own accord, but will adopt various plans to make him drunk. One plan is, to make bets on their slaves, as to who can drink the most whisky without getting drunk; and in this way they succeed in getting whole multitudes to drink to excess. Thus, when the slave asks for virtuous freedom, the cunning slaveholder, knowing his ignorance, cheats him with a dose of vicious dissipation, artfully labelled with the name of liberty. The most of us used to drink it down, and the result was just what might be supposed: many of us were led to think that there was little to choose between liberty and slavery. We felt, and very properly too, that we had almost as well be slaves to man as to rum. So, when the holidays ended, we staggered up from the filth of our wallowing, took a long breath, and marched to the field,—feeling, upon the whole, rather glad to go, from what our master had deceived us into a belief was freedom, back to the arms of slavery.

I have said that this mode of treatment is a part of the whole system of fraud and inhumanity of slavery. It is so. The mode here adopted to disgust the slave with freedom, by allowing him to see only the abuse of it, is carried out in other things. For instance, a slave loves molasses; he steals some. His master, in many cases, goes off to town, and buys a large quantity; he returns, takes his whip, and commands the slave to eat the molasses, until the poor fellow is made sick at the very mention of it. The same mode is sometimes adopted to make the slaves refrain from asking for more food than their regular allowance. A slave runs through his allowance, and applies for more. His master is enraged at him; but, not willing to send him off without food, gives him more than is necessary, and compels him to eat it within a given time. Then, if he complains that he cannot eat it, he is said to be satisfied neither full or fasting, and is whipped for being hard to please! I have an abundance of such illustrations of the same principle, drawn from my own observation, but think the cases I have cited sufficient. The practice is a very common one.

On the first of January, 1834, I left Mr. Covey, and went to live with Mr. William Freeland, who lived about three miles from St. Michael's. I soon found Mr. Freeland a very different man from Mr. Covey. Though not rich, he was what would be called an educated southern gentleman. Mr. Covey, as I have shown, was a well-trained negro-breaker and slavedriver. The former (slaveholder though he was) seemed to possess some regard for honor, some reverence for justice, and some respect for humanity. The latter seemed totally insensible to all such sentiments. Mr. Freeland had many of the faults peculiar to slaveholders, such as being very passionate and fretful; but I must do him the justice to say, that he was exceedingly free from those degrading vices to which Mr. Covey was constantly addicted. The one was open and frank, and we always knew where to find him. The other was a most artful deceiver, and could be understood only by such as were skilful enough to detect his cunningly-devised frauds. Another advantage I gained in my new master was, he made no pretensions to, or profession of, religion; and this, in my opinion, was truly a great advantage. I assert most unhesitatingly, that the religion of the south is a mere covering for the most horrid crimes,—a justifier of the most appalling barbarity,—a sanctifier of the most hateful frauds,—and a dark shelter under, which the darkest, foulest, grossest, and most infernal deeds of slaveholders find the strongest protection. Were I to be again reduced to the chains of slavery, next to that enslavement, I should regard being the slave of a religious master the greatest calamity that could befall me. For of all slaveholders with whom I have ever met, religious slaveholders are the worst. I have ever found them the meanest and basest, the most cruel and cowardly, of all others. It was my unhappy lot not only to belong to a religious slaveholder, but to live in a community of such religionists. Very near Mr. Freeland lived the Rev. Daniel Weeden, and in the same neighborhood lived the Rev. Rigby Hopkins. These were members and ministers in the Reformed Methodist Church. Mr. Weeden owned, among others, a woman slave, whose name I have forgotten. This woman's back, for weeks, was kept literally raw, made so by the lash of this merciless, *religious* wretch. He used to hire hands. His maxim was, Behave well or behave ill, it is the duty of a master occasionally to whip a slave, to remind him of his master's authority. Such was his theory, and such his practice.

Mr. Hopkins was even worse than Mr. Weeden. His chief boast was his ability to manage slaves. The peculiar feature of his government was that of whipping slaves in advance of deserving it. He always managed to have one or more of his slaves to whip every Monday morning. He did this to alarm their fears, and strike terror into those who escaped. His plan was to whip for the smallest offences, to prevent the commission of large ones. Mr. Hopkins could always find some excuse for whipping a slave. It would astonish one, unaccustomed to a slaveholding life, to see with what wonderful ease a slaveholder can find things, of which to make occasion to whip a slave. A mere look, word, or motion,—a mistake, accident, or want of power,—are all matters for which a slave may be whipped at any time. Does a slave look dissatisfied? It is said, he has the devil in him, and it must be whipped out. Does he speak loudly when spoken to by his master? Then he is getting high-minded, and should be taken down a button-hole lower. Does he forget to pull off his hat at the approach of a white person? Then he is wanting in reverence, and should be whipped for it. Does he ever venture to vindicate his conduct, when censured for it? Then he is guilty of impudence,—one of the greatest crimes of which a slave can be guilty. Does he ever venture to suggest a different mode of doing things from that pointed out by his master? He is indeed presumptuous, and getting above himself; and nothing less than a flogging will do for him. Does he, while ploughing, break a plough,—or, while hoeing, break a hoe? It is owing to his carelessness, and for it a slave must always be whipped. Mr. Hopkins could always find something of this sort to justify the use of the lash, and he seldom failed to embrace such opportunities. There was not a man in the whole county, with whom the slaves who had the getting their own home, would not prefer to live, rather than with this Rev. Mr. Hopkins. And yet there was not a man any where round, who made higher professions of religion, or was more active in revivals,—more attentive to the class, love-feast, prayer and preaching meetings, or more devotional in his family,—that prayed earlier, later, louder, and longer,—than this same reverend slave-driver, Rigby Hopkins.

But to return to Mr. Freeland, and to my experience while in his employment. He, like Mr. Covey, gave us enough to eat; but, unlike Mr. Covey, he also gave us sufficient time to take our meals. He worked us hard, but always between sunrise and sunset. He required a good deal of work to be done, but gave us good tools with which to work. His farm was large, but he employed hands enough to work it, and with ease, compared with many of his neighbors. My treatment, while in his employment, was heavenly, compared with what I experienced at the hands of Mr. Edward Covey.

Mr. Freeland was himself the owner of but two slaves. Their names were Henry Harris and John Harris. The rest of his hands he hired. These consisted of myself,

Sandy Jenkins,* and Handy Caldwell. Henry and John were quite intelligent, and in a very little while after I went there, I succeeded in creating in them a strong desire to learn how to read. This desire soon sprang up in the others also. They very soon mustered up some old spelling-books, and nothing would do but that I must keep a Sabbath school. I agreed to do so, and accordingly devoted my Sundays to teaching these my loved fellow-slaves how to read. Neither of them knew his letters when I went there. Some of the slaves of the neighboring farms found what was going on, and also availed themselves of this little opportunity to learn to read. It was understood, among all who came, that there must be as little display about it as possible. It was necessary to keep our religious masters at St. Michael's unacquainted with the fact, that, instead of spending the Sabbath in wrestling, boxing, and drinking whisky, we were trying to learn how to read the will of God; for they had much rather see us engaged in those degrading sports, than to see us behaving like intellectual, moral, and accountable beings. My blood boils as I think of the bloody manner in which Messrs. Wright Fairbanks and Garrison West, both class-leaders, in connection with many others, rushed in upon us with sticks and stones, and broke up our virtuous little Sabbath school, at St. Michael's—all calling themselves Christians! humble followers of the Lord Jesus Christ! But I am again digressing.

I held my Sabbath school at the house of a free colored man, whose name I deem it imprudent to

*This is the same man who gave me the roots to prevent my being whipped by Mr. Covey. He was "a clever soul." We used frequently to talk about the fight with Covey, and as often as we did so, he would claim my success as the result of the roots which he gave me. This superstition is very common among the more ignorant slaves. A slave seldom dies but that his death is attributed to trickery.

mention; for should it be known, it might embarrass him greatly, though the crime of holding the school was committed ten years ago. I had at one time over forty scholars, and those of the right sort, ardently desiring to learn. They were of all ages, though mostly men and women. I look back to those Sundays with an amount of pleasure not to be expressed. They were great days to my soul. The work of instructing my dear fellow-slaves was the sweetest engagement with which I was ever blessed. We loved each other, and to leave them at the close of the Sabbath was a severe cross indeed. When I think that these precious souls are to-day shut up in the prison-house of slavery, my feelings overcome me, and I am almost ready to ask, "Does a righteous God govern the universe? and for what does he hold the thunders in his right hand, if not to smite the oppressor, and deliver the spoiled out of the hand of the spoiler?" These dear souls came not to Sabbath school because it was popular to do so, nor did I teach them because it was reputable to be thus engaged. Every moment they spent in that school, they were liable to be taken up, and given thirty-nine lashes. They came because they wished to learn. Their minds had been starved by their cruel masters. They had been shut up in mental darkness. I taught them, because it was the delight of my soul to be doing something that looked like bettering the condition of my race. I kept up my school nearly the whole year I lived with Mr. Freeland; and, beside my Sabbath school, I devoted three evenings in the week, during the winter, to teaching the slaves at home. And I have the happiness to know, that several of those who came to Sabbath school learned how to read; and that one, at least, is now free through my agency.

The year passed off smoothly. It seemed only about half as long as the year which preceded it. I went through it without receiving a single blow. I will give Mr.

Freeland the credit of being the best master I ever had, *till I became my own master.* For the ease with which I passed the year, I was, however, somewhat indebted to the society of my fellow-slaves. They were noble souls; they not only possessed loving hearts, but brave ones. We were linked and interlinked with each other. I loved them with a love stronger than any thing I have experienced since. It is sometimes said that we slaves do not love and confide in each other. In answer to this assertion, I can say, I never loved any or confided in any people more than my fellow-slaves, and especially those with whom I lived at Mr. Freeland's. I believe we would have died for each other. We never undertook to do any thing, of any importance, without a mutual consultation. We never moved separately. We were one; and as much so by our tempers and dispositions, as by the mutual hardships to which we were necessarily subjected by our condition as slaves.

At the close of the year 1834, Mr. Freeland again hired me of my master, for the year 1835. But, by this time, I began to want to live *upon free land* as well as *with Freeland;* and I was no longer content, therefore, to live with him or any other slaveholder. I began, with the commencement of the year, to prepare myself for a final struggle, which should decide my fate one way or the other. My tendency was upward. I was fast approaching manhood, and year after year had passed, and I was still a slave. These thoughts roused me—I must do something. I therefore resolved that 1835 should not pass without witnessing an attempt, on my part, to secure my liberty. But I was not willing to cherish this determination alone. My fellow-slaves were dear to me. I was anxious to have them participate with me in this, my life-giving determination. I therefore, though with great prudence, commenced early to ascertain their views and feelings in regard to their condition, and to imbue their minds with thoughts of freedom. I bent myself to devising ways and means for our escape, and meanwhile strove, on all fitting occasions, to impress them with the gross fraud and inhumanity of slavery. I went first to Henry, next to John, then to the others. I found, in them all, warm hearts and noble spirits. They were ready to hear, and ready to act when a feasible plan should be proposed. This was what I wanted. I talked to them of our want of manhood, if we submitted to our enslavement without at least one noble effort to be free. We met often, and consulted frequently, and told our hopes and fears, recounted the difficulties, real and imagined, which we should be called on to meet. At times we were almost disposed to give up, and try to content ourselves with our wretched lot; at others, we were firm and unbending in our determination to go. Whenever we suggested any plan, there was shrinking—the odds were fearful. Our path was beset with the greatest obstacles; and if we succeeded in gaining the end of it, our right to be free was yet questionable—we were yet liable to be returned to bondage. We could see no spot this side of the ocean, where we could be free. We knew nothing about Canada. Our knowledge of the north did not extend farther than New York; and to go there, and be forever harassed with the frightful liability of being returned to slavery—with the certainty of being treated tenfold worse than before—the thought was truly a horrible one, and one which it was not easy to overcome. The case sometimes stood thus: At every gate through which we were to pass, we saw a watchman—at every ferry a guard—on every bridge a sentinel—and in every wood a patrol. We were hemmed in upon every side. Here were the difficulties, real or imagined—the good to be sought, and the evil to be shunned. On the one hand, there stood slavery, a stern reality, glaring frightfully upon us,—its robes already crimsoned with the blood of millions, and even now feasting itself greedily upon our own flesh. On the other hand, away back in the dim distance, under the flickering light of the north star, behind some craggy hill or snow-covered mountain, stood a doubtful freedom—half frozen—beckoning us to come and share its hospitality. This in itself was sometimes enough to stagger us; but when we permitted ourselves to survey the road, we were frequently appalled. Upon either side we saw grim death, assuming the most horrid shapes. Now it was starvation, causing us to eat our own flesh;—now we were contending with the waves, and were drowned;—now we were overtaken, and torn to pieces by the fangs of the terrible bloodhound. We were stung by scorpions, chased by wild beasts, bitten by snakes, and finally, after having nearly reached the desired spot,—after swimming rivers, encountering wild beasts, sleeping in the woods, suffering hunger and nakedness,—we were overtaken by our pursuers, and, in our resistance, we were shot dead upon the spot! I say, this picture sometimes appalled us, and made us

> "rather bear those ills we had,
> Than fly to others, that we knew not of."

In coming to a fixed determination to run away, we did more than Patrick Henry, when he resolved upon liberty or death. With us it was a doubtful liberty at most, and almost certain death if we failed. For my part, I should prefer death to hopeless bondage.

Sandy, one of our number, gave up the notion, but still encouraged us. Our company then consisted of Henry Harris, John Harris, Henry Bailey, Charles Roberts, and myself. Henry Bailey was my uncle, and belonged to my master. Charles married my aunt: he belonged to my master's father-in-law, Mr. William Hamilton.

The plan we finally concluded upon was, to get a large canoe belonging to Mr. Hamilton, and upon the Saturday night previous to Easter holidays, paddle directly up the Chesapeake Bay. On our arrival at the head of the bay, a distance of seventy or eighty miles from where we lived, it was our purpose to turn our canoe adrift, and follow the guidance of the north star till we got beyond the limits of Maryland. Our reason for taking the water route was, that we were less liable to be suspected as runaways; we hoped to be regarded as fishermen; whereas, if we should take the land route, we should be subjected to interruptions of almost every kind. Any one having a white face, and being so disposed, could stop us, and subject us to examination.

The week before our intended start, I wrote several protections, one for each of us. As well as I can remember, they were in the following words, to wit:—

"THIS is to certify that I, the undersigned, have given the bearer, my servant, full liberty to go to Baltimore, and spend the Easter holidays. Written with mine own hand, &c., 1835.

"WILLIAM HAMILTON,

"Near St. Michael's, in Talbot county, Maryland."

We were not going to Baltimore; but, in going up the bay, we went toward Baltimore, and these protections were only intended to protect us while on the bay.

As the time drew near for our departure, our anxiety became more and more intense. It was truly a matter of life and death with us. The strength of our determination was about to be fully tested. At this time, I was very active in explaining every difficulty, removing every doubt, dispelling every fear, and inspiring all with the firmness indispensable to success in our undertaking; assuring them that half was gained the instant we made the move; we had talked long enough; we were now ready to move; if not now, we never should be; and if we did not intend to move now, we had as well fold our arms, sit down, and acknowledge ourselves fit only to be slaves. This, none of us were prepared to acknowledge. Every man stood firm; and at our last meeting, we pledged ourselves afresh, in the most solemn manner, that, at the time appointed, we would certainly start in pursuit of freedom. This was in the middle of the week, at the end of which we were to be off. We went, as usual, to our several fields of labor, but with bosoms highly agitated with thoughts of our truly hazardous undertaking. We tried to conceal our feelings as much as possible; and I think we succeeded very well.

After a painful waiting, the Saturday morning, whose night was to witness our departure, came. I hailed it with joy, bring what of sadness it might. Friday night was a sleepless one for me. I probably felt more anxious than the rest, because I was, by common consent, at the head of the whole affair. The responsibility of success or failure lay heavily upon me. The glory of the one, and the confusion of the other, were alike mine. The first two hours of that morning were such as I never experienced before, and hope never to again. Early in the morning, we went, as usual, to the field. We were spreading manure: and all at once, while thus engaged, I was overwhelmed with an indescribable feeling, in the fulness of which I turned to Sandy, who was near by, and said, "We are betrayed!" "Well," said he, "that thought has this moment struck me." We said no more. I was never more certain of any thing.

The horn was blown as usual, and we went up from the field to the house for breakfast. I went for the form, more than for want of any thing to eat that morning. Just as I got to the house, in looking out at the lane gate, I saw four white men, with two colored men. The white men were on horseback, and the colored ones were walking behind, as if tied. I watched them a few moments till they got up to our lane gate. Here they halted, and tied the colored men to the gate-post. I was not yet certain as to what the matter was. In a few moments, in rode Mr. Hamilton, with a speed betokening great excitement. He came to the door, and inquired if Master William was in. He was told he was at the barn. Mr. Hamilton, without dismounting, rode up to the barn with extraordinary speed. In a few moments, he and Mr. Freeland returned to the house. By this time, the three constables rode up, and in great haste dismounted, tied their horses, and met Master William and Mr. Hamilton returning from the barn; and after talking awhile, they all walked up to the kitchen door. There was no one in the kitchen but myself and John. Henry and Sandy were up at the barn. Mr. Freeland put his head in at the door, and called me by name, saying, there were some gentlemen at the door who wished to see me. I stepped to the door, and inquired what they wanted. They at once seized me, and, without giving me any satisfaction, tied me—lashing my hands closely together. I insisted upon knowing what the matter was. They at length said, that they had learned I had been in a "scrape," and that I was to be examined before my master; and if their information proved false, I should not be hurt.

In a few moments, they succeeded in tying John. They then turned to Henry, who had by this time returned, and commanded him to cross his hands. "I won't!" said Henry, in a firm tone, indicating his readiness to meet the consequences of his refusal. "Won't you?" said Tom Graham, the constable. "No. I won't!" said Henry, in a still stronger tone. With this, two of the constables pulled out their shining pistols, and swore, by their Creator, that they would make him cross his hands or kill him. Each cocked his pistol, and, with fingers on the trigger, walked up to Henry, saying, at the same time, if he did not cross his hands, they would blow his damned heart out. "Shoot me! shoot me!" said Henry; "you can't kill me but once. Shoot, shoot,—and be damned! *I won't be tied!*" This he said in a tone of loud defiance; and at the same time, with a motion as quick as lightning, he with one single stroke dashed the pistols from the hand of each constable. As he did this, all hands fell upon him, and, after beating him some time, they finally overpowered him, and got him tied.

During the scuffle, I managed, I know not how, to get my pass out, and, without being discovered, put it into the fire. We were all now tied; and just as we were to leave for Easton jail, Betsy Freeland, mother of William Freeland, came to the door with her hands full of biscuits, and divided them between Henry and John. She then delivered herself of a speech, to the following effect:—addressing herself to me, she said, *"You devil! You yellow devil!* it was you that put it into the heads of Henry and John to run away. But for you, you long-legged mulatto devil! Henry nor John would never have thought of such a thing." I made no reply, and was immediately hurried off towards St. Michael's. Just a moment previous to the scuffle with Henry, Mr. Hamilton suggested the propriety of making a search for the protections which he had understood Frederick had written for himself and the rest. But, just at the moment he was about carrying his proposal into effect, his aid was needed in helping to tie Henry; and the excitement attending the scuffle caused them either to forget, or to deem it unsafe, under the circumstances, to search. So we were not yet convicted of the intention to run away.

When we got about half way to St. Michael's, while the constables having us in charge were looking ahead, Henry inquired of me what he should do with his pass. I told him to eat it with his biscuit, and own nothing; and we passed the word around, *"Own nothing;"* and *"Own nothing!"* said we all. Our confidence in each other was unshaken. We were resolved to succeed or fail together, after the calamity had befallen us as much as before. We were now prepared for any thing. We were to be dragged that morning fifteen miles behind horses, and then to be placed in the Easton jail. When we reached St. Michael's, we underwent a sort of examination. We all denied that we ever intended to run away. We did this more to bring out the evidence against us, than from any hope of getting clear of being sold; for, as I have said, we were ready for that. The fact was, we cared but little where we went, so we went together. Our greatest concern was about separation. We dreaded that more than any thing this side of death. We found the evidence against us to be the testimony of one person; our master would not tell who it was; but we came to a unanimous decision among ourselves as to who their informant was. We were sent off to the jail at Easton. When we got there, we were delivered up to the sheriff, Mr. Joseph Graham, and by him placed in jail. Henry, John, and myself, were placed in one room together—Charles, and Henry Bailey, in another. Their object in separating us was to hinder concert.

We had been in jail scarcely twenty minutes, when a swarm of slave traders, and agents for slave traders, flocked into jail to look at us, and to ascertain if we were for sale. Such a set of beings I never saw before! I felt myself surrounded by so many fiends from perdition. A band of pirates never looked more like their father, the devil. They laughed and grinned over us, saying, "Ah, my boys! we have got you, haven't we." And after taunting us in various ways, they one by one went into an examination of us, with intent to ascertain our value. They would impudently ask us if we would not like to have them for our masters. We would make them no answer, and leave them to find out as best they could. Then they would curse and swear at us, telling us that they could take the devil out of us in a very little while, if we were only in their hands.

While in jail, we found ourselves in much more comfortable quarters than we expected when we went there. We did not get much to eat, nor that which was very good; but we had a good clean room, from the windows of which we could see what was going on in the street, which was very much better than though we had been placed in one of the dark, damp cells. Upon the whole, we got along very well, so far as the jail and its keeper were concerned. Immediately after the holidays were over, contrary to all our expectations, Mr. Hamilton and Mr. Freeland came up to Easton, and took Charles, the two Henrys, and John, out of jail, and carried them home, leaving me alone. I regarded this separation as a final one. It caused me more pain than any thing else in the whole transaction. I was ready for any thing rather than separation. I supposed that they had consulted together, and had decided that, as I was the whole cause of the intention of the others to run away, it was hard to make the innocent suffer with the guilty; and that they had, therefore, concluded to take the others home, and sell me, as a warning to the others that remained. It is due to the noble Henry to say, he seemed almost as reluctant at leaving the prison as at leaving home to come to the prison. But we knew we should, in all probability, be separated, if we were sold; and since he was in their hands, he concluded to go peaceably home.

I was now left to my fate. I was all alone, and within the walls of a stone prison. But a few days before, and I was full of hope. I expected to have been safe in a land of freedom; but now I was covered with gloom, sunk down to the utmost despair. I thought the possibility of freedom was gone. I was kept in this way about one week, at the end of which, Captain Auld, my master, to my surprise and utter astonishment, came up, and took me out, with the intention of sending me, with a gentleman of his acquaintance, into Alabama. But, from some cause or other, he did not send me to Alabama, but concluded to send me back to Baltimore, to live again with his brother Hugh, and to learn a trade.

Thus, after an absence of three years and one month, I was once more permitted to return to my old home at Baltimore. My master sent me away, because there existed against me a very great prejudice in the community, and he feared I might be killed.

In a few weeks after I went to Baltimore, Master Hugh hired me to Mr. William Gardner, an extensive ship-builder, on Fell's Point. I was put there to learn how to calk. It, however, proved a very unfavorable place for the accomplishment of this object. Mr. Gardner was engaged that spring in building two large man-of-war brigs, professedly for the Mexican government. The vessels were to be launched in the July of that year, and in failure thereof, Mr. Gardner was to lose a considerable sum; so that when I entered, all was hurry. There was no time to learn any thing. Every man had to do that which he knew how to do. In entering the ship-yard, my orders from Mr. Gardner were, to do whatever the carpenters commanded me to do. This was placing me at the beck and call of about seventy-five men. I was to regard all these as masters. Their word was to be my law. My situation was a most trying one. At times I needed a dozen pair of hands. I was called a dozen ways in the space of a single minute. Three or four voices would strike my ear at the same moment. It was—"Fred., come help me to cant this timber here."—"Fred., come carry this timber yonder."—"Fred., bring that roller here."—"Fred., go get a fresh can of water."—"Fred., come help saw off the end of this timber."—"Fred., go quick, and get the crowbar."—"Fred., hold on the end of this fall."—"Fred., go to the blacksmith's shop, and get a new punch."—"Hurra, Fred! run and bring me a cold chisel."—"I say, Fred., bear a hand, and get up a fire as quick as lightning under that steam-box."—"Halloo, nigger! come, turn this grindstone."—"Come, come! move, move! and *bowse* this timber forward."—"I say, darky, blast your eyes, why don't you heat up some pitch?"—"Halloo! halloo! halloo! (Three voices at the same time.) "Come here!—Go there!—Hold on where you are! Damn you, if you move, I'll knock your brains out!"

This was my school for eight months; and I might have remained there longer, but for a most horrid fight I had with four of the white apprentices, in which my left eye was nearly knocked out, and I was horribly mangled in other respects. The facts in the case were these: Until a very little while after I went there, white and black ship-carpenters worked side by side, and no one seemed to see any impropriety in it. All hands seemed to be very well satisfied. Many of the black carpenters were freemen. Things seemed to be going on very well. All at once, the white carpenters knocked off, and said they would not work with free colored workmen. Their reason for this, as alleged, was, that if free colored carpenters were encouraged, they would soon take the trade into their own hands, and poor white men would be thrown out of employment. They therefore felt called upon at once to put a stop to it. And, taking advantage of Mr. Gardner's necessities, they broke off, swearing they would work no longer, unless he would discharge his black carpenters. Now, though this did not extend to me in form, it did reach me in fact. My fellow-apprentices very soon began to feel it degrading to them to work with me. They began to put on airs, and talk about the "niggers" taking the country, saying we all ought to be killed; and, being encouraged by the journeymen, they commenced making my condition as hard as they could, by hectoring me around, and sometimes striking me. I, of course, kept the vow I made after the fight with Mr. Covey, and struck back again, regardless of consequences; and while I kept them from combining, I succeeded very well; for I could whip the whole of them, taking them separately. They, however, at length combined, and came upon me, armed with sticks, stones, and heavy handspikes. One came in front with a half brick. There was one at each side of me, and one behind me. While I was attending to those in front, and on either side, the one behind ran up with the handspike, and struck me a heavy blow upon the head. It stunned me. I fell, and with this they all ran upon me, and fell to beating me with their fists. I let them lay on for a while, gathering strength. In an instant, I gave a sudden surge, and rose to my hands and knees. Just as I did that, one of their number gave me, with his heavy boot, a powerful kick in the left eye. My eyeball seemed to have burst. When they saw my eye closed, and badly swollen, they left me. With this I seized the handspike, and for a time pursued them. But here the carpenters interfered, and I thought I might as well give it up. It was impossible to stand my hand against so many. All this took place in sight of not less than fifty white ship-carpenters, and not one interposed a friendly word; but some cried, "Kill the damned nigger! Kill him! kill him! He struck a white person." I found my only chance for life was in flight. I succeeded in getting away without an additional blow, and barely so; for to strike a white man is death by Lynch law,—and that was the law in Mr. Gardner's ship-yard; nor is there much of any other out of Mr. Gardner's ship-yard.

I went directly home, and told the story of my wrongs to Master Hugh; and I am happy to say of him, irreligious as he was, his conduct was heavenly, compared with that of his brother Thomas under similar circumstances. He listened attentively to my narration of the circumstances leading to the savage outrage, and gave many proofs of his strong indignation at it. The heart of my once overkind mistress was again melted into pity. My puffed-out eye and blood-covered face moved her to tears. She took a chair by me, washed the blood from my face, and, with a mother's tenderness, bound up my head, covering the wounded eye with a lean piece of fresh beef. It was almost compensation for my suffering to witness, once more, a manifestation of kindness from this, my once affectionate old mistress. Master Hugh was very much enraged. He gave expression to his feelings by pouring out curses upon the heads of those who did the deed. As soon as I got a little the better of my bruises, he took me with him to Esquire Watson's, on Bond Street, to see what could be done about the matter. Mr. Watson inquired who saw the assault committed. Master Hugh told him it was done in Mr. Gardner's ship-yard, at midday, where there were a large company of men at work. "As to that," he said, "the deed was done, and there was no question as to who did it." His answer was, he could do nothing in the case, unless some white man would come forward and testify. He could issue no warrant on my word. If I had been killed in the presence of a thousand colored people, their testimony combined would have been insufficient to have arrested one of the murderers. Master Hugh, for once, was compelled to say this state of things was too bad. Of course, it was impossible to get any white man to volunteer his testimony in my behalf, and against the white young men. Even those who may have sympathized with me were not prepared to do this. It required a degree of courage unknown to them to do so; for just at that time, the slightest manifestation of humanity toward a colored person was denounced as abolitionism, and that name subjected its bearer to frightful liabilities. The watchwords of the bloody-minded in that region, and in those days, were, "Damn the abolitionists!" and "Damn the niggers!" There was nothing done, and probably nothing would have been done if I had been killed. Such was, and such remains, the state of things in the Christian city of Baltimore.

Master Hugh, finding he could get no redress, refused to let me go back again to Mr. Gardner. He kept me himself, and his wife dressed my wound till I was again restored to health. He then took me into the ship-yard of which he was foreman, in the employment of Mr. Walter Price. There I was immediately set to calking, and very soon learned the art of using my mallet and irons. In the course of one year from the time I left Mr. Gardner's, I was able to command the highest wages given to the most experienced calkers. I was now of some importance to my master. I was bringing him from six to seven dollars per week. I sometimes brought him nine dollars per week: my wages were a dollar and a half a day. After learning how to calk, I sought my own employment, made my own contracts, and collected the money which I earned. My pathway became much more smooth than before; my condition was now much more comfortable. When I could get no calking to do, I did nothing. During these leisure times, those old notions about freedom would steal over me again. When in Mr. Gardner's employment, I was kept in such a perpetual whirl of excitement, I could think of nothing, scarcely, but my life; and in thinking of my life, I almost forgot my liberty. I have observed this in my experience of slavery,—that whenever my condition was improved, instead of its increasing my contentment, it only increased my desire to be free, and set me to thinking of plans to gain my freedom. I have found that, to make a contented slave, it is necessary to make a thoughtless one. It is necessary to darken his moral and mental vision, and, as far as possible, to annihilate the power of reason. He must be able to detect no inconsistencies in slavery; he must be made to feel that slavery is right; and he can be brought to that only when he ceases to be a man.

I was now getting, as I have said, one dollar and fifty cents per day. I contracted for it; I earned it; it was paid to me; it was rightfully my own; yet, upon each returning Saturday night, I was compelled to deliver every cent of that money to Master Hugh. And why? Not because he earned it,—not because he had any hand in earning it,—not because I owed it to him,—not because he possessed the slightest shadow of a right to it; but solely because he had the power to compel me to give it up. The right of the grim-visaged pirate upon the high seas is exactly the same.

## CHAPTER XI

I now come to that part of my life during which I planned, and finally succeeded in making, my escape from slavery. But before narrating any of the peculiar circumstances, I deem it proper to make known my intention not to state all the facts connected with the transaction. My reasons for pursuing this course may be understood from the following: First, were I to give a minute statement of all the facts, it is not only possible, but quite probable, that others would thereby be involved in the most embarrassing difficulties. Secondly, such a statement would most undoubtedly induce greater vigilance on the part of slaveholders than has existed heretofore among them; which would, of course be the means of guarding a door whereby some dear brother bondman might escape his galling chains. I deeply regret the necessity that impels me to suppress any thing of importance connected with my experience in slavery. It would afford me great pleasure indeed, as well as materially add to the interest of my narrative, were I at liberty to gratify a curiosity, which I know exists in the minds of many, by an accurate statement of all the facts pertaining to my most fortunate escape. But I must deprive myself of this pleasure, and the curious of the gratification which such a statement would afford. I would allow myself to suffer under the greatest imputations which evil-minded men might suggest, rather than exculpate myself, and thereby run the hazard of closing the slightest avenue by which a brother slave might clear himself of the chains and fetters of slavery.

I have never approved of the very public manner in which some of our western friends have conducted what they call the *underground railroad*, but which, I think, by their open declarations, has been made most emphatically the *upperground railroad*. I honor those good men and women for their noble daring, and applaud them for willingly subjecting themselves to bloody persecution, by openly avowing their participation in the escape of slaves. I, however, can see very little good resulting from such a course, either to themselves or the slaves escaping; while, upon the other hand, I see and feel assured that those open declarations are a positive evil to the slaves remaining, who are seeking to escape. They do nothing towards enlightening the slave, whilst they do much towards enlightening the master. They stimulate him to greater watchfulness, and enhance his power to capture his slave. We owe something to the slaves south of the line as well as to those north of it; and in aiding the latter on their way to freedom, we should be careful to do nothing which would be likely to hinder the former from escaping from slavery. I would keep the merciless slaveholder profoundly ignorant of the means of flight adopted by the slave. I would leave him to imagine himself surrounded by myriads of invisible tormentors, ever ready to snatch from his infernal grasp his trembling prey. Let him be left to feel his way in the dark; let darkness commensurate with his crime hover over him; and let him feel that at every step he takes, in pursuit of the flying bondman, he is running the frightful risk of having his hot brains dashed out by an invisible agency. Let us render the tyrant no aid; let us not hold the light by which he can trace the footprints of our flying brother. But enough of this. I will now proceed to the statement of those facts, connected with my escape, for which I am alone responsible, and for which no one can be made to suffer but myself.

In the early part of the year 1838, I became quite restless. I could see no reason why I should, at the end of each week, pour the reward of my toil into the purse of my master. When I carried to him my weekly wages, he would, after counting the money, look me in the face with a robber-like fierceness, and ask, "Is this all?" He was satisfied with nothing less than the last cent. He would, however, when I made him six dollars, sometimes give me six cents, to encourage me. It had the opposite effect. I regarded it as a sort of admission of my right to the whole. The fact that he gave me any part of my wages was proof, to my mind, that he believed me entitled to the whole of them. I always felt worse for having received any thing; for I feared that the giving me a few cents would ease his conscience, and make him feel himself to be a pretty honorable sort of robber. My discontent grew upon me. I was ever on the look-out for means of escape; and, finding no direct means, I determined to try to hire my time, with a view of getting money with which to make my escape. In the spring of 1838, when Master Thomas came to Baltimore to purchase his spring goods, I got an opportunity, and applied to him to allow me to hire my time. He unhesitatingly refused my request, and told me this was another stratagem by which to escape. He told me I could go nowhere but that he could get me; and that, in the event of my running away, he should spare no pains in his efforts to catch me. He exhorted me to content myself, and be obedient. He told me, if I would be happy, I must lay out no plans for the future. He said, if I behaved myself properly, he would take care of me. Indeed, he advised me to complete thoughtlessness of the future, and taught me to depend solely upon him for happiness. He seemed to see fully the pressing necessity of setting aside my intellectual nature, in order to contentment in slavery. But in spite of him, and even in spite of myself, I continued to think, and to think about the injustice of my enslavement, and the means of escape.

About two months after this, I applied to Master

Hugh for the privilege of hiring my time. He was not acquainted with the fact that I had applied to Master Thomas, and had been refused. He too, at first, seemed disposed to refuse; but, after some reflection, he granted me the privilege, and proposed the following term: I was to be allowed all my time, make all contracts with those for whom I worked, and find my own employment; and, in return for this liberty, I was to pay him three dollars at the end of each week; find myself in calking tools, and in board and clothing. My board was two dollars and a half per week. This, with the wear and tear of clothing and calking tools, made my regular expenses about six dollars per week. This amount I was compelled to make up, or relinquish the privilege of hiring my time. Rain or shine, work or no work, at the end of each week the money must be forthcoming, or I must give up my privilege. This arrangement, it will be perceived, was decidedly in my master's favor. It relieved him of all need of looking after me. His money was sure. He received all the benefits of slaveholding without its evils; while I endured all the evils of a slave, and suffered all the care and anxiety of a freeman. I found it a hard bargain. But, hard as it was, I thought it better than the old mode of getting along. It was a step towards freedom to be allowed to bear the responsibilities of a freeman, and I was determined to hold on upon it. I bent myself to the work of making money. I was ready to work at night as well as day, and by the most untiring perseverance and industry, I made enough to meet my expenses, and lay up a little money every week. I went on thus from May till August. Master Hugh then refused to allow me to hire my time longer. The ground for his refusal was a failure on my part, one Saturday night, to pay him for my week's time. This failure was occasioned by my attending a camp meeting about ten miles from Baltimore. During the week, I had entered into an engagement with a number of young friends to start from Baltimore to the camp ground early Saturday evening; and being detained by my employer, I was unable to get down to Master Hugh's without disappointing the company. I knew that Master Hugh was in no special need of the money that night. I therefore decided to go to camp meeting, and upon my return pay him the three dollars. I staid at the camp meeting one day longer than I intended when I left. But as soon as I returned, I called upon him to pay him what he considered his due. I found him very angry; he could scarce restrain his wrath. He said he had a great mind to give me a severe whipping. He wished to know how I dared go out of the city without asking his permission. I told him I hired my time, and while I paid him the price which he asked for it, I did not know that I was bound to ask him when and where I should go. This reply troubled him; and, after reflecting a few moments, he turned to me, and said I should hire my time no longer; that the next thing he should know of, I would be running away. Upon the same plea, he told me to bring my tools and clothing home forthwith. I did so; but instead of seeking work, as I had been accustomed to do previously to hiring my time, I spent the whole week without the performance of a single stroke of work. I did this in retaliation. Saturday night, he called upon me as usual for my week's wages. I told him I had no wages; I had done no work that week. Here we were upon the point of coming to blows. He raved, and swore his determination to get hold of me. I did not allow myself a single word; but was resolved, if he laid the weight of his hand upon me, it should be blow for blow. He did not strike me, but told me that he would find me in constant employment in future. I thought the matter over during the next day, Sunday, and finally resolved upon the third day of September, as the day upon which I would make a second attempt to secure my freedom. I now had three weeks during which to prepare for my journey. Early on Monday morning, before Master Hugh had time to make any engagement for me, I went out and got employment of Mr. Butler, at his ship-yard near the drawbridge, upon what is called the City Block, thus making it unnecessary for him to seek employment for me. At the end of the week, I brought him between eight and nine dollars. He seemed very well pleased, and asked me why I did not do the same the week before. He little knew what my plans were. My object in working steadily was to remove any suspicion he might entertain of my intent to run away; and in this I succeeded admirably. I suppose he thought I was never better satisfied with my condition than at the very time during which I was planning my escape. The second week passed, and again I carried him my full wages; and so well pleased was he, that he gave me twenty-five cents, (quite a large sum for a slaveholder to give a slave,) and bade me to make a good use of it. I told him I would.

Things went on without very smoothly indeed, but within there was trouble. It is impossible for me to describe my feelings as the time of my contemplated start drew near. I had a number of warm-hearted friends in Baltimore,—friends that I loved almost as I did my life,—and the thought of being separated from them forever was painful beyond expression. It is my opinion that thousands would escape from slavery, who now remain, but for the strong cords of affection that bind them to their friends. The thought of leaving my friends was decidedly the most painful thought with which I had to contend. The love of them was my tender point, and shook my decision more than all things else. Besides the pain of separation, the dread and apprehension of a failure exceeded what I had experienced at my first attempt. The appalling defeat I then sustained returned to torment me. I felt assured that, if I failed in this attempt, my case would be a hopeless one—it would seal my fate as a slave forever. I could not hope to get off with any thing less than the severest punishment, and being placed beyond the means of escape. It required no very vivid imagination to depict the most frightful scenes through which I should have to pass, in case I failed. The wretchedness of slavery, and the blessedness of freedom, were perpetually before me. It was life and death with me. But I remained firm, and, according to my resolution, on the third day of September, 1838, I left my chains, and succeeded in reaching New York without the slightest interruption of any kind. How I did so,—what means I adopted,—what direction I travelled, and by what mode of conveyance,—I must leave unexplained, for the reasons before mentioned.

I have been frequently asked how I felt when I found myself in a free State. I have never been able to answer the question with any satisfaction to myself. It was a moment of the highest excitement I ever experienced. I suppose I felt as one may imagine the unarmed mariner to feel when he is rescued by a friendly man-of-war from the pursuit of a pirate. In writing to a dear friend, immediately after my arrival at New York, I said I felt like one who had escaped a den of hungry lions. This state of mind, however, very soon subsided; and I was again seized with a feeling of great insecurity and loneliness. I was yet liable to be taken back, and subjected to all the tortures of slavery. This in itself was enough to damp the ardor of my enthusiasm. But the loneliness overcame me. There I was in the midst of thousands, and yet a perfect stranger; without home and without friends, in the midst of thousands of my own brethren—children of a common Father, and yet I dared not to unfold to any one of them my sad condition. I was afraid to speak to any one for fear of speaking to the wrong one, and thereby falling into the hands of money-loving kidnappers, whose business it was to lie in wait for the panting fugitive, as the ferocious beasts of the forest lie in wait for their prey. The motto which I adopted when I started from slavery was this—"Trust no man!" I saw in every white man an enemy, and in almost every colored man cause for distrust. It was a most painful situation; and, to understand it, one must needs experience it, or imagine himself in similar circumstances. Let him be a fugitive slave in a strange land—a land given up to be the hunting-ground for slaveholders—whose inhabitants are legalized kidnappers—where he is every moment subjected to the terrible liability of being seized upon by his fellowmen, as the hideous crocodile seizes upon his prey!—I say, let him place himself in my situation—without home or friends—without money or credit—wanting shelter, and no one to give it—wanting bread, and no money to buy it,—and at the same time let him feel that he is pursued by merciless men-hunters, and in total darkness as to what to do, where to go, or where to stay,—perfectly helpless both as to the means of defence and means of escape,—in the midst of plenty, yet suffering the terrible gnawings of hunger,—in the midst of houses, yet having no home,—among fellow-men, yet feeling as if in the midst of wild beasts, whose greediness to swallow up the trembling and half-famished fugitive is only equalled by that with which the monsters of the deep swallow up the helpless fish upon which they subsist,—I say, let him be placed in this most trying situation,—the situation in which I was placed,—then, and not till then, will he fully appreciate the hardships of, and know how to sympathize with, the toil-worn and whip-scarred fugitive slave.

Thank Heaven, I remained but a short time in this distressed situation. I was relieved from it by the humane hand of Mr. DAVID RUGGLES, whose vigilance, kindness, and perseverance, I shall never forget. I am glad of an opportunity to express, as far as words can, the love and gratitude I bear him. Mr. Ruggles is now afflicted with blindness, and is himself in need of the same kind offices which he was once so forward in the performance of toward others. I had been in New York but a few days, when Mr. Ruggles sought me out, and very kindly took me to his boarding-house at the corner of Church and Lespenard Streets. Mr. Ruggles was then very deeply engaged in the memorable *Darg* case, as well as attending to a number of other fugitive slaves, devising ways and means for their successful escape; and, though watched and hemmed in on almost every side, he seemed to be more than a match for his enemies.

Very soon after I went to Mr. Ruggles, he wished to know of me where I wanted to go; as he deemed it unsafe for me to remain in New York. I told him I was a calker, and should like to go where I could get work. I thought of going to Canada; but he decided against it, and in favor of my going to New Bedford, thinking I should be able to get work there at my trade. At this time, Anna,* my intended wife, came on; for I wrote to her immediately after my arrival at New York, (notwithstanding my homeless, houseless, and helpless condition,) informing her of my successful flight, and wishing her to come on forthwith. In a few days after her arrival, Mr. Ruggles called in the Rev. J. W. C. Pennington, who, in the presence of Mr. Ruggles, Mrs. Michaels, and two or three others, performed the marriage ceremony, and gave us a certificate, of which the following is an exact copy:—

"THIS may certify, that I joined together in holy

*She was free.

matrimony Frederick Johnson† and Anna Murray, as man and wife, in the presence of Mr. David Ruggles and Mrs. Michaels.

"JAMES W. C. PENNINGTON.

"*New York, Sept.* 15, 1838."

Upon receiving this certificate, and a five-dollar bill from Mr. Ruggles, I shouldered one part of our baggage, and Anna took up the other, and we set out forthwith to take passage on board of the steamboat John W. Richmond for Newport, on our way to New Bedford. Mr. Ruggles gave me a letter to a Mr. Shaw in Newport, and told me, in case my money did not serve me to New Bedford, to stop in Newport and obtain further assistance; but upon our arrival at Newport, we were so anxious to get to a place of safety, that, notwithstanding we lacked the necessary money to pay our fare, we decided to take seats in the stage, and promise to pay when we got to New Bedford. We were encouraged to do this by two excellent gentlemen, residents of New Bedford, whose names I afterward ascertained to be Joseph Ricketson and William C. Taber. They seemed at once to understand our circumstances, and gave us such assurance of their friendliness as put us fully at ease in their presence. It was good indeed to meet with such friends, at such a time. Upon reaching New Bedford, we were directed to the house of Mr. Nathan Johnson, by whom we were kindly received, and hospitably provided for. Both Mr. and Mrs. Johnson took a deep and lively interest in our welfare. They proved themselves quite worthy of the name of abolitionists. When the stage-driver found us unable to pay our fare, he held on upon our baggage as security for

†I had changed my name from Frederick *Bailey* to that of *Johnson.*

the debt. I had but to mention the fact to Mr. Johnson, and he forthwith advanced the money.

We now began to feel a degree of safety, and to prepare ourselves for the duties and responsibilities of a life of freedom. On the morning after our arrival at New Bedford, while at the breakfast-table, the question arose as to what name I should be called by. The name given me by my mother was, "Frederick Augustus Washington Bailey." I, however, had dispensed with the two middle names long before I left Maryland so that I was generally known by the name of "Frederick Bailey." I started from Baltimore bearing the name of "Stanley." When I got to New York, I again changed my name to "Frederick Johnson," and thought that would be the last change. But when I got to New Bedford, I found it necessary again to change my name. The reason of this necessity was, that there were so many Johnsons in New Bedford, it was already quite difficult to distinguish between them. I gave Mr. Johnson the privilege of choosing me a name, but told him he must not take from me the name of "Frederick." I must hold on to that, to preserve a sense of my identity. Mr. Johnson had just been reading the "Lady of the Lake," and at once suggested that my name be "Douglass." From that time until now I have been called "Frederick Douglass;" and as I am more widely known by that name than by either of the others, I shall continue to use it as my own.

I was quite disappointed at the general appearance of things in New Bedford. The impression which I had received respecting the character and condition of the people of the north, I found to be singularly erroneous. I had very strangely supposed, while in slavery, that few of the comforts, and scarcely any of the luxuries, of life were enjoyed at the north, compared with what were enjoyed by the slaveholders of the south. I probably came to this conclusion from the fact that northern people owned no slaves. I supposed that they were about upon a level with the non-slaveholding population of the south. I knew *they* were exceedingly poor, and I had been accustomed to regard their poverty as the necessary consequence of their being non-slaveholders. I had somehow imbibed the opinion that, in the absence of slaves, there could be no wealth, and very little refinement. And upon coming to the north, I expected to meet with a rough, hard-handed, and uncultivated population, living in the most Spartan-like simplicity, knowing nothing of the ease, luxury, pomp, and grandeur of southern slaveholders. Such being my conjectures, any one acquainted with the appearance of New Bedford may very readily infer how palpably I must have seen my mistake.

In the afternoon of the day when I reached New Bedford, I visited the wharves, to take a view of the shipping. Here I found myself surrounded with the strongest proofs of wealth. Lying at the wharves, and riding in the stream, I saw many ships of the finest model, in the best order, and of the largest size. Upon the right and left, I was walled in by granite warehouses of the widest dimensions, stowed to their utmost capacity with the necessaries and comforts of life. Added to this, almost every body seemed to be at work, but noiselessly so, compared with what I had been accustomed to in Baltimore. There were no loud songs heard from those engaged in loading and unloading ships. I heard no deep oaths or horrid curses on the laborer. I saw no whipping of men; but all seemed to go smoothly on. Every man appeared to understand his work, and went at it with a sober, yet cheerful earnestness, which betokened the deep interest which he felt in what he was doing, as well as a sense of his own dignity as a man. To me this looked exceedingly strange. From the wharves I strolled around and over the town, gazing with wonder and admiration at the splendid churches, beautiful dwellings, and finely-cultivated gardens; evincing an amount of wealth, comfort, taste, and refinement, such as I had never seen in any part of slaveholding Maryland.

Every thing looked clean, new and beautiful. I saw few or no dilapidated houses, with poverty-stricken inmates; no half-naked children and barefooted women, such as I had been accustomed to see in Hillsborough, Easton, St. Michael's, and Baltimore. The people looked more able, stronger, healthier, and happier, than those of Maryland. I was for once made glad by a view of extreme wealth, without being saddened by seeing extreme poverty. But the most astonishing as well as the most interesting thing to me was the condition of the colored people, a great many of whom, like myself, had escaped thither as a refuge from the hunters of men. I found many, who had not been seven years out of their chains, living in finer houses, and evidently enjoying more of the comforts of life, than the average of slaveholders in Maryland. I will venture to assert that my friend Mr. Nathan Johnson (of whom I can say with a grateful heart, "I was hungry, and he gave me meat; I was thirsty, and he gave me drink; I was a stranger, and he took me in") lived in a neater house; dined at a better table; took, paid for, and read, more newspapers; better understood the moral, religious, and political character of the nation,—than nine tenths of the slaveholders in Talbot county, Maryland. Yet Mr. Johnson was a working man. His hands were hardened by toil, and not his alone, but those also of Mrs. Johnson. I found the colored people much more spirited than I had supposed they would be. I found among them a determination to protect each other from the blood-thirsty kidnapper, at all hazards. Soon after my arrival, I was told of a circumstance which illustrated their spirit. A colored man and a fugitive slave were on unfriendly terms. The former was heard to threaten the latter with informing his master of his whereabouts. Straightway a meeting was called among the colored people, under the stereotyped notice, "Business of importance!" The betrayer was invited to attend. The people came at the appointed hour, and organized the meeting by appointing a very religious old gentleman as president, who, I believe, made a prayer, after which he addressed the meeting as follows: *"Friends, we have got him here, and I would recommend that you young men just take him outside the door, and kill him!"* With this, a number of them bolted at him; but they were intercepted by some more timid than themselves, and the betrayer escaped their vengeance, and has not been seen in New Bedford since. I believe there have been no more such threats, and should there be hereafter, I doubt not that death would be the consequence.

I found employment, the third day after my arrival, in stowing a sloop with a load of oil. It was new, dirty, and hard work for me; but I went at it with a glad heart and a willing hand. I was now my own master. It was a happy moment, the rapture of which can be understood only by those who have been slaves. It was the first work, the reward of which was to be entirely my own. There was no Master Hugh standing ready, the moment I earned the money, to rob me of it. I worked that day with a pleasure I had never before experienced. I was at work for myself and newly-married wife. It was to me the starting-point of a new existence. When I got through with that job, I went in pursuit of a job of calking; but such was the strength of prejudice against color, among the white calkers, that they refused to work with me, and of course I could get no employment.* Finding my trade

*I am told that colored persons can now get employment at calking in New Bedford—a result of anti-slavery effort.

of no immediate benefit, I threw off my calking habiliments, and prepared myself to do any kind of work I could get to do. Mr. Johnson kindly let me have his wood-horse and saw, and I very soon found myself a plenty of work. There was no work too hard—none too dirty. I was ready to saw wood, shovel coal, carry the hod, sweep the chimney, or roll oil casks,—all of which I did for nearly three years in New Bedford, before I became known to the antislavery world.

In about four months after I went to New Bedford, there came a young man to me, and inquired if I did not wish to take the "Liberator." I told him I did; but, just having made my escape from slavery, I remarked that I was unable to pay for it then. I, however, finally became a subscriber to it. The paper came, and I read it from week to week with such feelings as it would be quite idle for me to attempt to describe. The paper became my meat and my drink. My soul was set all on fire. Its sympathy for my brethren in bonds—its scathing denunciations of slaveholders—its faithful exposures of slavery—and its powerful attacks upon the upholders of the institution—sent a thrill of joy through my soul, such as I had never felt before!

I had not long been a reader of the "Liberator," before I got a pretty correct idea of the principles, measures and spirit of the anti-slavery reform. I took right hold of the cause. I could do but little; but what I could, I did with a joyful heart, and never felt happier than when in an anti-slavery meeting. I seldom had much to say at the meetings, because what I wanted to say was said so much better by others. But, while attending an anti-slavery convention at Nantucket, on the 11th of August, 1841, I felt strongly moved to speak, and was at the same time much urged to do so by Mr. William C. Coffin, a gentleman who had heard me speak in the colored people's meeting at New Bedford. It was a severe cross, and I took it up reluctantly. The truth was, I felt myself a slave, and the idea of speaking to white people weighed me down. I spoke but a few moments, when I felt a degree of freedom, and said what I desired with considerable ease. From that time until now, I have been engaged in pleading the cause of my brethren—with what success, and with what devotion, I leave those acquainted with my labors to decide.

## *Appendix*

I find, since reading over the foregoing Narrative that I have, in several instances, spoken in such a tone and manner, respecting religion, as may possibly lead those unacquainted with my religious views to suppose me an opponent of all religion. To remove the liability of such misapprehension, I deem it proper to append the following brief explanation. What I have said respecting and against religion, I mean strictly to apply to the *slaveholding religion* of this land, and with no possible reference to Christianity proper; for, between the Christianity of this land, and the Christianity of Christ, I recognize the widest possible difference—so wide, that to receive the one as good, pure, and holy, is of necessity to reject the other as bad, corrupt, and wicked. To be the friend of the one, is of necessity to be the enemy of the other. I love the pure, peaceable, and impartial Christianity of Christ: I therefore hate the corrupt, slaveholding, women-whipping, cradle-plundering, partial and hypocritical Christianity of this land. Indeed, I can see no reason, but the most deceitful one, for calling the religion of this land Christianity. I look upon it as the climax of all misnomers, the boldest of all frauds, and the grossest of all libels. Never was there a clearer case of "stealing the livery of the court of heaven to serve the devil in." I am filled with unutterable loathing when I contemplate the religious pomp and show, together with the horrible inconsistencies, which every where surround me. We have men-stealers for ministers, women-whippers for missionaries, and cradle-plunderers for church members. The man who wields the blood-clotted cowskin during the week fills the pulpit on Sunday, and claims to be a minister of the meek and lowly Jesus. The man who robs me of my earnings at the end of each week meets me as a class-leader on Sunday morning, to show me the way of life, and the path of salvation. He who sells my sister, for purposes of prostitution, stands forth as the pious advocate of purity. He who proclaims it a religious duty to read the Bible denies me the right of learning to read the name of the God who made me. He who is the religious advocate of marriage robs whole millions of its sacred influence, and leaves them to the ravages of wholesale pollution. The warm defender of the sacredness of the family relation is the same that scatters whole families,—sundering husbands and wives, parents and children, sisters and brothers,—leaving the hut vacant, and the hearth desolate. We see the thief preaching against theft, and the adulterer against adultery. We have men sold to build churches, women sold to support the gospel, and babes sold to purchase Bibles for the *poor heathen! all for the glory of God and the good of souls!* The slave auctioneer's bell and the church-going bell chime in with each other, and the bitter cries of the heart-broken slave are drowned in the religious shouts of his pious master. Revivals of religion and revivals in the slave-trade go hand in hand together. The slave prison and the church stand near each other. The clanking of fetters and the rattling of chains in the prison, and the pious psalm and solemn prayer in the church, may be heard at the same time. The dealers in the bodies and souls of men erect their stand in the presence of the pulpit, and they mutually help each other. The dealer gives his blood-stained gold to support the pulpit, and the pulpit, in return, covers his infernal business with the garb of Christianity. Here we have religion and robbery the allies of each other—devils dressed in angels' robes, and hell presenting the semblance of paradise.

"Just God! and these are they,
Who minister at thine altar, God of right!
Men who their hands, with prayer and blessing, lay
On Israel's ark of light.

"What! preach, and kidnap men?
Give thanks, and rob thy own afflicted poor?
Talk of thy glorious liberty, and then
Bolt hard the captive's door?

"What! servants of thy own
Merciful Son, who came to seek and save
The homeless and the outcast, fettering down
The tasked and plundered slave!

"Pilate and Herod friends!
Chief priests and rulers, as of old, combine!
Just God and holy! is that church which lends
Strength to the spoiler thine?"

The Christianity of America is a Christianity, of whose votaries it may be as truly said, as it was of the ancient scribes and Pharisees, "They bind heavy burdens, and grievous to be borne, and lay them on men's shoulders, but they themselves will not move them with one of their fingers. All their works they do for to be seen of men.——They love the uppermost rooms at feasts, and the chief seats in the synagogues, . . . and to be called of men, Rabbi, Rabbi.——But woe unto you, scribes and Pharisees, hypocrites! for ye shut up the kingdom of heaven against men; for ye neither go in yourselves, neither suffer ye them that are entering to go in. Ye devour widows' houses, and for a pretence make long prayers; therefore ye shall receive the greater damnation. Ye compass sea and land to make one proselyte, and when he is made, ye make him twofold more the child of hell than yourselves.——Woe unto you, scribes and Pharisees, hypocrites! for ye pay tithe of mint, and anise, and cumin, and have omitted the weightier matters of the law, judgment, mercy, and faith; these ought ye to have done, and not to leave the other undone. Ye blind guides! which strain at a gnat, and swallow a camel. Woe unto you, scribes and Pharisees, hypocrites! for ye make clean the outside of the cup and of the platter; but within, they are full of extortion and excess.——Woe unto you, scribes and Pharisees, hypocrites! for ye are like unto whited sepulchres, which indeed appear beautiful outward, but are within full of dead men's bones, and of all uncleanness. Even so ye also outwardly appear righteous unto men, but within ye are full of hypocrisy and iniquity."

Dark and terrible as is this picture, I hold it to be strictly true of the overwhelming mass of professed Christians in America. They strain at a gnat, and swallow a camel. Could any thing be more true of our churches? They would be shocked at the proposition of fellowshipping a *sheep*-stealer; and at the same time they hug to their communion a *man*-stealer, and brand me with being an infidel, if I find fault with them for it. They attend with Pharisaical strictness to the outward forms of religion, and at the same time neglect the weightier matters of the law, judgment, mercy, and faith. They are always ready to sacrifice, but seldom to show mercy. They are they who are represented as professing to love God whom they have not seen, whilst they hate their brother whom they have seen. They love the heathen on the other side of the globe. They can pray for him, pay money to have the Bible put into his hand, and missionaries to instruct him; while they despise and totally neglect the heathen at their own doors.

Such is, very briefly, my view of the religion of this land; and to avoid any misunderstanding, growing out of the use of general terms, I mean, by the religion of this land, that which is revealed in the words, deeds, and actions, of those bodies, north and south, calling themselves Christian churches, and yet in union with slaveholders. It is against religion, as presented by these bodies, that I have felt it my duty to testify.

I conclude these remarks by copying the following portrait of the religion of the south, (which is, by communion and fellowship, the religion of the north,) which I soberly affirm is "true to the life," and without caricature or the slightest exaggeration. It is said to have been drawn, several years before the present anti-slavery agitation began, by a northern Methodist preacher, who, while residing at the south, had an opportunity to see slaveholding morals, manners, and piety, with his own eyes. "Shall I not visit for these things? saith the Lord. Shall not my soul be avenged on such a nation as this?"

"A PARODY.

"Come, saints and sinners, hear me tell
How pious priests whip Jack and Nell,
And women buy and children sell,
And preach all sinners down to hell,
And sing of heavenly union.

"They'll bleat and baa, dona like goats,
Gorge down black sheep, and strain at motes,
Array their backs in fine black coats,
Then seize their negroes by their throats,
And choke, for heavenly union.

"They'll church you if you sip a dram,
And damn you if you steal a lamb;
Yet rob old Tony, Doll, and Sam,
Of human rights, and bread and ham;
Kidnapper's heavenly union.

"They'll loudly talk of Christ's reward,
And bind his image with a cord,
And scold, and swing the lash abhorred,
And sell their brother in the Lord
To handcuffed heavenly union.

"They'll read and sing a sacred song,
And make a prayer both loud and long,
And teach the right and do the wrong,
Hailing the brother, sister throng,
  With words of heavenly union.

"We wonder how such saints can sing,
Or praise the Lord upon the wing,
Who roar, and scold, and whip, and sting,
And to their slaves and mammon cling,
  In guilty conscience union.

"They'll raise tobacco, corn, and rye,
And drive, and thieve, and cheat, and lie,
And lay up treasures in the sky,
By making switch and cowskin fly,
  In hope of heavenly union.

"They'll crack old Tony on the skull,
And preach and roar like Bashan bull,
Or braying ass, of mischief full,
Then seize old Jacob by the wool,
  And pull for heavenly union.

"A roaring, ranting, sleek man-thief,
Who lived on mutton, veal, and beef,
Yet never would afford relief
To needy, sable sons of grief,
  Was big with heavenly union.

"'Love not the world,' the preacher said,
And winked his eye, and shook his head;
He seized on Tom, and Dick, and Ned,
Cut short their meat, and clothes, and bread,
  Yet still loved heavenly union.

"Another preacher whining spoke
Of One whose heart for sinners broke:
He tied old Nanny to an oak,
And drew the blood at every stroke,
  And prayed for heavenly union.

"Two others oped their iron jaws,
And waved their children-stealing paws;
There sat their children in gewgaws;
By stinting negroes' backs and maws,
  They kept up heavenly union.

"All good from Jack another takes,
And entertains their flirts and rakes,
Who dress as sleek as glossy snakes,
And cram their mouths with sweetened cakes;
  And this goes down for union."

Sincerely and earnestly hoping that this little book may do something toward throwing light on the American slave system, and hastening the glad day of deliverance to the millions of my brethren in bonds—faithfully relying upon the power of truth, love, and justice, for success in my humble efforts—and solemnly pledging myself anew to the sacred cause,—I subscribe myself,

FREDERICK DOUGLASS.

LYNN, *Mass., April* 28, 1845.

THE END.

# MY BONDAGE AND MY FREEDOM

Ten years after the publication of the *Narrative,* Douglass published a revised and enlarged version of his autobiography. *My Bondage and My Freedom* provides additional details and also records his activities as an abolitionist in the North, his lecture tours in Great Britain, and his efforts to establish an antislavery newspaper. The excerpts that follow offer vignettes of Douglass' life as a slave and as a free man. Chapter XVII is reproduced in its entirety because it permits a stylistic comparison with Douglass' account of his battle with Covey in Chapter X of the *Narrative*. Chapter XXV is also reproduced in full; the "various incidents" of this final chapter suggest the less unified nature of *My Bondage and My Freedom* as compared with the *Narrative*.

## *[The Master's House]*

The close-fisted stinginess that fed the poor slave on coarse corn-meal and tainted meat; that clothed him in crashy tow-linen, and hurried him on to toil through the field, in all weathers, with wind and rain beating through his tattered garments; that scarcely gave even the young slave-mother time to nurse her hungry infant in the fence corner; wholly vanishes on approaching the sacred precincts of the great house, the home of the Lloyds. There the scriptural phrase finds an exact illustration; the highly favored inmates of this mansion are literally arrayed "in purple and fine linen," and fare sumptuously every day! The table groans under the heavy and blood-bought luxuries gathered with pains-taking care, at home and abroad. Fields, forests, rivers and seas, are made tributary here. Immense wealth, and its lavish expenditure, fill the great house with all that can please the eye, or tempt the taste. Here, appetite, not food, is the great *desideratum.* Fish, flesh and fowl, are here in profusion. Chickens, of all breeds; ducks, of all kinds, wild and tame, the common, and the huge Muscovite; Guinea fowls, turkeys, geese, and pea fowls, are in their several pens, fat and fatting for the destined vortex. The graceful swan, the mongrels, the black-necked wild goose; partridges, quails, pheasants and pigeons; choice water fowl, with all their strange varieties, are caught in this huge family net. Beef, veal, mutton and venison, of the most select kinds and quality, roll bounteously to this grand consumer. The teeming riches of the Chesapeake bay, its rock, perch, drums, crocus, trout, oysters, crabs, and terrapin, are drawn hither to adorn the glittering table of the great house. The dairy, too, probably the finest on the Eastern Shore of Maryland—supplied by cattle of the best English stock, imported for the purpose, pours its rich donations of fragrant cheese, golden butter, and delicious cream, to heighten the attraction of the gorgeous, unending round of feasting. Nor are the fruits of the earth forgotten or neglected. The fertile garden, many acres in size, constituting a separate establishment, distinct from the common farm—with its scientific gardener, imported from Scotland, (a Mr. McDermott,) with four men under his direction, was not behind, either in the abundance or in the delicacy of its contributions to the same full board. The tender asparagus, the succulent celery, and the delicate cauliflower; egg plants, beets, lettuce, parsnips, peas, and French beans, early and late; radishes, cantelopes, melons of all kinds; the fruits and flowers of all climes and of all descriptions, from the hardy apple of the north, to the lemon and orange of the south, culminated at this point. Baltimore gathered figs, raisins, almonds and juicy grapes from Spain. Wines and brandies from France; teas of various flavor, from China; and rich, aromatic coffee from Java, all conspired to swell the tide of high life, where pride and indolence rolled and lounged in magnificence and satiety.

Behind the tall-backed and elaborately wrought chairs, stand the servants, men and maidens—fifteen in number—discriminately selected, not only with a view to their industry and faithfulness, but with special regard to their personal appearance, their graceful agility and captivating address. Some of these are armed with fans, and are fanning reviving breezes toward the over-heated brows of the alabaster ladies; others watch with eager eye, and with fawn-like step anticipate and supply, wants before they are sufficiently formed to be announced by word or sign.

These servants constituted a sort of black aristocracy on Col. Lloyd's plantation. They resembled the field hands in nothing, except in color, and in this they held the advantage of a velvet-like glossiness, rich and beautiful. The hair, too, showed the same advantage. The delicate colored maid rustled in the scarcely worn silk of her young mistress, while the servant men were equally well attired from the overflowing wardrobe of their young masters; so that, in dress, as well as in form and feature, in manner and speech, in tastes and habits, the distance between these favored few, and the sorrow and hunger-smitten multitudes of the quarter and the field, was immense; and this is seldom passed over.

Let us now glance at the stables and the carriage house, and we shall find the same evidence of pride and luxurious extravagance. Here are three splendid coaches, soft within and lustrous without. Here, too, are gigs, phætons, barouches, sulkeys and sleighs. Here are saddles and harnesses—beautifully wrought and silver mounted—kept with every care. In the stable you will find, kept only for pleasure, full thirty-five horses, of the most approved blood for speed and beauty. There are two men here constantly employed in taking care of these horses. One of these men must be always in the stable, to answer every call from the great house. Over the way from the stable, is a house built expressly for the hounds—a pack of twenty-five or thirty—whose fare would have made glad the heart of a dozen slaves. Horses and hounds are not the only consumers of the slave's toil. There was practiced, at the Lloyd's, a hospitality which would have astonished and charmed any health-seeking northern divine or merchant, who might have chanced to share it. Viewed from his own table, and *not* from the field, the colonel was a model of generous hospitality. His house was, literally, a hotel, for weeks during the summer months. At these times, especially, the air was freighted with the rich fumes of baking, boiling, roasting and broiling. The odors I shared with the winds; but the meats were under a more stringent monopoly—except that, occasionally, I got a cake from Mas' Daniel. In Mas' Daniel I had a friend at court, from whom I learned many things which my eager curiosity was excited to know. I always knew when company was expected, and who they were, although I was an outsider, being the property, not of Col. Lloyd, but of a servant of the wealthy colonel. On these occasions, all that pride, taste and money could do, to dazzle and charm, was done.

Who could say that the servants of Col. Lloyd were not well clad and cared for, after witnessing one of his magnificent entertainments? Who could say that they did not seem to glory in being the slaves of such a master? Who, but a fanatic, could get up any sympathy for persons whose every movement was agile, easy and graceful, and who evinced a consciousness of high superiority? And who would ever venture to suspect that Col. Lloyd was subject to the troubles of ordinary mortals? Master and slave seem alike in their glory here? Can it all be seeming? Alas! it may only be a sham at last! This immense wealth; this gilded splendor; this profusion of luxury; this exemption from toil; this life of ease; this sea of plenty; aye, what of it all? Are the pearly gates of happiness and sweet content flung open to such suitors? *far from it!* The poor slave, on his hard, pine plank, but scantily covered with his thin blanket, sleeps more soundly than the feverish voluptuary who reclines upon his feather bed and downy pillow. Food, to the indolent lounger, is poison, not sustenance. Lurking beneath all their dishes, are invisible spirits of evil, ready to feed the self-deluded gormandizers with aches, pains, fierce temper, uncontrolled passions, dyspepsia, rheumatism, lumbago and gout; and of these the Lloyds got their full share. To the pampered love of ease, there is no resting place. What is pleasant to-day, is repulsive to-morrow; what is soft now, is hard at another time; what is sweet in the morning, is bitter in the evening. Neither to the wicked, nor to the idler, is there any solid peace: *"Troubled, like the restless sea."*

## [The Slave's Right to Steal]

For, in all the changes of Master Hugh's family, there was no change in the bountifulness with which they supplied me with food. Not to give a slave enough to eat, is meanness intensified, and it is so recognized among slaveholders generally, in Maryland. The rule is, no matter how coarse the food, only let there be enough of it. This is the theory, and—in the part of Maryland I came from—the general practice accords with this theory. Lloyd's plantation was an exception, as was, also, the house of Master Thomas Auld.

All know the lightness of Indian corn-meal, as an article of food, and can easily judge from the following facts whether the statements I have made of the stinginess of Master Thomas, are borne out. There were four slaves of us in the kitchen, and four whites in the great house—Thomas Auld, Mrs. Auld, Hadaway Auld, (brother of Thomas Auld,) and little Amanda. The names of the slaves in the kitchen, were Eliza, my sister; Priscilla, my aunt; Henny, my cousin; and myself. There were eight persons in the family. There was, each week, one half bushel of corn-meal brought from the mill; and in the kitchen, corn-meal was almost our exclusive food, for very little else was allowed us. Out of this half bushel of corn-meal, the family in the great house had a small loaf every morning; thus leaving us, in the kitchen, with not quite a half a peck of meal per week, apiece. This allowance was less than half the allowance of food on Lloyd's plantation. It was not enough to subsist upon; and we were, therefore, reduced to the wretched necessity of living at the expense of our neighbors. We were compelled either to beg, or to steal, and we did both. I frankly confess, that while I hated everything like stealing, *as such*, I nevertheless did not hesitate to take food, when I was hungry, wherever I could find it. Nor was this practice the mere result of an unreasoning instinct; it was, in my case, the result of a clear apprehension of the claims of morality. I weighed and considered the matter closely, before I ventured to satisfy my hunger by such means. Considering that my labor and person were the property of Master Thomas, and that I was by him deprived of the necessaries of life—necessaries obtained by my own labor—it was easy to deduce the right to supply myself with what was my own. It was simply appropriating what was my own to the use of my master, since the health and strength derived from such food were exerted in *his* service. To be sure, this was stealing, according to the law and gospel I heard from St. Michael's pulpit; but I had already begun to attach less importance to what dropped from that quarter, on that point, while, as yet, I retained my reverence for religion. It was not always convenient to steal from master, and the same reason why I might, innocently, steal from him, did not seem to justify me in stealing from others. In the case of my master, it was only a question of *removal*—the taking his meat out of one tub, and putting it into another; the ownership of the meat was not affected by the transaction. At first, he owned it in the *tub*, and last, he owned it in *me*. His meat house was not always open. There was a strict watch kept on that point, and the key was on a large bunch in Rowena's pocket. A great many times have we, poor creatures, been severely pinched with hunger, when meat and bread have been moulding under the lock, while the key was in the pocket of our mistress. This had been so when she *knew* we were nearly half starved; and yet, that mistress, with saintly air, would kneel with her husband, and pray each morning that a merciful God would bless them in basket and in store, and save them, at last, in his kingdom. But I proceed with the argument.

It was necessary that the right to steal from *others* should be established; and this could only rest upon a wider range of generalization than that which supposed the right to steal from my master.

It was sometime before I arrived at this clear right. The reader will get some idea of my train of reasoning, by a brief statement of the case. "I am," thought I, "not only the slave of Master Thomas, but I am the slave of society at large. Society at large has bound itself, in form and in fact, to assist Master Thomas in robbing me of my rightful liberty, and of the just reward of my labor; therefore, whatever rights I have against Master Thomas, I have, equally, against those confederated with him in robbing me of liberty. As society has marked me out as privileged plunder, on the principle of self-preservation I am justified in plundering in turn. Since each slave belongs to all; all must, therefore, belong to each."

I shall here make a profession of faith which may shock some, offend others, and be dissented from by all. It is this: Within the bounds of his just earnings, I hold that the slave is fully justified in helping himself to the *gold and silver, and the best apparel of his master, or that of any other slaveholder; and that such taking is not stealing in any just sense of that word.*

The morality of *free* society can have no application to *slave* society. Slaveholders have made it almost impossible for the slave to commit any crime, known either to the laws of God or to the laws of man. If he steals, he takes his own; if he kills his master, he imitates only the heroes of the revolution. Slaveholders I hold to be individually and collectively responsible for all the evils which grow out of the horrid relation, and I believe they will be so held at the judgment, in the sight of a just God. Make a man a slave, and you rob him of moral responsibility.

## XVII

# *The Last Flogging*

Sleep itself does not always come to the relief of the weary in body, and the broken in spirit; especially when past troubles only foreshadow coming disasters. The last hope had been extinguished. My master, who I did not venture to hope would protect me as *a man*, had even now refused to protect me as *his property;* and had cast me back, covered with reproaches and bruises, into the hands of a stranger to that mercy which was the soul of the religion he professed. May the reader never spend such a night as that allotted to me, previous to the morning which was to herald my return to the den of horrors from which I had made a temporary escape.

I remained all night—sleep I did not—at St. Michael's; and in the morning (Saturday) I started off, according to the order of Master Thomas, feeling that I had no friend on earth, and doubting if I had one in heaven. I reached Covey's about nine o'clock; and just as I stepped into the field, before I had reached the house, Covey, true to his snakish habits, darted out at me from a fence corner, in which he had secreted himself, for the purpose of securing me. He was amply provided with a cowskin and a rope; and he evidently intended to *tie me up*, and to wreak his vengeance on me to the fullest extent. I should have been an easy prey, had he succeeded in getting his hands upon me, for I had taken no refreshment since noon on Friday; and this, together with the pelting, excitement, and the loss of blood, had reduced my strength. I, however, darted back into the woods, before the ferocious hound could get hold of me, and buried myself in a thicket, where he lost sight of me. The corn-field afforded me cover, in getting to the woods. But for the tall corn, Covey would have overtaken me, and made me his captive. He seemed very much chagrined that he did not catch me, and gave up the chase, very reluctantly; for I could see his angry movements, toward the house from which he had sallied, on his foray.

Well, now I am clear of Covey, and of his wrathful lash, for the present. I am in the wood, buried in its somber gloom, and hushed in its solemn silence; hid from all human eyes; shut in with nature and nature's God, and absent from all human contrivances. Here was a good place to pray; to pray for help for deliverance—a prayer I had often made before. But how could I pray? Covey could pray—Capt. Auld could pray—I would fain pray; but doubts (arising partly from my own neglect of the means of grace, and partly from the sham religion which everywhere prevailed, cast in my mind a doubt upon all religion, and led me to the conviction that prayers were unavailing and delusive) prevented my embracing the opportunity, as a religious one. Life, in itself, had almost become burdensome to me. All my outward relations were against me; I must stay here and starve, (I was already hungry,) or go home to Covey's, and have my flesh torn to pieces, and my spirit humbled under the cruel lash of Covey. This was the painful alternative presented to me. The day was long and irksome. My physical condition was deplorable. I was weak, from the toils of the previous day, and from the want of food and rest; and had been so little concerned about my appearance, that I had not yet washed the blood from my garments. I was an object of horror, even to myself. Life, in Baltimore, when most oppressive, was a paradise to this. What had I done, what had my parents done, that such a life as this should be mine? That day, in the woods, I would have exchanged my manhood for the brutehood of an ox.

Night came. I was still in the woods, unresolved what to do. Hunger had not yet pinched me to the point of going home, and I laid myself down in the leaves to rest; for I had been watching for hunters all day, but not being molested during the day, I expected no disturbance during the night. I had come to the conclusion that Covey relied upon hunger to drive me home; and in this I was quite correct—the facts showed that he had made no effort to catch me, since morning.

During the night, I heard the step of a man in the woods. He was coming toward the place where I lay. A person lying still has the advantage over one walking in the woods, in the day time, and this advantage is much greater at night. I was not able to engage in a physical struggle, and I had recourse to the common resort of the weak. I hid myself in the leaves to prevent discovery. But, as the night rambler in the woods drew nearer, I found him to be a *friend*, not an enemy; it was a slave of Mr. William Groomes, of Easton, a kind hearted fellow, named "Sandy." Sandy lived with Mr. Kemp that year, about four miles from St. Michael's. He, like myself, had been hired out by the year; but, unlike myself, had not been hired out to be broken. Sandy was the husband of a free woman, who lived in the lower part of "*Pot-pie Neck,*" and he was now on his way through the woods, to see her, and to spend the Sabbath with her.

As soon as I had ascertained that the disturber of my solitude was not an enemy, but the good-hearted Sandy—a man as famous among the slaves of the neighborhood for his good nature, as for his good sense—I came out from my hiding place, and made myself known to him. I explained the circumstances of the past two days, which had driven me to the woods, and he deeply compassionated my distress. It was a bold thing for him to shelter me, and I could not ask him to do so; for, had I been found in his hut, he would have suffered the penalty of thirty-nine lashes on his bare back, if not something worse. But, Sandy was too generous to permit the fear of punishment to prevent his relieving a brother bondman from hunger and exposure; and, therefore, on his own motion, I accompanied him to his home, or rather to the home of his wife—for the house and lot were hers. His wife was called up—for it was now about midnight—a fire was made, some Indian meal was soon mixed with salt and water, and an ash cake was baked in a hurry to relieve my hunger. Sandy's wife was not behind him in kindness—both seemed to esteem it a privilege to succor me; for, although I was hated by Covey and by my master, I was loved by the colored people, because *they* thought I was hated for my knowledge, and persecuted because I was feared. I was the *only* slave *now* in that region who could read and write. There had been one other man, belonging to Mr. Hugh Hamilton, who could read, (his name was "Jim,") but he, poor fellow, had, shortly after my coming into the neighborhood, been sold off to the far south. I saw Jim ironed, in the cart, to be carried to Easton for sale,—pinioned like a yearling for the slaughter. My knowledge was now the pride of my brother slaves; and, no doubt, Sandy felt something of the general interest in me on that account. The supper was soon ready, and though I have feasted since, with honorables, lord mayors and aldermen, over the sea, my supper on ash cake and cold water, with Sandy, was the meal, of all my life, most sweet to my taste, and now most vivid in my memory.

Supper over, Sandy and I went into a discussion of what was *possible* for me, under the perils and hardships which now overshadowed my path. The question was, must I go back to Covey, or must I now attempt to run away? Upon a careful survey, the latter was found to be impossible; for I was on a narrow neck of land, every avenue from which would bring me in sight of pursuers.

There was the Chesapeake bay to the right, and "Pot-pie" river to the left, and St. Michael's and its neighborhood occupying the only space through which there was any retreat.

I found Sandy an old adviser. He was not only a religious man, but he professed to believe in a system for which I have no name. He was a genuine African, and had inherited some of the so called magical powers, said to be possessed by African and eastern nations. He told me that he could help me; that, in those very woods, there was an herb, which in the morning might be found, possessing all the powers required for my protection, (I put his thoughts in my own language;) and that, if I would take his advice, he would procure me the root of the herb of which he spoke. He told me further, that if I would take that root and wear it on my right side, it would be impossible for Covey to strike me a blow; that with this root about my person, no white man could whip me. He said he had carried it for years, and that he had fully tested its virtues. He had never received a blow from a slaveholder since he carried it; and he never expected to receive one, for he always meant to carry that root as a protection. He knew Covey well, for Mrs. Covey was the daughter of Mr. Kemp; and he (Sandy) had heard of the barbarous treatment to which I was subjected, and he wanted to do something for me.

Now all this talk about the root, was, to me, very absurd and ridiculous, if not positively sinful. I at first rejected the idea that the simple carrying a root on my right side, (a root, by the way, over which I walked every time I went into the woods,) could possess any such magic power as he ascribed to it, and I was, therefore, not disposed to cumber my pocket with it. I had a positive aversion to all pretenders to "*divination.*" It was beneath one of my intelligence to countenance such dealings with the devil, as this power implied. But, with all my learning—it was really precious little—Sandy was more than a match for me. "My book learning," he said, "had not kept Covey off me," (a powerful argument just then,) and he entreated me, with flashing eyes, to try this. If it did me no good, it could do me no harm, and it would cost me nothing, any way. Sandy was so earnest, and so confident of the good qualities of this weed, that, to please him, rather than from any conviction of its excellence, I was induced to take it. He had been to me the good Samaritan, and had, almost providentially, found me, and helped me when I could not help myself; how did I know but that the hand of the Lord was in it? With thoughts of this sort, I took the roots from Sandy, and put them in my right hand pocket

This was, of course, Sunday morning. Sandy now urged me to go home, with all speed, and to walk up bravely to the house, as though nothing had happened. I saw in Sandy too deep an insight into human nature, with all his superstition, not to have some respect for his advice; and perhaps, too, a slight gleam or shadow of his superstition had fallen upon me. At any rate, I started off toward Covey's, as directed by Sandy. Having, the previous night, poured my griefs into Sandy's ears, and got him enlisted in my behalf, having made his wife a sharer in my sorrows, and having, also, become well refreshed by sleep and food, I moved off, quite courageously, toward the much dreaded Covey's. Singularly enough, just as I entered his yard gate, I met him and his wife, dressed in their Sunday best—looking as smiling as angels—on their way to church. The manner of Covey astonished me. There was something really benignant in his countenance. He spoke to me as never before; told me that the pigs had got into the lot, and he wished me to drive them out; inquired how I was, and seemed an altered man. This extraordinary conduct of

Covey, really made me begin to think that Sandy's herb had more virtue in it than I, in my pride, had been willing to allow; and, had the day been other than Sunday, I should have attributed Covey's altered manner solely to the magic power of the root. I suspected, however, that the *Sabbath*, and not the *root*, was the real explanation of Covey's manner. His religion hindered him from breaking the Sabbath, but not from breaking my skin. He had more respect for the *day* than for the *man*, for whom the day was mercifully given; for while he would cut and slash my body during the week, he would not hesitate, on Sunday, to teach me the value of my soul, or the way of life and salvation by Jesus Christ.

All went well with me till Monday morning; and then, whether the root had lost its virtue, or whether my tormentor had gone deeper into the black art than myself, (as was sometimes said of him,) or whether he had obtained a special indulgence, for his faithful Sabbath day's worship, it is not necessary for me to know, or to inform the reader; but, this much I *may* say,—the pious and benignant smile which graced Covey's face on *Sunday*, wholly disappeared on *Monday*. Long before daylight, I was called up to go and feed, rub, and curry the horses. I obeyed the call, and I would have so obeyed it, had it been made at an earlier hour, for I had brought my mind to a firm resolve, during that Sunday's reflection, viz: to obey every order, however unreasonable, if it were possible, and, if Mr. Covey should then undertake to beat me, to defend and protect myself to the best of my ability. My religious views on the subject of resisting my master, had suffered a serious shock, by the savage persecution to which I had been subjected, and my hands were no longer tied by my religion. Master Thomas's indifference had severed the last link. I had now to this extent "backslidden" from this point in the slave's religious creed; and I soon had occasion to make my fallen state known to my Sunday-pious brother, Covey.

Whilst I was obeying his order to feed and get the horses ready for the field, and when in the act of going up the stable loft for the purpose of throwing down some blades, Covey sneaked into the stable, in his peculiar snake-like way, and seizing me suddenly by the leg, he brought me to the stable floor, giving my newly mended body a fearful jar. I now forgot my *roots*, and remembered my pledge to *stand up in my own defense.* The brute was endeavoring skillfully to get a slip-knot on my legs, before I could draw up my feet. As soon as I found what he was up to, I gave a sudden spring, (my two days' rest had been of much service to me,) and by that means, no doubt, he was able to bring me to the floor so heavily. He was defeated in his plan of tying me. While down, he seemed to think he had me very securely in his power. He little thought he was—as the rowdies say—"in" for a "rough and tumble" fight; but such was the fact. Whence came the daring spirit necessary to grapple with a man who, eight-and-forty hours before, could, with his slightest word have made me tremble like a leaf in a storm, I do not know; at any rate, *I was resolved to fight*, and, what was better still, I was actually hard at it. The fighting madness had come upon me, and I found my strong fingers firmly attached to the throat of my cowardly tormentor; as heedless of consequences, at the moment, as though we stood as equals before the law. The very color of the man was forgotten. I felt as supple as a cat, and was ready for the snakish creature at every turn. Every blow of his was parried, though I dealt no blows in turn. I was strictly on the *defensive*, preventing him from injuring me, rather than trying to injure him. I flung him on the ground several times, when he meant to have hurled me there. I held him so firmly by the throat, that his blood followed my nails. He held me, and I held him.

All was fair, thus far, and the contest was about equal. My resistance was entirely unexpected, and Covey was taken all aback by it, for he trembled in every limb. "*Are you going to resist*, you scoundrel?" said he. To which, I returned a polite "*yes sir*"; steadily gazing my interrogator in the eye, to meet the first approach or dawning of the blow, which I expected my answer would call forth. But, the conflict did not long remain thus equal. Covey soon cried out lustily for help; not that I was obtaining any marked advantage over him, or was injuring him, but because he was gaining none over me, and was not able, single handed, to conquer me. He called for his cousin Hughes, to come to his assistance, and now the scene was changed. I was compelled to give blows, as well as to parry them; and, since I was, in any case, to suffer for resistance, I felt (as the musty proverb goes) that "I might as well be hanged for an old sheep as a lamb." I was still *defensive* toward Covey, but *aggressive* toward Hughes; and, at the first approach of the latter, I dealt a blow, in my desperation, which fairly sickened my youthful assailant. He went off, bending over with pain, and manifesting no disposition to come within my reach again. The poor fellow was in the act of trying to catch and tie my right hand, and while flattering himself with success, I gave him the kick which sent him staggering away in pain, at the same time that I held Covey with a firm hand.

Taken completely by surprise, Covey seemed to have lost his usual strength and coolness. He was frightened, and stood puffing and blowing, seemingly unable to command words or blows. When he saw that poor Hughes was standing half bent with pain—his courage quite gone—the cowardly tyrant asked if I "meant to persist in my resistance." I told him "I *did mean to resist,* come what might;" that I had been by him treated like a *brute*, during the last six months; and that I should stand it *no longer*. With that, he gave me a shake, and attempted to drag me toward a stick of wood, that was lying just outside the stable door. He meant to knock me down with it; but, just as he leaned over to get the stick, I seized him with both hands by the collar, and, with a vigorous and sudden snatch, I brought my assailant harmlessly, his full length, on the *not over* clean ground—for we were now in the cow yard. He had selected the place for the fight, and it was but right that he should have all the advantages of his own selection.

By this time, Bill, the hired man, came home. He had been to Mr. Hemsley's, to spend the Sunday with his nominal wife, and was coming home on Monday morning, to go to work. Covey and I had been skirmishing from before daybreak, till now, that the sun was almost shooting his beams over the eastern woods, and we were still at it. I could not see where the matter was to terminate. He evidently was afraid to let me go, lest I should again make off to the woods; otherwise, he would probably have obtained arms from the house, to frighten me. Holding me, Covey called upon Bill for assistance. The scene here, had something comic about it. "Bill," who knew *precisely* what Covey wished him to do, affected ignorance, and pretended he did not know what to do. "What shall I do, Mr. Covey," said Bill. "Take hold of him—take hold of him!" said Covey. With a toss of his head, peculiar to Bill, he said, "indeed, Mr. Covey, I want to go to work." "*This is* your work," said Covey; "take hold of him." Bill replied, with spirit, "My master hired me here, to work, and *not* to help you whip Frederick." It was now my turn to speak. "Bill," said I, "don't put your hands on me." To which he replied, "MY GOD! Frederick, I aint goin' to tech ye," and Bill walked off, leaving Covey and myself to settle our matters as best we might.

But, my present advantage was threatened when I saw Caroline (the slave-woman of Covey) coming to the cow yard to milk, for she was a powerful woman, and could have mastered me very easily, exhausted as I now was. As soon as she came into the yard, Covey attempted to rally her to his aid. Strangely—and, I may add, fortunately—Caroline was in no humor to take a hand in any such sport. We were all in open rebellion, that morning. Caroline answered the command of her master to "*take hold of me*," precisely as Bill had answered, but in *her*, it was at greater peril so to answer; she was the slave of Covey, and he could do what he pleased with her. It was *not* so with Bill, and Bill knew it. Samuel Harris, to whom Bill belonged, did not allow his slaves to be beaten, unless they were guilty of some crime which the law would punish. But, poor Caroline, like myself, was at the mercy of the merciless Covey; nor did she escape the dire effects of her refusal. He gave her several sharp blows.

Covey at length (two hours had elapsed) gave up the contest. Letting me go, he said,—puffing and blowing at a great rate—"now, you scoundrel, go to your work; I would not have whipped you half so much as I have had you not resisted." The fact was, *he had not whipped me at all.* He had not, in all the scuffle, drawn a single drop of blood from me. I had drawn blood from him; and, even without this satisfaction, I should have been victorious, because my aim had not been to injure him, but to prevent his injuring me.

During the whole six months that I lived with Covey, after this transaction, he never laid on me the weight of his finger in anger. He would, occasionally, say he did not want to have to get hold of me again—a declaration which I had no difficulty in believing; and I had a secret feeling, which answered, "you need not wish to get hold of me again, for you will be likely to come off worse in a second fight than you did in the first."

Well, my dear reader, this battle with Mr. Covey,—undignified as it was, and as I fear my narration of it is—was the turning point in my "*life as a slave.*" It rekindled in my breast the smouldering embers of liberty; it brought up my Baltimore dreams, and revived a sense of my own manhood. I was a changed being after that fight. I was *nothing* before; I WAS A MAN NOW. It recalled to life my crushed self-respect and my self-confidence, and inspired me with a renewed determination to be A FREEMAN. A man, without force, is without the essential dignity of humanity. Human nature is so constituted, that it cannot *honor* a helpless man, although it can *pity* him; and even this it cannot do long, if the signs of power do not arise.

He only can understand the effect of this combat on my spirit, who has himself incurred something, hazarded something, in repelling the unjust and cruel aggressions of a tyrant. Covey was a tyrant, and a cowardly one, withal. After resisting him, I felt as I had never felt before. It was a resurrection from the dark and pestiferous tomb of slavery, to the heaven of comparative freedom. I was no longer a servile coward, trembling under the frown of a brother worm of the dust, but, my long-cowed spirit was roused to an attitude of manly independence. I had reached the point, at which I was *not afraid to die.* This spirit made me a freeman in *fact*, while I remained a slave in *form*. When a slave cannot be flogged he is more than half free. He has a domain as broad as his own manly heart to defend, and he is really "*a power on earth.*" While slaves prefer their lives, with flogging, to instant death, they will always find christians enough, like unto Covey, to accommodate that preference. From this time, until that of my escape from slavery, I was never fairly whipped. Several attempts were made to whip me, but they were always unsuccessful. Bruises I did get, as I shall hereafter inform the reader; but the case I have been describing, was the end of the brutification to which slavery had subjected me.

The reader will be glad to know why, after I had so grievously offended Mr. Covey, he did not have me taken in hand by the authorities; indeed, why the law of Maryland, which assigns hanging to the slave who resists his master, was not put in force against me; at any rate, why I was not taken up, as is usual in such cases, and publicly whipped, for an example to other slaves, and as a means of deterring me from committing the same offense again. I confess, that the easy manner in which I got off, was, for a long time, a surprise to me, and I cannot, even now, fully explain the cause.

The only explanation I can venture to suggest, is the fact, that Covey was, probably, ashamed to have it known and confessed that he had been mastered by a boy of sixteen. Mr. Covey enjoyed the unbounded and very valuable reputation, of being a first rate overseer and *negro breaker*. By means of this reputation, he was able to procure his hands for *very trifling* compensation, and with very great ease. His interest and his pride mutually suggested the wisdom of passing the matter by, in silence. The story that he had undertaken to whip a lad, and had been resisted, was, of itself, sufficient to damage him; for his bearing should, in the estimation of slaveholders, be of that imperial order that should make such an occurrence *impossible*. I judge from these circumstances, that Covey deemed it best to give me the go-by. It is, perhaps, not altogether creditable to my natural temper, that, after this conflict with Mr. Covey, I did, at times, purposely aim to provoke him to an attack, by refusing to keep with the other hands in the field, but I could never bully him to another battle. I had made up my mind to do him serious damage, if he ever again attempted to lay violent hands on me.

> "Hereditary bondmen, know ye not
> Who would be free, themselves must strike the blow?"

## *[Floggable Offenses]*

The reader might imagine a difficulty in finding faults enough for such frequent whipping. But this is because you have no idea how easy a matter it is to offend a man who is on the look-out for offenses. The man, unaccustomed to slaveholding, would be astonished to observe how many *floggable* offenses there are in the slaveholder's catalogue of crimes; and how easy it is to commit any one of them, even when the slave least intends it. A slaveholder, bent on finding fault, will hatch up a dozen a day, if he chooses to do so, and each one of these shall be of a punishable description. A mere look, word, or motion, a mistake, accident, or want of power, are all matters for which a slave may be whipped at any time. Does a slave look dissatisfied with his condition? It is said, that he has the devil in him, and it must be whipped out. Does he answer *loudly*, when spoken to by his master, with an air of self-consciousness? Then, must he be taken down a button-hole lower, by the lash, well laid on. Does he forget, and omit to pull off his hat, when approaching a white person? Then, he must, or may be, whipped for his bad manners. Does he ever venture to vindicate his conduct, when harshly and unjustly accused? Then, he is guilty of impudence, one of the greatest crimes in the social catalogue of southern society. To allow a slave to escape punishment, who has impudently attempted to exculpate himself from unjust charges, preferred against him by some white person, is to be guilty of great dereliction of duty. Does a slave ever venture to suggest a better way of doing a thing, no matter what? he is, altogether, too officious—wise above what is written—and he deserves, even if he does not get, a flogging for his presumption. Does he, while plowing, break a plow, or while hoeing, break a hoe, or while chopping, break an ax? no matter what were the imperfections of the implement broken, or the natural liabilities for breaking, the slave can be whipped for carelessness. The *reverend* slaveholder could always find something of this sort, to justify him in using the lash several times during the week.

## [*The* Liberator *and William Lloyd Garrison*]

In four or five months after reaching New Bedford, there came a young man to me, with a copy of the "Liberator," the paper edited by WILLIAM LLOYD GARRISON, and published by ISAAC KNAPP, and asked me to subscribe for it. I told him I had but just escaped from slavery, and was of course very poor, and remarked further, that I was unable to pay for it then; the agent, however, very willingly took me as a subscriber, and appeared to be much pleased with securing my name to his list. From this time I was brought in contact with the mind of William Lloyd Garrison. His paper took its place with me next to the bible.

The Liberator was a paper after my own heart. It detested slavery—exposed hypocrisy and wickedness in high places—made no truce with the traffickers in the bodies and souls of men; it preached human brotherhood, denounced oppression, and, with all the solemnity of God's word, demanded the complete emancipation of my race. I not only liked—I *loved* this paper, and its editor. He seemed a match for all the opponents of emancipation, whether they spoke in the name of the law, or the gospel. His words were few, full of holy fire, and straight to the point. Learning to love him, through his paper, I was prepared to be pleased with his presence. Something of a hero worshiper, by nature, here was one, on first sight, to excite my love and reverence.

Seventeen years ago, few men possessed a more heavenly countenance than William Lloyd Garrison, and few men evinced a more genuine or a more exalted piety. The bible was his text book—held sacred, as the word of the Eternal Father—sinless perfection—complete submission to insults and injuries—literal obedience to the injunction, if smitten on one side to turn the other also. Not only was Sunday a Sabbath, but all days were Sabbaths, and to be kept holy. All sectarism false and mischievous—the regenerated, throughout the world, members of one body, and the HEAD Christ Jesus. Prejudice against color was rebellion against God. Of all men beneath the sky, the slaves, because most neglected and despised, were nearest and dearest to his great heart. Those ministers who defended slavery from the bible, were of their "father the devil;" and those churches which fellowshiped slaveholders as christians, were synagogues of Satan, and our nation was a nation of liars. Never loud or noisy—calm and serene as a summer sky, and as pure. "You are the man, the Moses, raised up by God, to deliver his modern Israel from bondage," was the spontaneous feeling of my heart, as I sat away back in the hall and listened to his mighty words; mighty in truth—mighty in their simple earnestness.

I had not long been a reader of the Liberator, and listener to its editor, before I got a clear apprehension of the principles of the anti-slavery movement. I had already the spirit of the movement, and only needed to understand its principles and measures. These I got from the Liberator, and from those who believed in that paper. My acquaintance with the movement increased my hope for the ultimate freedom of my race, and I united with it from a sense of delight, as well as duty.

Every week the Liberator came, and every week I made myself master of its contents. All the anti-slavery meetings held in New Bedford I promptly attended, my heart burning at every true utterance against the slave system, and every rebuke of its friends and supporters. Thus passed the first three years of my residence in New

Bedford. I had not then dreamed of the possibility of my becoming a public advocate of the cause so deeply imbedded in my heart. It was enough for me to listen—to receive and applaud the great words of others, and only whisper in private, among the white laborers on the wharves, and elsewhere, the truths which burned in my breast.

## [Abolitionist Lecturer]

In the summer of 1841, a grand anti-slavery convention was held in Nantucket, under the auspices of Mr. Garrison and his friends. Until now, I had taken no holiday since my escape from slavery. Having worked very hard that spring and summer, in Richmond's brass foundery—sometimes working all night as well as all day—and needing a day or two of rest, I attended this convention, never supposing that I should take part in the proceedings. Indeed, I was not aware that any one connected with the convention even so much as knew my name. I was, however, quite mistaken. Mr. William C. Coffin, a prominent abolitionist in those days of trial, had heard me speaking to my colored friends, in the little schoolhouse on Second street, New Bedford, where we worshiped. He sought me out in the crowd, and invited me to say a few words to the convention. Thus sought out, and thus invited, I was induced to speak out the feelings inspired by the occasion, and the fresh recollection of the scenes through which I had passed as a slave. My speech on this occasion is about the only one I ever made, of which I do not remember a single connected sentence. It was with the utmost difficulty that I could stand erect, or that I could command and articulate two words without hesitation and stammering. I trembled in every limb. I am not sure that my embarrassment was not the most effective part of my speech, if speech it could be called. At any rate, this is about the only part of my performance that I now distinctly remember. But excited and convulsed as I was, the audience, though remarkably quiet before, became as much excited as myself. Mr. Garrison followed me, taking me as his text; and now, whether I had made an eloquent speech in behalf of freedom or not, his was one never to be forgotten by those who heard it. Those who had heard Mr. Garrison oftenest, and had known him longest, were astonished. It was an effort of unequaled power, sweeping down, like a very tornado, every opposing barrier, whether of sentiment or opinion. For a moment, he possessed that almost fabulous inspiration, often referred to but seldom attained, in which a public meeting is transformed, as it were, into a single individuality—the orator wielding a thousand heads and hearts at once, and by the simple majesty of his all controlling thought, converting his hearers into the express image of his own soul. That night there were at least one thousand Garrisonians in Nantucket! At the close of this great meeting, I was duly waited on by Mr. John A. Collins—then the general agent of the Massachusetts anti-slavery society—and urgently solicited by him to become an agent of that society, and to publicly advocate its anti-slavery principles. I was reluctant to take the proffered position. I had not been quite three years from slavery—was honestly distrustful of my ability—wished to be excused; publicity exposed me to discovery and arrest by my master; and other objections came up, but Mr. Collins was not to be put off, and I finally consented to go out for three months, for I supposed that I should have got to the end of my story and my usefulness, in that length of time.

Here opened upon me a new life—a life for which I had had no preparation. I was a "graduate from the peculiar institution," Mr. Collins used to say, when introducing me, "*with my diploma written on my back!*" The three years of my freedom had been spent in the hard school of adversity. My hands had been furnished by nature with something like a solid leather coating, and I had bravely marked out for myself a life of rough labor, suited to the hardness of my hands, as a means of supporting myself and rearing my children.

Now what shall I say of this fourteen years' experience as a public advocate of the cause of my enslaved brothers and sisters? The time is but as a speck, yet large enough to justify a pause for retrospection—and a pause it must only be.

Young, ardent, and hopeful, I entered upon this new life in the full gush of unsuspecting enthusiasm. The cause was good; the men engaged in it were good; the means to attain its triumph, good; Heaven's blessing must attend all, and freedom must soon be given to the pining millions under a ruthless bondage. My whole heart went with the holy cause, and my most fervent prayer to the Almighty Disposer of the hearts of men, were continually offered for its early triumph. "Who or what," thought I, "can withstand a cause so good, so holy, so indescribably glorious. The God of Israel is with us. The might of the Eternal is on our side. Now let but the truth be spoken, and a nation will start forth at the sound!" In this enthusiastic spirit, I dropped into the ranks of freedom's friends, and went forth to the battle. For a time I was made to forget that my skin was dark and my hair crisped. For a time I regretted that I could not have shared the hardships and dangers endured by the earlier workers for the slave's release. I soon, however, found that my enthusiasm had been extravagant; that hardships and dangers were not yet passed; and that the life now before me, had shadows as well as sunbeams.

Among the first duties assigned me, on entering the ranks, was to travel, in company with Mr. George Foster, to secure subscribers to the "Anti-slavery Standard" and the "Liberator." With him I traveled and lectured through the eastern counties of Massachusetts. Much interest was awakened—large meetings assembled.

Many came, no doubt, from curiosity to hear what a negro could say in his own cause. I was generally introduced as a "*chattel*"—a "*thing*"—a piece of southern "*property*"—the chairman assuring the audience that *it* could speak. Fugitive slaves, at that time, were not so plentiful as now; and as a fugitive slave lecturer, I had the advantage of being a "*brand new fact*"—the first one out. Up to that time, a colored man was deemed a fool who confessed himself a runaway slave, not only because of the danger to which he exposed himself of being retaken, but because it was a confession of a very *low* origin! Some of my colored friends in New Bedford thought very badly of my wisdom for thus exposing and degrading myself. The only precaution I took, at the beginning, to prevent Master Thomas from knowing where I was, and what I was about, was the withholding of my former name, my master's name, and the name of the state and county from which I came. During the first three or four months, my speeches were almost exclusively made up of narrations of my own personal experience as a slave. "Let us have the facts," said the people. So also said Friend George Foster, who always wished to pin me down to my simple narrative. "Give us the facts," said Collins, "we will take care of the philosophy." Just here arose some embarrassment. It was impossible for me to repeat the same old story month after month, and to keep up my interest in it. It was new to the people, it is true, but it was an old story to me; and to go through with it night after night, was a task altogether too mechanical for my nature. "Tell your story, Frederick," would whisper my then revered friend, William Lloyd Garrison, as I stepped upon the platform. I could not always obey, for I was now reading and thinking. New views of the subject were presented to my mind. It did not entirely satisfy me to *narrate* wrongs; I *felt* like *denouncing* them. I could not always curb my moral indignation for the perpetrators of slaveholding villainy, long enough for a circumstantial statement of the facts which I felt almost everybody must know. Besides, I was growing, and needed room. "People won't believe you ever was a slave, Frederick, if you keep on this way," said Friend Foster. "Be yourself," said Collins, "and tell your story." It was said to me, "Better have a *little* of the plantation manner of speech than not; 'tis not best that you seem too learned." These excellent friends were actuated by the best of motives, and were not altogether wrong in their advice; and still I must speak just the word that seemed to *me* the word to be spoken *by* me.

At last the apprehended trouble came. People doubted if I ever had been a slave. They said I did not talk like a slave, look like a slave, nor act like a slave, and that they believed I had never been south of Mason and Dixon's line. "He don't tell us where he came from—what his master's name was—how he got away—nor the story of his experience. Besides, he is educated, and is, in this, a contradiction of all the facts we have concerning the ignorance of the slaves." Thus, I was in a pretty fair way to be denounced as an impostor. The committee of the Massachusetts anti-slavery society knew all the facts in my case, and agreed with me in the prudence of keeping them private. They, therefore, never doubted my being a genuine fugitive; but going down the aisles of the churches in which I spoke, and hearing the free spoken Yankees saying, repeatedly, "*He's never been a slave, I'll warrant ye,*" I resolved to dispel all doubt, at no distant day, by such a revelation of facts as could not be made by any other than a genuine fugitive.

In a little less than four years, therefore, after becoming a public lecturer, I was induced to write out the leading facts connected with my experience in slavery, giving names of persons, places, and dates—

thus putting it in the power of any who doubted, to ascertain the truth or falsehood of my story of being a fugitive slave. This statement soon became known in Maryland, and I had reason to believe that an effort would be made to recapture me.

## XXV

## *Various Incidents*

I have now given the reader an imperfect sketch of nine years' experience in freedom—three years as a common laborer on the wharves of New Bedford, four years as a lecturer in New England, and two years of semi-exile in Great Britain and Ireland. A single ray of light remains to be flung upon my life during the last eight years, and my story will be done.

A trial awaited me on my return from England to the United States, for which I was but very imperfectly prepared. My plans for my then future usefulness as an anti-slavery advocate were all settled. My friends in England had resolved to raise a given sum to purchase for me a press and printing materials; and I already saw myself wielding my pen, as well as my voice, in the great work of renovating the public mind, and building up a public sentiment which should, at least, send slavery and oppression to the grave, and restore to "liberty and the pursuit of happiness" the people with whom I had suffered, both as a slave and as a freeman. Intimation had reached my friends in Boston of what I intended to do, before my arrival, and I was prepared to find them favorably disposed toward my much cherished enterprise. In this I was mistaken. I found them very earnestly opposed to the idea of my starting a paper, and for several reasons. First, the paper was not needed; secondly, it would interfere with my usefulness as a lecturer; thirdly, I was better fitted to speak than to write; fourthly, the paper could not succeed. This opposition, from a quarter so highly esteemed, and to which I had been accustomed to look for advice and direction, caused me not only to hesitate, but inclined me to abandon the enterprise. All previous attempts to establish such a journal having failed, I felt that probably I should but add another to the list of failures, and thus contribute another proof of the mental and moral deficiencies of my race. Very much that was said to me in respect to my imperfect literary acquirements, I felt to be most painfully true. The unsuccessful projectors of all the previous colored newspapers were my superiors in point of education, and if they failed, how could I hope for success? Yet I did hope for success, and persisted in the undertaking. Some of my English friends greatly encouraged me to go forward, and I shall never cease to be grateful for their words of cheer and generous deeds.

I can easily pardon those who have denounced me as ambitious and presumptuous, in view of my persistence in this enterprise. I was but nine years from slavery. In point of mental experience, I was but nine years old. That one, in such circumstances, should aspire to establish a printing press, among an educated people, might well be considered, if not ambitious, quite silly. My American friends looked at me with astonishment! "A wood-sawyer" offering himself to the public as an editor! A slave, brought up in the very depths of ignorance, assuming to instruct the highly civilized people of the north in the principles of liberty, justice, and humanity! The thing looked absurd. Nevertheless, I persevered. I felt that the want of education, great as it was, could be overcome by study, and that knowledge would come by experience; and further, (which was perhaps the most controlling consideration,) I thought that an intelligent public, knowing my early history, would easily pardon a large share of the deficiencies which I was sure that my paper would exhibit. The most distressing thing, however, was the offense which I was about to give my Boston friends, by what seemed to them a reckless disregard of their sage advice. I am not sure that I was not under the influence of something like a slavish adoration of my Boston friends, and I labored hard to convince them of the wisdom of my undertaking, but without success. Indeed, I never expect to succeed, although time has answered all their original objections. The paper has been successful. It is a large sheet, costing eighty dollars per week—has three thousand subscribers—has been published regularly nearly eight years—and bids fair to stand eight years longer. At any rate, the eight years to come are as full of promise as were the eight that are past.

It is not to be concealed, however, that the maintenance of such a journal, under the circumstances, has been a work of much difficulty; and could all the perplexity, anxiety, and trouble attending it, have been clearly foreseen, I might have shrunk from the undertaking. As it is, I rejoice in having engaged in the enterprise, and count it joy to have been able to suffer, in many ways, for its success, and for the success of the cause to which it has been faithfully devoted. I look upon the time, money, and labor bestowed upon it, as being amply rewarded, in the development of my own mental and moral energies, and in the corresponding development of my deeply injured and oppressed people.

From motives of peace, instead of issuing my paper in Boston, among my New England friends, I came to Rochester, Western New York, among strangers, where the circulation of my paper could not interfere with the local circulation of the Liberator and the Standard; for at that time I was, on the anti-slavery question, a faithful disciple of William Lloyd Garrison, and fully committed to his doctrine touching the pro-slavery character of the constitution of the United States, and the *non-voting principle*, of which he is the known and distinguished advocate. With Mr. Garrison, I held it to be the first duty of the non-slaveholding states to dissolve the union with the slaveholding states; and hence my cry, like his, was, "No union with slaveholders." With these views, I came into Western New York; and during the first four years of my labor here, I advocated them with pen and tongue, according to the best of my ability.

About four years ago, upon a reconsideration of the whole subject, I became convinced that there was no necessity for dissolving the "union between the northern and southern states;" that to seek this dissolution was no part of my duty as an abolitionist; that to abstain from voting, was to refuse to exercise a legitimate and powerful means for abolishing slavery; and that the constitution of the United States not only contained no guarantees in favor of slavery, but, on the contrary, it is, in its letter and spirit, an anti-slavery instrument, demanding the abolition of slavery as a condition of its own existence, as the supreme law of the land.

Here was a radical change in my opinions, and in the action logically resulting from that change. To those with whom I had been in agreement and in sympathy, I was now in opposition. What they held to be a great and important truth, I now looked upon as a dangerous error. A very painful, and yet a very natural, thing now happened. Those who could not see any honest reasons for changing their views, as I had done, could not easily see any such reasons for my change, and the common punishment of apostates was mine.

The opinions first entertained were naturally derived and honestly entertained, and I trust that my present opinions have the same claims to respect. Brought directly, when I escaped from slavery, into contact with a class of abolitionists regarding the constitution as a slaveholding instrument, and finding their views supported by the united and entire history of every department of the government, it is not strange that I assumed the constitution to be just what their interpretation made it. I was bound, not only by their superior knowledge, to take their opinions as the true ones, in respect to the subject, but also because I had no means of showing their unsoundness. But for the responsibility of conducting a public journal, and the necessity imposed upon me of meeting opposite views from abolitionists in this state, I should in all probability have remained as firm in my disunion views as any other disciple of William Lloyd Garrison.

My new circumstances compelled me to re-think the whole subject, and to study, with some care, not only the just and proper rules of legal interpretation, but the origin, design, nature, rights, powers, and duties of civil government, and also the relations which human beings sustain to it. By such a course of thought and reading, I was conducted to the conclusion that the constitution of the United States—inaugurated "to form a more perfect union, establish justice, insure domestic tranquillity, provide for the common defense, promote the general welfare, and secure the blessings of liberty"—could not well have been designed at the same time to maintain and perpetuate a system of rapine and murder like slavery; especially, as not one word can be found in the constitution to authorize such a belief. Then, again, if the declared purposes of an instrument are to govern the meaning of all its parts and details, as they clearly should, the constitution of our country is our warrant for the abolition of slavery in every state in the American Union. I mean, however, not to argue, but simply to state my views. It would require very many pages of a volume like this, to set forth the arguments demonstrating the unconstitutionality and the complete illegality of slavery in our land; and as my experience, and not my arguments, is within the scope and contemplation of this volume, I omit the latter and proceed with the former.

I will now ask the kind reader to go back a little in my story, while I bring up a thread left behind for convenience sake, but which, small as it is, cannot be properly omitted altogether; and that thread is American prejudice against color, and its varied illustrations in my own experience.

When I first went among the abolitionists of New England, and began to travel, I found this prejudice very strong and very annoying. The abolitionists themselves were not entirely free from it, and I could see that they were nobly struggling against it. In their eagerness, sometimes, to show their contempt for the feeling, they proved that they had not entirely recovered from it; often illustrating the saying, in their conduct, that a man may "stand up so straight as to lean backward." When it was said to me, "Mr. Douglass, I will walk to meeting with you; I am not afraid of a black man," I could not help thinking—seeing nothing very frightful in my appearance—"And why should you be?" The children at the north had all been educated to believe that if they were bad, the old *black* man—not the old *devil*—would get them; and it was evidence of some courage, for any so educated to get the better of their fears.

The custom of providing separate cars for the accommodation of colored travelers, was established on nearly all the railroads of New England, a dozen years ago. Regarding this custom as fostering the spirit of caste, I made it a rule to seat myself in the cars for the accommodation of passengers generally. Thus seated, I was sure to be called upon to betake myself to the "*Jim Crow car.*" Refusing to obey, I was often dragged out of my seat, beaten, and severely bruised, by conductors and brakemen. Attempting to start from Lynn, one day, for Newburyport, on the Eastern railroad, I went, as my custom was, into one of the best railroad carriages on the road. The seats were very luxuriant and beautiful. I was soon waited upon by the conductor, and ordered out; whereupon I demanded the reason for my invidious removal. After a good deal of parleying, I was told that it was because I was black. This I denied, and appealed to the company to sustain my denial; but they were evidently unwilling to commit themselves, on a point so delicate, and requiring such nice powers of discrimination, for they remained as dumb as death. I was soon waited on by half a dozen fellows of the baser sort, (just such as would volunteer to take a bull-dog out of a meeting-house in time of public worship,) and told that I must move out of that seat, and if I did not, they would drag me out. I refused to move, and they clutched me, head, neck, and shoulders. But, in anticipation of the stretching to which I was about to be subjected, I had interwoven myself among the seats. In dragging me out, on this occasion, it must have cost the company twenty-five or thirty dollars, for I tore up seats and all. So great was the excitement in Lynn, on the subject, that the superintendent, Mr. Stephen A. Chase, ordered the trains to run through Lynn without stopping, while I remained in that town; and this ridiculous farce was enacted. For several days the trains went dashing through Lynn without stopping. At the same time that they excluded a free colored man from their cars, this same company allowed slaves, in company with their masters and mistresses, to ride unmolested.

After many battles with the railroad conductors, and being roughly handled in not a few instances, proscription was at last abandoned; and the "Jim Crow car"—set up for the degradation of colored people—is nowhere found in New England. This result was not brought about without the intervention of the people, and the threatened enactment of a law compelling railroad companies to respect the rights of travelers. Hon. Charles Francis Adams performed signal service in the Massachusetts legislature, in bringing about this reformation; and to him the colored citizens of that state are deeply indebted.

Although often annoyed, and sometimes outraged, by this prejudice against color, I am indebted to it for many passages of quiet amusement. A half-cured subject of it is sometimes driven into awkward straits, especially if he happens to get a genuine specimen of the race into his house.

In the summer of 1843, I was traveling and lecturing, in company with William A. White, Esq., through the state of Indiana. Anti-slavery friends were not very abundant in Indiana, at that time, and beds were not more plentiful than friends. We often slept out, in preference to sleeping in the houses, at some points. At the close of one of our meetings, we were invited home with a kindly-disposed old farmer, who, in the generous enthusiasm of the moment, seemed to have forgotten that he had but one spare bed, and that his guests were an ill-matched pair. All went on pretty well, till near bed time, when signs of uneasiness began to show themselves, among the unsophisticated sons and daughters. White is remarkably fine looking, and very evidently a born gentleman; the idea of putting us in the same bed was hardly to be tolerated; and yet, there we were, and but the one bed for us, and that, by the way, was in the same room occupied by the other members of the family. White, as well as I, perceived the difficulty, for yonder slept the old folks, there the sons, and a little farther along slept the daughters; and but one other bed remained. Who should have this bed, was the puzzling question. There was some whispering between the old folks, some confused looks among the young, as the time for going to bed approached. After witnessing the confusion as long as I liked, I relieved the kindly-disposed family by playfully saying, "Friend White, having got entirely rid of my prejudice against color, I think, as a proof of it, I must allow you to sleep with me to-night." White kept up the joke, by seeming to esteem himself the favored party, and thus the difficulty was removed. If we went to a hotel, and called for dinner, the landlord was sure to set one table for White and another for me, always taking him to be master, and me the servant. Large eyes were generally made when the order was given to remove the dishes from my table to that of White's. In those days, it was thought strange that a white man and a colored man could dine peaceably at the same table, and in some parts the strangeness of such a sight has not entirely subsided.

Some people will have it that there is a natural, an inherent, and an invincible repugnance in the breast of the white race toward dark-colored people; and some very intelligent colored men think that their proscription is owing solely to the color which nature has given them. They hold that they are rated according to their color, and that it is impossible for white people ever to look upon dark races of men, or men belonging to the African race, with other than feelings of aversion. My experience, both serious and mirthful, combats this conclusion. Leaving out of sight, for a moment, grave facts, to this point, I will state one or two, which illustrate a very interesting feature of American character as well as American prejudice. Riding from Boston to Albany, a few years ago, I found myself in a large car, well filled with passengers. The seat next to me was about the only vacant one. At every stopping place we took in new passengers, all of whom, on reaching the seat next to me, cast a disdainful glance upon it, and passed to another car, leaving me in the full enjoyment of a whole form. For a time, I did not know but that my riding there was prejudicial to the interest of the railroad company. A circumstance occurred, however, which gave me an elevated position at once. Among the passengers on this train was Gov. George N. Briggs. I was not acquainted with him, and had no idea that I was known to him. Known to him, however, I was, for upon observing me, the governor left his place, and making his way toward me, respectfully asked the privilege of a seat by my side; and upon introducing himself, we entered into a conversation very pleasant and instructive to me. The despised seat now became honored. His excellency had removed all the prejudice against sitting by the side of a negro; and upon his leaving it, as he did, on reaching Pittsfield, there were at least one dozen applicants for the place. The governor had, without changing my skin a single shade, made the place respectable which before was despicable.

A similar incident happened to me once on the Boston and New Bedford railroad, and the leading party to it has since been governor of the state of Massachusetts. I allude to Col. John Henry Clifford. Lest the reader may fancy I am aiming to elevate myself, by claiming too much intimacy with great men, I must state that my only acquaintance with Col. Clifford was formed while I was *his hired servant* during the first winter of my escape from slavery. I owe it him to say, that in that relation I found him always kind and gentlemanly. But to the incident. I entered a car at Boston, for New Bedford, which, with the exception of a single seat, was full, and found I must occupy this, or stand up, during the journey. Having no mind to do this, I stepped up to the man having the next seat, and who had a few parcels on the seat, and gently asked leave to take a seat by his side. My fellow-passenger gave me a look made up of reproach and indignation, and asked me why I should come to that particular seat. I assured him, in the gentlest manner, that of all others this was the seat for me. Finding that I was actually about to sit down, he sang out, "O! stop, stop! and let me get out!" Suiting the action to the word, up the agitated man got, and sauntered to the other end of the car, and was compelled to stand for most of the way thereafter. Half-way to New Bedford, or more, Col. Clifford, recognizing me, left his seat, and not having seen me before since I had ceased to wait on him, (in everything except hard arguments against his pro-slavery position,) apparently forgetful of his rank, manifested, in greeting me, something of the feeling of an old friend. This demonstration was not lost on the gentleman whose dignity I had, an hour before, most seriously offended. Col. Clifford was known to be about the most aristocratic gentleman in Bristol county; and it was evidently thought that I must be somebody, else I should not have been thus noticed, by a person so distinguished. Sure enough, after Col. Clifford left me, I found myself surrounded with friends; and among the number, my offended friend stood nearest, and with an apology for his rudeness, which I could not resist, although it was one of the lamest ever offered. With such facts as these before me—and I have many of them—I am inclined to think that pride and fashion have much to do with the treatment commonly extended to colored people in the United States. I once heard a very plain man say, (and he was cross-eyed, and awkwardly flung together in other respects,) that he should be a handsome man when public opinion shall be changed.

Since I have been editing and publishing a journal devoted to the cause of liberty and progress, I have had my mind more directed to the condition and circumstances of the free colored people than when I was the agent of an abolition society. The result has been a corresponding change in the disposition of my time and labors. I have felt it to be a part of my mission—under a gracious Providence—to impress my sable brothers in this country with the conviction that, notwithstanding the ten thousand discouragements and the powerful hinderances, which beset their existence in this country—notwithstanding the blood-written history of Africa, and her children, from whom we have descended, or the clouds and darkness, (whose stillness and gloom are made only more awful by wrathful thunder and lightning,) now overshadowing them—progress is yet possible, and bright skies shall yet shine upon their pathway; and that "Ethiopia shall yet reach forth her hand unto God."

Believing that one of the best means of emancipating the slaves of the south is to improve and elevate the character of the free colored people of the north I shall labor in the future, as I have labored in the past, to promote the moral, social, religious, and intellectual elevation of the free colored people; never forgetting my own humble origin, nor refusing, while Heaven lends me ability, to use my voice, my pen, or my vote, to advocate the great and primary work of the universal and unconditional emancipation of my entire race.

# LIFE AND TIMES OF FREDERICK DOUGLASS

Douglass published his third autobiography, the *Life and Times of Frederick Douglass*, in 1881, covering his experiences to that date as well as recounting the periods included in the *Narrative* (1845) and *My Bondage and My Freedom* (1855). In 1892, three years before his death, he published a revised, expanded edition of *Life and Times*, from which the following excerpts are drawn. Douglass presents himself in this final autobiography as a successful public figure appointed to high offices by a succession of administrations. More revealing, however, than descriptions of his official public roles or his European travels are the details provided in the following excerpts, which range from an explanation of how he actually escaped from slavery to a retrospective view of his life as an attempt to articulate the concerns of blacks in the United States.

## *[Details of His Escape from Slavery]*

In the first narrative of my experience in slavery, written nearly forty years ago, and in various writings since, I have given the public what I considered very good reasons for withholding the manner of my escape. In substance these reasons were, first, that such publication at any time during the existence of slavery might be used by the master against the slave, and prevent the future escape of any who might adopt the same means that I did. The second reason was, if possible, still more binding to silence—for publication of details would certainly have put in peril the persons and property of those who assisted. Murder itself was not more sternly and certainly punished in the State of Maryland than was the aiding and abetting the escape of a slave. Many colored men, for no other crime than that of giving aid to a fugitive slave, have, like Charles T. Torrey, perished in prison. The abolition of slavery in my native State and throughout the country, and the lapse of time, render the caution hitherto observed no longer necessary. But, even since the abolition of slavery, I have sometimes thought it well enough to baffle curiosity by saying that while slavery existed there were good reasons for not telling the manner of my escape, and since slavery had ceased to exist there was no reason for telling it. I shall now, however, cease to avail myself of this formula, and, as far as I can, endeavor to satisfy this very natural curiosity. I should perhaps have yielded to that feeling sooner, had there been anything very heroic or thrilling in the incidents connected with my escape, for I am sorry to say I have nothing of that sort to tell; and yet the courage that could risk betrayal and the bravery which was ready to encounter death if need be, in pursuit of freedom, were essential features in the undertaking. My success was due to address rather than to courage; to good luck rather than to bravery. My means of escape were provided for me by the very men who were making laws to hold and bind me more securely in slavery. It was the custom in the State of Maryland to require of the free colored people to have what were called free papers. This instrument they were required to renew very often, and by charging a fee for this writing, considerable sums from time to time were collected by the State. In these papers the name, age, color, height and form of the free man were described, together with any scars or other marks upon his person which could assist in his identification. This device of slaveholding ingenuity, like other devices of wickedness, in some measure defeated itself—since more than one man could be found to answer the same general description. Hence many slaves could escape by personating the owner of one set of papers; and this was often done as follows: A slave nearly or sufficiently answering the description set forth in the papers, would borrow or hire them till he could by their means escape to a free state, and then, by mail or otherwise, return them to the owner. The operation was a hazardous one for the lender as well as for the borrower. A failure on the part of the fugitive to send back the papers would imperil his benefactor, and the discovery of the papers in possession of the wrong man would imperil both the fugitive and his friend. It was therefore an act of supreme trust on the part of a freeman of color thus to put in jeopardy his own liberty that another might be free. It was, however, not unfrequently bravely done, and was seldom discovered. I was not so fortunate as to sufficiently resemble any of my free acquaintances as to answer the description of their papers. But I had one friend—a sailor—who owned a sailor's protection, which answered somewhat the purpose of free papers—describing his person and certifying to the fact that he was a free American sailor. The instrument had at its head the American eagle, which at once gave it the appearance of an authorized document. This protection did not, when in my hands, describe its bearer very accurately. Indeed, it called for a man much darker than myself, and close examination of it would have caused my arrest at the start. In order to avoid this fatal scrutiny on the part of the railroad official, I had arranged with Isaac Rolls, a hackman, to bring my baggage to the train just on the moment of starting, and jumped upon the car myself when the train was already in motion. Had I gone into the station and offered to purchase a ticket, I should have been instantly and carefully examined, and undoubtedly arrested. In choosing this plan upon which to act, I considered the jostle of the train, and the natural haste of the conductor in a train crowded with passengers, and relied upon my skill and address in playing the sailor as described in my protection, to do the rest. One element in my favor was the kind feeling which prevailed in Baltimore and other seaports at the time, towards "those who go down to the sea in ships." "Free trade and sailors' rights" expressed the sentiment of the country just then. In my clothing I was rigged out in sailor style. I had on a red shirt and a tarpaulin hat and black cravat, tied in sailor fashion, carelessly and loosely about my neck. My knowledge of ships and sailor's talk came much to my assistance, for I knew a ship from stem to stern, and from keelson to cross-trees, and could talk sailor like an "old salt." On sped the train, and I was well on the way to Havre de Grace before the conductor came into the negro car to collect tickets and examine the papers of his black passengers. This was a critical moment in the drama. My whole future depended upon the decision of this conductor. Agitated I was while this ceremony was proceeding, but still, externally at least, I was apparently calm and self-possessed. He went on with his duty—examining several colored passengers before reaching me. He was somewhat harsh in tone and peremptory in manner until he reached me, when, strangely enough, and to my surprise and relief, his whole manner changed. Seeing that I did not readily produce my free papers, as the other colored persons in the car had done, he said to me in a friendly contrast with that observed towards the others: "I suppose you have your free papers?" To which I answered: "No, sir; I never carry my free papers to sea with me." "But you have something to show that you are a free man, have you not?" "Yes, sir," I answered; "I have a paper with the American eagle on it, that will carry me round the world." With this I drew from my deep sailor's pocket my seaman's protection, as before described. The merest glance at the paper satisfied him, and he took my fare and went on about his business. This moment of time was one of the most anxious I ever experienced. Had the conductor looked closely at the paper, he could not have failed to discover that it called for a very different looking person from myself, and in that case it would have been his duty to arrest me on the instant and send me back to Baltimore from the first station. When he left me with the assurance that I was all right, though much relieved, I realized that I was still in great danger: I was still in Maryland, and subject to arrest at any moment. I saw on the train several persons who would have known me in any other clothes, and I feared they might recognize me, even in my sailor "rig," and report me to the conductor, who would then subject me to a closer examination, which I knew well would be fatal to me.

Though I was not a murderer fleeing from justice, I felt, perhaps, quite as miserable as such a criminal. The train was moving at a very high rate of speed for that time of railroad travel, but to my anxious mind, it was moving far too slowly. Minutes were hours, and hours were days during this part of my flight. After Maryland I was to pass through Delaware—another slave State, where slavecatchers generally awaited their prey, for it was not in the interior of the State, but on its borders, that these human hounds were most vigilant and active. The border lines between slavery and freedom were the dangerous ones, for the fugitives. The heart of no fox or deer, with hungry hounds on his trail, in full chase, could have beaten more anxiously or noisily than did mine from the time I left Baltimore till I reached Philadelphia. The passage of the Susquehanna river at Havre de Grace was at that time made by ferry-boat, on board of which I met a young colored man by the name of Nichols, who came very near betraying me. He was a "hand" on the boat, but instead of minding his business, he insisted upon knowing me, and asking me dangerous questions as to where I was going, and when I was coming back, etc. I got away from my old and inconvenient acquaintance as soon as I could decently do so, and went to another part of the boat. Once across the river I encountered a new danger. Only a few days before I had been at work on a revenue cutter, in Mr. Price's shipyard, under the care of Captain McGowan. On the meeting at this point of the two trains, the one going south stopped on the track just opposite to the one going north, and it so happened that this Captain McGowan sat at a window where he could see me very distinctly, and would certainly have recognized me had he looked at me but for a second. Fortunately, in the hurry of the moment, he did not see me, and the trains soon passed each other on their respective ways. But this was not the only hair-breadth escape. A German blacksmith, whom I knew well, was on the train with me, and looked at me very intently, as if he thought he had seen me somewhere before in his travels. I really believe he knew me, but had no heart to betray me. At any rate he saw me escaping and held his peace.

The last point of imminent danger, and the one I dreaded most, was Wilmington. Here we left the train and took the steamboat for Philadelphia. In making the change I again apprehended arrest, but no one disturbed me, and I was soon on the broad and beautiful Delaware, speeding away to the Quaker City. On reaching Philadelphia in the afternoon I inquired of a colored man how I could get on to New York? He directed me to the Willow street depot, and thither I went, taking the train that night. I reached New York Tuesday morning, having completed the journey in less than twenty-four hours. Such is briefly the manner of my escape from slavery—and the end of my experience as a slave.

## *[John Brown]*

About the time I began my enterprise in Rochester I chanced to spend a night and a day under the roof of a man whose character and conversation, and whose objects and aims in life, made a very deep impression upon my mind and heart. His name had been mentioned to me by several prominent colored men, among whom were the Rev. Henry Highland Garnet and J. W. Loguen. In speaking of him their voices would drop to a whisper, and what they said of him made me very eager to see and to know him. Fortunately, I was invited to see him in his own house. At the time to which I now refer this man was a respectable merchant in a populous and thriving city, and our first place of meeting was at his store. This was a substantial brick building on a prominent, busy street. A glance at the interior, as well as at the massive walls without, gave me the impression that the owner must be a man of considerable wealth. My welcome was all that I could have asked. Every member of the family, young and old, seemed glad to see me, and I was made much at home in a very little while. I was, however, a little disappointed with the appearance of the house and its location. After seeing the fine store I was prepared to see a fine residence in an eligible locality, but this conclusion was completely dispelled by actual observation. In fact, the house was neither commodious nor elegant, nor its situation desirable. It was a small wooden building on a back street, in a neighborhood chiefly occupied by laboring men and mechanics; respectable enough, to be sure, but not quite the place, I thought, where one would look for the residence of a flourishing and successful merchant. Plain as was the outside of this man's house, the inside was plainer. Its furniture would have satisfied a Spartan. It would take longer to tell what was not in this house than what was in it. There was an air of plainness about it which almost suggested destitution. My first meal passed under the misnomer of tea, though there was nothing about it resembling the usual significance of that term. It consisted of beef-soup, cabbage, and potatoes—a meal such as a man might relish after following the plow all day or performing a forced march of a dozen miles over a rough road in frosty weather. Innocent of paint, veneering, varnish, or table-cloth, the table announced itself unmistakably of pine and of the plainest workmanship. There was no hired help visible. The mother, daughters, and sons did the serving, and did it well. They were evidently used to it, and had no thought of any impropriety or degradation in being their own servants. It is said that a house in some measure reflects the character of its occupants; this one certainly did. In it there were no disguises, no illusions, no make-believes. Everything implied stern truth, solid purpose, and rigid economy. I was not long in company with the master of this house before I discovered that he was indeed the master of it, and was likely to become mine too if I stayed long enough with him. He fulfilled St. Paul's idea of the head of the family. His wife believed in him, and his children observed him with reverence. Whenever he spoke his words commanded earnest attention. His arguments, which I ventured at some points to oppose, seemed to convince all; his appeals touched all, and his will impressed all. Certainly I never felt myself in the presence of a stronger religious influence than while in this man's house.

In person he was lean, strong, and sinewy, of the best New England mold, built for times of trouble and fitted to grapple with the flintiest hardships. Clad in plain American woolen, shod in boots of cowhide leather, and wearing a cravat of the same substantial material, under six feet high, less than 150 pounds in weight, aged about fifty, he presented a figure straight and symmetrical as a mountain pine. His bearing was singularly impressive. His head was not large, but compact and high. His hair was coarse, strong, slightly gray and closely trimmed, and grew low on his forehead. His face was smoothly shaved, and revealed a strong, square mouth, supported by a broad and prominent chin. His eyes were bluish-gray, and in conversation they were full of light and fire. When on the street, he moved with a long, springing, race-horse step, absorbed by his own reflections, neither seeking nor shunning observation. Such was the man whose name I had heard in whispers: such was the spirit of his house and family; such was the house in which he lived; and such was Captain John Brown, whose name has now passed into history, as that of one of the most marked characters and greatest heroes known to American fame.

After the strong meal already described, Captain Brown cautiously approached the subject which he wished to bring to my attention; for he seemed to apprehend opposition to his views. He denounced slavery in look and language fierce and bitter, thought that slaveholders had forfeited their right to live, that the slaves had the right to gain their liberty in any way they could, did not believe that moral suasion would ever liberate the slave, or that political action would abolish the system. He said that he had long had a plan which could accomplish this end, and he had invited me to his house to lay that plan before me. He said he had been for some time looking for colored men to whom he could safely reveal his secret, and at times he had almost despaired of finding such men; but that now he was encouraged, for he saw heads of such rising up in all directions. He had observed my course at home and abroad, and he wanted my coöperation. His plan as it then lay in his mind had much to commend it. It did not, as some suppose, contemplate a general rising among the slaves, and a general slaughter of the slave-masters. An insurrection, he thought, would only defeat the object; but his plan did contemplate the creating of an armed force which should act in the very heart of the South. He was not averse to the shedding of blood, and thought the practice of carrying arms would be a good one for the colored people to adopt, as it would give them a sense of their manhood. No people, he said, could have self-respect, or be respected, who would not fight for their freedom. He called my attention to a map of the United States, and pointed out to me the far-reaching Alleghanies, which stretch away from the borders of New York into the Southern States. "These mountains," he said, "are the basis of my plan. God has given the strength of the hills to freedom; they were placed here for the emancipation of the negro race; they are full of natural forts, where one man for defense will be equal to a hundred for attack; they are full also of good hiding-places, where large numbers of brave men could be concealed, and baffle and elude pursuit for a long time. I know these mountains well, and could take a body of men into them and keep them there despite of all the efforts of Virginia to dislodge them. The true object to be sought is first of all to destroy the money value of slave property; and that can only be done by rendering such property insecure. My plan, then, is to take at first about twenty-five picked men, and begin on a small scale; supply them with arms and ammunition and post them in squads of fives on a line of twenty-five miles. The most persuasive and judicious of these shall go down to the fields from time to time, as opportunity offers, and induce the slaves to join them, seeking and selecting the most restless and daring."

He saw that in this part of the work the utmost care must be used to avoid treachery and disclosure. Only the most conscientious and skillful should be sent on this perilous duty. With care and enterprise he thought he could soon gather a force of one hundred hardy men, men who would be content to lead the free and adventurous life to which he proposed to train them; when these were properly drilled, and each man had found the place for which he was best suited, they would begin work in earnest; they would run off the slaves in large numbers, retain the brave and strong ones in the mountains, and send the weak and timid to the north by the underground railroad. His operations would be enlarged with increasing numbers and would not be confined to one locality.

When I asked him how he would support these men, he said emphatically that he would subsist them upon the enemy. Slavery was a state of war, and the slave had a right to anything necessary to his freedom. "But," said I, "suppose you succeed in running off a few slaves, and thus impress the Virginia slaveholders with a sense of insecurity in their slaves, the effect will be only to make them sell their slaves further south." "That," said he, "will be what I want first to do; then I would follow them up. If we could drive slavery out of *one county*, it would be a great gain; it would weaken the system throughout the State." "But they would employ bloodhounds to hunt you out of the mountains." "That they might attempt," said he, "but the chances are, we should whip them, and when we should have whipped one squad, they would be careful how they pursued." "But you might be surrounded and cut off from your provisions or means of subsistence." He thought that this could not be done so they could not cut their way out, but even if the worst came he could but be killed, and he had no better use for his life than to lay it down in the cause of the slave. When I suggested that we might convert the slaveholders, he became much excited, and said that could never be, "he knew their proud hearts and that they would never be induced to give up their slaves, until they felt a big stick about their heads." He observed that I might have noticed the simple manner in which he lived, adding that he had adopted this method in order to save money to carry out his purposes. This was said in no boastful tone, for he felt that he had delayed already too long, and had no room to boast either his zeal or his self-denial. Had some men made such display of rigid virtue, I should have rejected it, as affected, false, and hypocritical, but in John Brown, I felt it to be real as iron or granite. From this night spent with John Brown in Springfield, Mass., 1847, while I continued to write and speak against slavery, I became all the same less hopeful of its peaceful abolition. My utterances became more and more tinged by the color of this man's strong impressions. Speaking at an anti-slavery convention in Salem, Ohio, I expressed this apprehension that slavery could only be destroyed by blood-shed, when I was suddenly and sharply interrupted by my good old friend Sojourner Truth with the question, "Frederick, is God dead?" "No," I answered, "and because God is not dead slavery can only end in blood." My quaint old sister was of the Garrison school of non-resistants, and was shocked at my sanguinary doctrine, but she too became an advocate of the sword, when the war for the maintenance of the Union was declared.

## *[Harriet Beecher Stowe and Free Blacks]*

In the midst of . . . fugitive slave troubles came the book known as Uncle Tom's Cabin, a work of marvelous depth and power. Nothing could have better suited the moral and humane requirements of the hour. Its effect was amazing, instantaneous, and universal. No book on the subject of slavery had so generally and favorably touched the American heart. It combined all the power and pathos of preceding publications of the kind, and was hailed by many as an inspired production. Mrs. Stowe at once became an object of interest and admiration. She had made fortune and fame at home, and had awakened a deep interest abroad. Eminent persons in England, roused to anti-slavery enthusiasm by her "Uncle Tom's Cabin," invited her to visit that country, and promised to give her a testimonial. Mrs. Stowe accepted the invitation and the proffered testimonial. Before sailing for England, however, she invited me from Rochester, N. Y., to spend a day at her house in Andover, Mass. Delighted with an opportunity to become personally acquainted with the gifted authoress, I lost no time in making my way to Andover. I was received at her home with genuine cordiality. There was no contradiction between the author and her book. Mrs. Stowe appeared in conversation equally as well as she appeared in her writing. She made to me a nice little speech in announcing her object in sending for me. "I have invited you here," she said, "because I wish to confer with you as to what can be done for the free colored people of the country. I am going to England and expect to have a considerable sum of money placed in my hands, and I intend to use it in some way for the permanent improvement of the free colored people, and especially for that class which has become free by their own exertions. In what way I can do this most successfully is the subject about which I wish to talk with you. In any event I desire to have some monument rise after Uncle Tom's Cabin, which shall show that it produced more than a transient influence." She said several plans had been suggested, among others an educational institution pure and simple, but that she thought favorably of the establishment of an industrial school; and she desired me to express my views as to what I thought would be the best plan by which to help the free colored people. I was not slow to tell Mrs. Stowe all I knew and had thought on the subject. As to a purely educational institution, I agreed with her that it did not meet our necessities. I argued against expending money in that way. I was also opposed to an ordinary industrial school where pupils should merely earn the means of obtaining an education in books. There were such schools, already. What I thought of as best was rather a series of workshops, where colored people could learn some of the handicrafts, learn to work in iron, wood, and leather, and where a plain English education could also be taught. I argued that the *want* of money was the root of all evil to the colored people. They were shut out from all lucrative employments and compelled to be merely barbers, waiters, coachmen, and the like, at wages so low that they could lay up little or nothing. Their poverty kept them ignorant and their ignorance kept them degraded. We needed more to learn how to make a good living than to learn Latin and Greek. After listening to me at considerable length, she was good enough to tell me that she favored my views, and would devote the money she expected to receive abroad to meeting the want I had described as the most important; by establishing an institution in which colored youth should learn trades as well as to read, write, and count.

When about to leave Andover, Mrs. Stowe asked me to put my views on the subject in the form of a letter, so that she could take it to England with her and show it to her friends there, that they might see to what their contributions were to be devoted. I acceded to her request and wrote her the following letter for the purpose named:

ROCHESTER, March 8, 1853.

MY DEAR MRS. STOWE:

You kindly informed me, when at your house a fortnight ago, that you designed to do something which should permanently contribute to the improvement and elevation of the free colored people in the United States. You especially expressed an interest in such of this class as had become free by their own exertions, and desired most of all to be of service to them. In what manner and by what means you can assist this class most successfully, is the subject upon which you have done me the honor to ask my opinion. . . . I assert, then, that *poverty, ignorance,* and *degradation* are the combined evils; or in other words, these constitute the social disease of the free colored people of the United States.

To deliver them from this triple malady is to improve and elevate them, by which I mean simply to put them on an equal footing with their white fellow-countrymen in the sacred right to "*Life, Liberty,* and the pursuit of happiness." I am for no fancied or artificial elevation, but only ask fair play. How shall this be obtained? I answer, first, not by establishing for our use high schools and colleges. Such institutions are, in my judgment, beyond our immediate occasions and are not adapted to our present most pressing wants. High schools and colleges are excellent institutions, and will in due season be greatly subservient to our progress; but they are the result, as well as they are the demand, of a point of progress which we as a people have not yet attained. Accustomed as we have been to the rougher and harder modes of living, and of gaining a livelihood, we cannot and we ought not to hope that in a single leap from our low condition, we can reach that of *Minsters, Lawyers, Doctors, Editors, Merchants,* etc. These will doubtless be attained by us; but this will only be when we have patiently and laboriously, and I may add successfully, mastered and passed through the intermediate gradations of agriculture and the mechanic arts. Besides, there are (and perhaps this is a better reason for my view of the case) numerous institutions of learning in this country, already thrown open to colored youth. To my thinking, there are quite as many facilities now afforded to the colored people as they can spare the time, from the sterner duties of life, to judiciously appropriate. In their present condition of poverty, they cannot spare their sons and daughters two or three years at boarding-schools or colleges, to say nothing of finding the means to sustain them while at such institutions. I take it, therefore, that we are well provided for in this respect; and that it may be fairly inferred from the fact, that the facilities for our education, so far as schools and colleges in the Free States are concerned, will increase quite in proportion with our future wants. Colleges have been open to colored youth in this country during the last dozen years. Yet few, comparatively, have acquired a classical education; and even this few have found themselves educated far above a living condition, there being no methods by which they could turn their learning to account. Several of this latter class have entered the ministry; but you need not be told that an educated people is needed to sustain an educated ministry. There must be a certain amount of cultivation among the people, to sustain such a ministry. At present we have not that cultivation amongst us, and, therefore, we value in the preacher strong lungs rather than high learning. I do not say that educated ministers are not needed amongst us, far from it! I wish there were more of them! but to increase their number is *not* the largest benefit you can bestow upon us.

We have two or three colored lawyers in this country; and I rejoice in the fact; for it affords very gratifying evidence of our progress. Yet it must be confessed that, in point of success, our lawyers are as great failures as our ministers. White people will not employ them to the obvious embarrassment of their causes, and the blacks, taking their *cue* from the whites, have not sufficient confidence in their abilities to employ them. Hence educated colored men, among the colored people, are at a very great discount. It would seem that education and emigration go together with us, for as soon as a man rises amongst us, capable, by his genius and learning, to do us great service, just so soon he finds that he can serve himself better by going elsewhere. In proof of this, I might instance the Russwurms, the Garnetts, the Wards, the Crummells, and others, all men of superior ability and attainments, and capable of removing mountains of prejudice against their race, by their simple presence in the country; but these gentlemen, finding themselves embarrassed here by the peculiar disadvantages to which I have referred, disadvantages in part growing out of their education, being repelled by ignorance on the one hand, and prejudice on the other, and having no taste to continue a contest against such odds, have sought more congenial climes, where they can live more peaceable and quiet lives. I regret their election, but I cannot blame them; for with an equal amount of education, and the hard lot which was theirs, I might follow their example. . . .

There is little reason to hope that any considerable number of the free colored people will ever be induced to leave this country, even if such a thing were desirable. The black man (*un*like the Indian) loves civilization. He does not make very great progress in civilization himself, but he likes to be in the midst of it, and prefers to share its most galling evils, to encountering barbarism. Then the love of country, the dread of isolation, the lack of adventurous spirit, and the thought of seeming to desert their "brethren in bonds," are a powerful check upon all schemes of colonization, which look to the removal of the colored people, without the slaves. The truth is, dear madam, we are *here*, and here we are likely to remain. Individuals emigrate—nations never. We have grown up with this republic, and I see nothing in her character, or even in the character of the American people, as yet, which compels the belief that we must leave the United States. If, then, we are to remain here, the question for the wise and good is precisely that which you have submitted to me—namely: What can be done to improve the condition of the free people of color in the United States? The plan which I humbly submit in answer to this inquiry (and in the hope that it may find favor with you, and with the many friends of humanity who honor, love and cooperate with you) is the establishment in Rochester, N. Y., or in some other part of the United States equally favorable to such an enterprise, of an INDUSTRIAL COLLEGE in which shall be taught several important branches of the mechanic arts. This college shall be open to colored youth. I will pass over the details of such an institution as I propose. . . . Never having had a day's schooling in all my life, I may not be expected to map out the details of a plan so comprehensive as that involved in the idea of a college. I repeat, then, that I leave the organization and administration of the institution to the superior wisdom of yourself and the friends who second your noble efforts. The argument in favor of an Industrial College (a college to be conducted by the best men, and the best workmen which the mechanic arts can afford: a college where colored youth can be instructed to use their hands, as well as their heads; where they can be put in possession of the means of getting a living whether their lot in after life may be cast among civilized or uncivilized men; whether they choose to stay here, or prefer to return to the land of their fathers) is briefly this: Prejudice against the free colored people in the United States has shown itself nowhere so invincible as among mechanics. The farmer and the professional man cherish no feeling so bitter as that cherished by these. The latter would starve us out of the country entirely. At this moment I can more easily get my son into a lawyer's office to study law than I can into a blacksmith's shop to blow the bellows and to wield the sledge-hammer. Denied the means of learning useful trades, we are pressed into the narrowest limits to obtain a livelihood. In times past we have been the hewers of wood and drawers of water for American society, and we once enjoyed a monopoly in menial employments, but this is so no longer. Even these employments are rapidly passing away out of our hands. The fact is (every day begins with the lesson, and ends with the lesson) that colored men must learn trades; must find new employments; new modes of usefulness to society, or that they must decay under the pressing wants to which their condition is rapidly bringing them

We must become mechanics; we must build as well as live in houses; we must make as well as use furniture; we must construct bridges as well as pass over them, before we can properly live or be respected by our fellow men. We need mechanics as well as ministers. We need workers in iron, clay, and leather. We have orators, authors, and other professional men, but these reach only a certain class, and get respect for our race in certain select circles. To live here as we ought we must fasten ourselves to our countrymen through their every-day, cardinal wants. We must not only be able to *black* boots, but to *make* them. At present we are, in the northern States, unknown as mechanics. We give no proof of genius or skill at the county, State, or national fairs. We are unknown at any of the great exhibitions of the industry of our fellow-citizens, and being unknown, we are unconsidered.

The fact that we make no show of our ability is held conclusive of our inability to make any, hence all the indifference and contempt with which incapacity is regarded fall upon us, and that too when we have had no means of disproving the infamous opinion of our natural inferiority. I have, during the last dozen years, denied before the Americans that we are an inferior race; but this has been done by arguments based upon admitted principles rather than by the presentation of facts. Now, firmly believing, as I do, that there are skill, invention, power, industry, and real mechanical genius among the colored people, which will bear favorable testimony for them, and which only need the means to develop them, I am decidedly in favor of the establishment of such a college as I have mentioned. The benefits of such an institution would not be confined to the Northern States, nor to the free colored people. They would extend over the whole Union. The slave not less than the freeman would be benefited by such an institution. It must be confessed that the most powerful argument now used by the southern slaveholder, and the one most soothing to his conscience, is that derived from the low condition of the free colored people of the North. I have long felt that too little attention has been given by our truest friends in this country to removing this stumbling-block out of the way of the slave's liberation.

The most telling, the most killing refutation of slavery is the presentation of an industrious, enterprising, thrifty, and intelligent free black population. Such a population I believe would rise in the Northern States under the fostering care of such a college as that supposed.

To show that we are capable of becoming mechanics I might adduce any amount of testimony; but, dear madam, I need not ring the changes on such a proposition. There is no question in the mind of any unprejudiced person that the Negro is capable of making a good mechanic. Indeed, even those who cherish the bitterest feelings toward us have admitted that the apprehension that negroes might be employed in their stead dictated the policy of excluding them from trades altogether. But I will not dwell upon this point, as I fear I have already trespassed too long upon your precious time, and written more than I ought to expect you to read. Allow me to say in conclusion that I believe every intelligent colored man in America will approve and rejoice at the establishment of some such institution as that now suggested. There are many respectable colored men, fathers of large families, having boys nearly grown up, whose minds are tossed by day and by night with the anxious inquiry, What shall I do with my boys? Such an institution would meet the wants of such persons. Then, too, the establishment of such an institution would be in character with the eminently practical philanthropy of your transatlantic friends. America could scarcely object to it as an attempt to agitate the public mind on the subject of slavery, or to *dissolve the Union.* It could not be tortured into a cause for hard words by the American people, but the noble and good of all classes would see in the effort an excellent motive, a benevolent object, temperately, wisely, and practically manifested.

Wishing you, dear madam, renewed health, a pleasant passage and safe return to your native land,

I am, most truly, your grateful friend,

FREDERICK DOUGLASS.

*Mrs. H. B. Stowe.*

I was not only requested to write the foregoing letter for the purpose indicated, but I was also asked, with admirable foresight, to see and ascertain, as far as possible, the views of the free colored people themselves in respect to the proposed measure for their benefit. This I was enabled to do in July, 1853, at the largest and most enlightened colored convention that, up to that time, had ever assembled in this country. This convention warmly approved the plan of a manual labor school, as already described, and expressed high appreciation of the wisdom and benevolence of Mrs. Stowe. This convention was held in Rochester, N. Y., and will long be remembered there for the surprise and gratification it caused our friends in that city. They were not looking for such exhibitions of enlightened zeal and ability as were there displayed in speeches, addresses, and resolutions, and in the conduct of the business for which it had assembled. Its proceedings attracted widespread attention at home and abroad.

While Mrs. Stowe was abroad she was, by the proslavery press of our country, so persistently and vigorously attacked for receiving money for her own private use, that the Rev. Henry Ward Beecher felt called upon to notice and reply to it in the columns of the New York *Independent*, of which he was then the editor. He denied that Mrs. Stowe was gathering British gold for herself and referred her assailants to me if they would learn what she intended to do with the money. In answer to her maligners, I denounced their accusations as groundless and through the columns of my paper, assured the public that the testimonial then being raised in England by Mrs. Stowe would be sacredly devoted to the establishment of an industrial school for colored youth. This announcement was circulated by other journals, and the attacks ceased. Nobody could well object to such application of the money received from any source, at home or abroad. After her return to this country I called again on Mrs. Stowe, and was much disappointed to learn from her that she had reconsidered her plan for the industrial school. I have never been able to see any force in the reasons for this change. It is enough, however, to say that they were sufficient for her, and that she no doubt acted conscientiously, though her change of purpose was a great disappointment, and placed me in an awkward position before the colored people of this country, as well as to friends abroad, to whom I had given assurances that the money would be appropriated in the manner I have described.

## *[John Brown's Raid on Harpers Ferry]*

On the evening when the news came that John Brown had taken and was then holding the town of Harper's Ferry, it so happened that I was speaking to a large audience in National Hall, Philadelphia. The announcement came upon us with the startling effect of an earthquake. It was something to make the boldest hold his breath. I saw at once that my old friend had attempted what he had long ago resolved to do, and I felt certain that the result must be his capture and destruction. As I expected, the next day brought the news that with two or three men he had fortified and was holding a small engine-house, but that he was surrounded by a body of Virginia militia, who, thus far, had not ventured to capture the insurgents, but that escape was impossible. A few hours later and word came that Colonel Robert E. Lee with a company of United States troops had made a breach in Capt. Brown's fort, and had captured him alive, though mortally wounded. His carpet-bag had been secured by Governor Wise, and it was found to contain numerous letters and documents which directly implicated Gerritt Smith, Joshua R. Giddings, Samuel G. Howe, Frank P. Sanborn, and myself. This intelligence was soon followed by a telegram saying that we were all to be arrested. Knowing that I was then in Philadelphia, stopping with my friend Thomas J. Dorsey, Mr. John Hern, the telegraph operator, came to me and, with others, urged me to leave the city by the first train, as it was known through the newspapers that I was then in Philadelphia, and officers might even then be on my track. To me there was nothing improbable in all this. My friends for the most part were appalled at the thought of my being arrested then or there, or while on my way across the ferry from Walnut street wharf to Camden, for there was where I felt sure the arrest would be made, and asked some of them to go so far as this with me merely to see what might occur; but, upon one ground or another, they all thought it best not to be found in my company at such a time, except dear old Franklin Turner—a true man. The truth is, that in the excitement which prevailed my friends had reason to fear that the very fact that they were with me would be a sufficient reason for their arrest with me. The delay in the departure of the steamer seemed unusually long to me, for I confess I was seized with a desire to reach a more northern latitude. My friend Frank did not leave my side till "all ashore" was ordered and the paddles began to move. I reached New York at night, still under the apprehension of arrest at any moment, but no signs of such an event being made, I went at once to the Barclay street ferry, took the boat across the river, and went direct to Washington street, Hoboken, the home of Mrs. Marks, where I spent the night, and I may add without undue profession of timidity, an *anxious* night. The morning papers brought no relief, for they announced that the government would spare no pains in ferreting out and bringing to punishment all who were connected with the Harper's Ferry outrage, and that search would be made for papers as well as persons. I was now somewhat uneasy from the fact that sundry letters and a constitution written by John Brown were locked up in my desk in Rochester. In order to prevent these papers from falling into the hands of the government of Virginia, I got my friend, Miss Ottilia Assing, to write at my dictation the following telegram to B. F. Blackall, the telegraph operator in Rochester, a friend and frequent visitor at my house, who would readily understand the meaning of the dispatch:

"B. F. BLACKALL, Esq.:

"Tell Lewis (my oldest son) to secure all the important papers in my high desk."

I did not sign my name, and the result showed that I had rightly judged that Mr. Blackall would understand and promptly attend to the request. The mark of the chisel with which the desk was opened is still on the drawer, and is one of the traces of the John Brown raid. Having taken measures to secure my papers, the trouble was to know just what to do with myself. To stay in Hoboken was out of the question, and to go to Rochester was to all appearance to go into the hands of the hunters, for they would naturally seek me at my home if they sought me at all. I, however, resolved to go home and risk my safety there. I felt sure that, once in the city, I could not be easily taken from there without a preliminary hearing upon the requisition, and not then if the people could be made aware of what was in progress. But how to get to Rochester was a serious question. It would not do to go to New York city and take the train, for that city was not less incensed against John Brown conspirators than many parts of the South. The course hit upon by my friends, Mr. Johnston and Miss Assing, was, to take me at night in a private conveyance from Hoboken to Paterson, where I could take the Erie railroad for home. This plan was carried out, and I reached home in safety, but had been there but a few moments when I was called upon by Samuel D. Porter, Esq., and my neighbor, Lieutenant-Governor Selden, who informed me that the governor of the State would certainly surrender me on a proper requisition from the governor of Virginia, and that while the people of Rochester would not permit me to be taken South, yet, in order to avoid collision with the government and consequent bloodshed, they advised me to quit the country, which I did—going to Canada. Governor Wise in the meantime, being advised that I had left Rochester for the State of Michigan, made requisition on the governor of that State for my surrender to Virginia.

The following letter from Governor Wise to President James Buchanan (which since the war was sent me by B. F. Lossing, the historian), will show by what means the governor of Virginia meant to get me into his power, and that my apprehensions of arrest were not altogether groundless:

[Confidential.]

RICHMOND, VA., NOV. 13, 1859.

*To His Excellency James Buchanan, President of the United States, and to the Honorable Postmaster-General of the United States:*

GENTLEMEN—I have information such as has caused me, upon proper affidavits, to make requisition upon the Executive of Michigan for the delivery up of the person of Frederick Douglass, a negro man, supposed now to be in Michigan, charged with murder, robbery, and inciting servile insurrection in the State of Virginia. My agents for the arrest and reclamation of the person so charged are Benjamin M. Morris and William N. Kelly. The latter has the requisition, and will wait on you to the end of obtaining nominal authority as post-office agents. They need be very secretive in this matter, and some pretext for traveling through the dangerous section for the execution of the laws in this behalf, and some protection against obtrusive, unruly, or lawless violence. If it be proper so to do, will the postmaster-general be pleased to give to Mr. Kelly, for each of these men, a permit and authority to act as detectives for the post-office department, without pay, but to pass and repass without question, delay, or hindrance?

Respectfully submitted by your obedient servant,

HENRY A. WISE.

There is no reason to doubt that James Buchanan afforded Governor Wise all the aid and coöperation for which he was asked. I have been informed that several United States marshals were in Rochester in search of me within six hours after my departure. I do not know that I can do better at this stage of my story than to insert the following letter, written by me to the Rochester *Democrat and American:*

CANADA WEST, Oct. 31, 1859.

MR. EDITOR:

I notice that the telegraph makes Mr. Cook (one of the unfortunate insurgents at Harper's Ferry, and now a prisoner in the hands of the thing calling itself the Government of Virginia, but which in fact is but an organized conspiracy by one part of the people against another and weaker) denounce me as a coward, and assert that I promised to be present in person at the Harper's Ferry insurrection. This is certainly a very grave impeachment, whether viewed in its bearings upon friends or upon foes, and you will not think it strange that I should take a somewhat serious notice of it. Having no acquaintance whatever with Mr. Cook, and never having exchanged a word with him about the Harper's Ferry insurrection, I am disposed to doubt if he could have used the language concerning me which the wires attribute to him. The lightning, when speaking for itself, is among the most direct, reliable, and truthful of things; but when speaking of the terror-stricken slaveholders at Harper's Ferry, it has been made the swiftest of liars. Under its nimble and trembling fingers it magnifies 17 men into 700, and has since filled the columns of the New York *Herald* for days with its interminable contradictions. But assuming that it has told only the simple truth as to the sayings of Mr. Cook in this instance, I have this answer to make to my accuser: Mr. Cook may be perfectly right in denouncing me as a coward; I have not one word to say in defense or vindication of my character for courage; I have always been more distinguished for running than fighting, and, tried by the Harper's-Ferry-insurrection-test, I am most miserably deficient in courage, even more so than Cook when he deserted his brave old captain and fled to the mountains. To this extent Mr. Cook is entirely right, and will meet no contradiction from me, or from anybody else. But wholly, grievously, and most unaccountably wrong is Mr. Cook when he asserts that I promised to be present in person at the Harper's Ferry insurrection. Of whatever other imprudence and indiscretion I may have been guilty, I have never made a promise so rash and wild as this. The taking of Harper's Ferry was a measure never encouraged by my word or by my vote. At any time or place, my wisdom or my cowardice has not only kept me from Harper's Ferry, but has equally kept me from making any promise to go there. I desire to be quite emphatic here, for of all guilty men, he is the guiltiest who lures his fellow-men to an undertaking of this sort, under promise of assistance which he afterwards fails to render. I therefore declare that there is no man living, and no man dead, who, if living, could truthfully say that I ever promised him, or anybody else, either conditionally, or otherwise, that I would be present in person at the

Harper's Ferry insurrection. My field of labor for the abolition of slavery has not extended to an attack upon the United States arsenal. In the teeth of the documents already published and of those which may hereafter be published, I affirm that no man connected with that insurrection, from its noble and heroic leader down, can connect my name with a single broken promise of any sort whatever. So much I deem it proper to say negatively. The time for a full statement of what I know and of ALL I know of this desperate but sublimely disinterested effort to emancipate the slaves of Maryland and Virginia from their cruel task-masters, has not yet come, and may never come. In the denial which I have now made, my motive is more a respectful consideration for the opinions of the slaves' friends than from my fear of being made an accomplice in the general conspiracy against slavery, when there is a reasonable hope for success. Men who live by robbing their fellow-men of their labor and liberty have forfeited their right to know anything of the thoughts, feelings, or purposes of those whom they rob and plunder. They have by the single act of slaveholding voluntarily placed themselves beyond the laws of justice and honor, and have become only fitted for companionship with thieves and pirates—the common enemies of God and of all mankind. While it shall be considered right to protect one's self against thieves, burglars, robbers, and assassins, and to slay a wild beast in the act of devouring his human prey, it can never be wrong for the imbruted and whip-scarred slaves, or their friends, to hunt, harass, and even strike down the traffickers in human flesh. If anybody is disposed to think less of me on account of this sentiment, or because I may have had a knowledge of what was about to occur, and did not assume the base and detestable character of an informer, he is a man whose good or bad opinion of me may be equally repugnant and despicable.

Entertaining these sentiments, I may be asked why I did not join John Brown—the noble old hero whose one right hand had shaken the foundation of the American Union, and whose ghost will haunt the bed-chambers of all the born and unborn slaveholders of Virginia through all their generations, filling them with alarm and consternation. My answer to this has already been given; at least impliedly given—"The tools to those who can use them!" Let every man work for the abolition of slavery in his own way. I would help all and hinder none. My position in regard to the Harper's Ferry insurrection may be easily inferred from these remarks, and I shall be glad if those papers which have spoken of me in connection with it would find room for this brief statement. I have no apology for keeping out of the way of those gentlemanly United States marshals, who are said to have paid Rochester a somewhat protracted visit lately, with a view to an interview with me. A government recognizing the validity of the *Dred Scott* decision at such a time as this, is not likely to have any very charitable feelings towards me, and if I am to meet its representatives I prefer to do so at least upon equal terms. If I have committed any offense against society I have done so on the soil of the State of New York, and I should be perfectly willing to be arraigned there before an impartial jury; but I have quite insuperable objections to being caught by the hounds of Mr. Buchanan, and *"bagged"* by Gov. Wise. For this appears to be the arrangement. Buchanan does the fighting and hunting, and Wise *"bags"* the game. Some reflections may be made upon my leaving on a tour to England just at this time. I have only to say that my going to that country has been rather delayed than hastened by the insurrection at Harper's Ferry. All know that I had intended to leave here in the first week of November.

FREDERICK DOUGLASS.

## *[Black Soldiers and the Union]*

From the first, I, for one, saw in this war the end of slavery; and truth requires me to say that my interest in the success of the North was largely due to this belief. True it is that this faith was many times shaken by passing events, but never destroyed. When Secretary Seward instructed our ministers to say to the governments to which they were accredited that, "terminate however it might, the status of no class of the people of the United States would be changed by the rebellion—that the slaves would be slaves still, and that the masters would be masters still"—when General McClellan and General Butler warned the slaves in advance that, "if any attempt was made by them to gain their freedom it would be suppressed with an iron hand"—when the government persistently refused to employ colored troops—when the emancipation proclamation of General John C. Fremont, in Missouri, was withdrawn—when slaves were being returned from our lines to their masters—when Union soldiers were stationed about the farm-houses of Virginia to guard and protect the master in holding his slaves—when Union soldiers made themselves more active in kicking colored men out of their camps than in shooting rebels—when even Mr. Lincoln could tell the poor negro that "he was the cause of the war," I still believed, and spoke as I believed, all over the North, that the mission of the war was the liberation of the slave, as well as the salvation of the Union; and hence from the first I reproached the North that they fought the rebels with only one hand, when they might strike effectually with two—that they fought with their soft white hand, while they kept their black iron hand chained and helpless behind them—that they fought the effect, while they protected the cause, and that the Union cause would never prosper till the war assumed an anti-slavery attitude, and the negro was enlisted on the loyal side. In every way possible—in the columns of my paper and on the platform, by letters to friends, at home and abroad, I did all that I could to impress this conviction upon this country. But nations seldom listen to advice from individuals, however reasonable. They are taught less by theories than by facts and events. There was much that could be said against making the war an abolition war—much that seemed wise and patriotic. "Make the war an abolition war," we were told, "and you drive the border States into the rebellion, and thus add power to the enemy and increase the number you will have to meet on the battle-field. You will exasperate and intensify southern feeling, making it more desperate, and put far away the day of peace between the two sections." "Employ the arm of the negro, and the loyal men of the North will throw down their arms and go home." "This is the white man's country and the white man's war." "It would inflict an intolerable wound upon the pride and spirit of white soldiers of the Union to see the negro in the United States uniform. Besides, if you make the negro a soldier, you cannot depend on his courage; a crack of his old master's whip will send him scampering in terror from the field." And so it was that custom, pride, prejudice, and the old-time respect for southern feeling, held back the government from an anti-slavery policy and from arming the negro. Meanwhile the rebellion availed itself of the negro most effectively. He was not only the stomach of the rebellion, by supplying its commissary department, but he built its forts, dug its intrenchments and performed other duties of the camp which left the rebel soldier more free to fight the loyal army than he could otherwise have been. It was the cotton and corn of the negro that made the rebellion sack stand on end and caused a continuance of the war. "Destroy these," was the burden of all my utterances during this part of the struggle, "and you cripple and destroy the rebellion." It is surprising how long and bitterly the government resisted and rejected this view of the situation. The abolition heart of the North ached over the delay, and uttered its bitter complaints, but the administration remained blind and dumb. Bull Run, Ball's Bluff, Big Bethel, Fredericksburg, and the Peninsula disasters were the only teachers whose authority was of sufficient importance to excite the attention or respect of our rulers, and they were even slow in being taught by these. An important point was gained, however, when General B. F. Butler, at Fortress Monroe, announced the policy of treating the slaves as "contrabands," to be made useful to the Union cause, and was sustained therein at Washington, and sentiments of a similar nature were expressed on the floor of Congress by Hon. A. G. Riddle of Ohio. A grand accession was made to this view of the case when Hon. Simon Cameron, then secretary of war, gave it his earnest support, and General David Hunter put the measure into practical operation in South Carolina. General Phelps from Vermont, in command at Carrollton, La., also advocated the same plan, though under discouragements which cost him his command. And many and grievous disasters on flood and field were needed to educate the loyal nation and President Lincoln up to the realization of the necessity, not to say justice, of this position, and many devices, intermediate steps, and make-shifts were suggested to smooth the way to the ultimate policy of freeing the slave, and arming the freedmen.

When at last the truth began to dawn upon the administration that the negro might be made useful to loyalty, as well as to treason, to the Union as well as to the

Confederacy, it began to consider in what way it could employ him which would the least shock and offend the popular prejudice against him. He was already in the army as a waiter, and in that capacity there was no objection to him; and so it was thought that as this was the case, the feeling which tolerated him as a waiter would not seriously object if he should be admitted to the army as a laborer, especially as no one under a southern sun cared to have a monopoly of digging and toiling in trenches. This was the first step in employing negroes in the United States service. The second step was to give them a peculiar costume which should distinguish them from soldiers, and yet mark them as a part of the loyal force. As the eyes of the loyal administration still further opened, it was proposed to give these laborers something better than spades and shovels with which to defend themselves in cases of emergency. Still later it was proposed to make them soldiers, but soldiers without the blue uniform, soldiers with a mark upon them to show that they were inferior to other soldiers; soldiers with a badge of degradation upon them. However, once in the army as a laborer, once there with a red shirt on his back and a pistol in his belt, the negro was not long in appearing on the field as a soldier. But still, he was not to be a soldier in the sense, and on an equal footing, with white soldiers. It was given out that he was not to be employed in the open field with white troops, under the inspiration of doing battle and winning victories for the Union cause, and in the face and teeth of his old masters, but that he should be made to garrison forts in yellow-fever and otherwise unhealthy localities of the South, to save the health of white soldiers; and, in order to keep up the distinction further, the black soldiers were to have only half the wages of the white soldiers, and were to be commanded entirely by white commissioned officers. While of course I was deeply pained and saddened by the estimate thus put upon my race, and grieved at the slowness of heart which marked the conduct of the loyal government, I was not discouraged, and urged every man who could, to enlist; to get an eagle on his button, a musket on his shoulder, and the star spangled banner over his head. Hence, as soon as Governor Andrew of Massachusetts received permission from Mr. Lincoln to raise two colored regiments, the 54th and 55th, I made the following address to the colored citizens of the North through my paper, then being published in Rochester, which was copied in the leading journals:

"MEN OF COLOR, TO ARMS!

"When first the rebel cannon shattered the walls of Sumter and drove away its starving garrison, I predicted that the war then and there inaugurated would not be fought out entirely by white men. Every month's experience during these dreary years has confirmed that opinion. A war undertaken and brazenly carried on for the perpetual enslavement of colored men, calls logically and loudly for colored men to help suppress it. Only a moderate share of sagacity was needed to see that the arm of the slave was the best defense against the arm of the slaveholder. Hence, with every reverse to the national arms, with every exulting shout of victory raised by the slaveholding rebels, I have implored the imperiled nation to unchain against her foe her powerful black hand. Slowly and reluctantly that appeal is beginning to be heeded. Stop not now to complain that it was not heeded sooner. That it should not may or may not have been best. This is not the time to discuss that question. Leave it to the future. When the war is over, the country saved, peace established and the black man's rights are secured, as they will be, history with an impartial hand will dispose of that and sundry other questions. Action! action! not criticism, is the plain duty of this hour. Words are now useful only as they stimulate to blows. The office of speech now is only to point out when, where, and how to strike to the best advantage. There is no time to delay. The tide is at its flood that leads on to fortune. From East to West, from North to South, the sky is written all over. 'NOW OR NEVER.' Liberty won by white men would lose half its luster. 'Who would be free themselves must strike the blow.' 'Better even die free, than to live slaves.' This is the sentiment of every brave colored man amongst us. There are weak and cowardly men in all nations. We have them amongst us. They tell you this is the 'white man's war'; that you 'will be no better off after than before the war'; that the getting of you into the army is to 'sacrifice you on the first opportunity.' Believe them not; cowards themselves, they do not wish to have their cowardice shamed by your brave example. Leave them to their timidity, or to whatever motive may hold them back. I have not thought lightly of the words I am now addressing you. The counsel I give comes of close observation of the great struggle now in progress, and of the deep conviction that this is your hour and mine. In good earnest, then, and after the best deliberation, I now, for the first time during this war, feel at liberty to call and counsel you to arms. By every consideration which binds you to your enslaved fellow-countrymen and to the peace and welfare of your country; by every aspiration which you cherish for the freedom and equality of yourselves and your children; by all the ties of blood and identity which make us one with the brave black men now fighting our battles in Louisiana and in South Carolina, I urge you to fly to arms, and smite with death the power that would bury the government and your liberty in the same hopeless grave. I wish I could tell you that the State of New York calls you to this high honor. For the moment her constituted authorities are silent on the subject. They will speak by and by, and doubtless on the right side: but we are not compelled to wait for her. We can get at the throat of treason and slavery through the State of Massachusetts. She was first in the War of Independence; first to break the chains of her slaves; first to make the black man equal before the law; first to admit colored children to her common schools, and she was first to answer with her blood the alarm-cry of the nation, when its capital was menaced by rebels. You know her patriotic governor, and you know Charles Sumner. I need not add more.

Massachusetts now welcomes you to arms as soldiers. She has but a small colored population from which to recruit. She has full leave of the general government to send one regiment to the war, and she has undertaken to do it. Go quickly and help fill up the first colored regiment from the North. I am authorized to assure you that you will receive the same wages, the same rations, the same equipments, the same protection, the same treatment, and the same bounty, secured to white soldiers. You will be led by able and skillful officers, men who will take especial pride in your efficiency and success. They will be quick to accord to you all the honor you shall merit by your valor, and to see that your rights and feelings are respected by other soldiers. I have assured myself on these points, and can speak with authority. More than twenty years of unswerving devotion to our common cause may give me some humble claim to be trusted at this momentous crisis. I will not argue. To do so implies hesitation and doubt, and you do not hesitate. You do not doubt. The day dawns; the morning star is bright upon the horizon! The iron gate of our prison stands half open. One gallant rush from the North will fling it wide open, while four millions of our brothers and sisters shall march out into liberty. The chance is now given you to end in a day the bondage of centuries, and to rise in one bound from social degradation to the place of common equality with all other varieties of men. Remember Denmark Vessey of Charleston; remember Nathaniel Turner of South Hampton; remember Shields Green and Copeland, who followed noble John Brown, and fell as glorious martyrs for the cause of the slave. Remember that in a contest with oppression, the Almighty has no attribute which can take sides with oppressors. The case is before you. This is our golden opportunity. Let us accept it, and forever wipe out the dark reproaches unsparingly hurled against us by our enemies. Let us win for ourselves the gratitude of our country, and the best blessings of our posterity through all time. The nucleus of this first regiment is now in camp at Readville, a short distance from Boston. I will undertake to forward to Boston all persons adjudged fit to be mustered into the regiment, who shall apply to me at any time within the next two weeks.

"ROCHESTER, March 2, 1863."

Immediately after authority had been given by President Lincoln to Governor John A. Andrew of Massachusetts, to raise and equip two regiments of colored men for the war, I received a letter from George L. Stearns of Boston, a noble worker for freedom in Kansas, and a warm friend of John Brown, earnestly entreating me to assist in raising the required number of men. It was presumed that by my labors in the anti-slavery cause, I had gained some influence with the colored men of the country, and that they would listen to me in this emergency; which supposition, I am happy to say, was supported by the results. There were fewer colored people in Massachusetts then than now, and it was necessary, in order to make up the full quota of these regiments, to recruit for them in other Northern States. The nominal conditions upon which colored men were asked to enlist were not satisfactory to me or to them; but assurances from Governor Andrew that they would in the end be made just and equal, together with my faith in the logic of events and my conviction that the wise thing for the colored man to do was to get into the army by any door open to him, no matter how narrow, made me accept with alacrity the work to which I was invited. The raising of these two regiments—the 54th and 55th—and their splendid behavior in South and North Carolina, was the beginning of great things for the colored people of the whole country; and not the least satisfaction I now have in contemplating my humble part in raising them, is the fact that my two sons, Charles and Lewis, were the first two in the State of New York to enlist in them. The 54th was not long in the field before it proved itself gallant and strong, worthy to rank with the most courageous of its white companions in arms. Its assault upon Fort Wagner, in which it was so fearfully cut to pieces, and lost nearly half its officers, including its beloved and trusted commander, Col, Shaw, at once gave it a name and a fame throughout the country. In that terrible battle, under the wing of night, more cavils in respect of the quality of negro manhood were set at rest than could have been during a century of ordinary life and observation. After that assault we heard no more of sending negroes to garrison forts and arsenals, to fight miasma, yellow-fever, and small-pox. Talk of his ability to meet the foe in the open field, and of his equal fitness with the white man to stop a bullet, then began to prevail. From this time (and the fact ought to be remembered) the colored troops were called upon to occupy positions which required the courage, steadiness, and endurance of veterans, and even their enemies were obliged to admit that they proved themselves worthy the confidence reposed in them. After the 54th and 55th Massachusetts colored regiments were placed in the field, and one of them had distinguished itself with so much credit in the hour of trial, the desire to send more such troops to the front became pretty general. Pennsylvania proposed to raise ten regiments. I was again called by my friend Mr. Stearns to assist in raising these regiments, and I set about the work with full purpose of heart, using every argument of which I was capable, to persuade every colored man able to bear arms to rally around the flag and help to save the country and the race. It was during this time that the attitude of the government at Washington caused me deep sadness and discouragement, and forced me in a measure to suspend my efforts in that direction. I had assured colored men that, once in the Union army, they would be put upon an equal footing with other soldiers; that they would be paid, promoted, and exchanged as prisoners of war, Jeff Davis's threat that they would be treated as felons, to the contrary notwithstanding. But thus far, the government had not kept its promise, or the promise made for it. The following letter which I find published in my paper of the same date will show the course I felt it my duty to take under the circumstances:

"ROCHESTER, August 1st, 1863.

"MAJOR GEORGE L. STEARNS:

"*My Dear Sir,*—Having declined to attend the meeting to promote enlistments, appointed for me at Pittsburgh, in present circumstances, I owe you a word of explanation. I have hitherto deemed it a duty, as it certainly has been a pleasure, to cooperate with you in the work of raising colored troops in the free States to fight the battles of the Republic against slaveholding rebels and traitors. Upon the first call you gave me to this work I responded with alacrity. I saw, or thought I saw, a ray of light, brightening the future of my whole race, as well as that of our war-troubled country, in arousing colored men to fight for the nation's life. I continue to believe in the black man's arm, and still have some hope in the integrity of our rulers. Nevertheless, I must for the present leave to others the work of persuading colored men to join the Union army. I owe it to my long-abused people, and especially to those already in the army, to expose their wrongs and plead their cause. I cannot do that in connection with recruiting. When I plead for recruits I want to do it with all my heart, without qualification. I cannot do that now. The impression settles upon me that colored men have much over-rated the enlightenment, justice, and generosity of our rulers at Washington. In my humble way I have contributed somewhat to that false estimate. You know that when the idea of raising colored troops was first suggested, the special duty to be assigned them was the garrisoning of forts and arsenals in certain warm, unhealthy, and miasmatic localities in the South. They were thought to be better adapted to that service than white troops. White troops trained to war, brave and daring, were to take fortifications, and the blacks were to hold them from falling again into the hands of the rebels. Three advantages were to arise out of this wise division of labor: 1st, The spirit and pride of white troops was not to waste itself in dull, monotonous inactivity in fort life; their arms were to be kept bright by constant use. 2d, The health of white troops was to be preserved, 3d, Black troops were to have the advantage of sound military training and to be otherwise useful, at the same time that they should be tolerably secure from capture by the rebels, who early avowed their determination to enslave and slaughter them in defiance of the laws of war. Two out of the three advantages were to accrue to the white troops. Thus far, however, I believe that no such duty as holding fortifications has been committed to colored troops. They have done far other and more important work than holding fortifications. I have no special complaint to make at this point, and I simply mention it to strengthen the statement that, from the beginning of this business, it was the confident belief among both the colored and white friends of colored enlistments that President Lincoln, as commander-in-chief of the army and navy, would certainly see to it that his colored troops should be so handled and disposed of as to be but little exposed to capture by the rebels, and that, if so exposed, as they have repeatedly been from the first, the president possessed both the disposition and the means for compelling the rebels to respect the rights of such as might fall into their hands. The piratical proclamation of Jefferson Davis, announcing slavery and assassination to colored prisoners, was before the country and the world. But men had faith in Mr. Lincoln and his advisers. He was silent, to be sure, but charity suggested that being a man of action rather than words he only waited for a case in which he should be required to act. This faith in the man enabled us to speak with warmth and effect in urging enlistments among colored men. That faith, my dear sir, is now nearly gone. Various occasions have arisen during the last six months for the exercise of his power in behalf of the colored men in his service. But no word comes to us from the war department, sternly assuring the rebel chief that inquisition shall yet be made for innocent blood. No word of retaliation when a black man is slain by a rebel in cold blood. No word was said when free men from Massachusetts were caught and sold into slavery in Texas. No word is said when brave black men, according to the testimony of both friend and foe, fought like heroes to plant the star-spangled banner on the blazing parapets of Fort Wagner and in so doing were captured, mutilated, killed, and sold into slavery. The same crushing silence reigns over this scandalous outrage as over that of the slaughtered teamsters at Murfreesboro; the same as over that at Milliken's Bend and Vicksburg. I am free to say, my dear sir, that the case looks as if the confiding colored soldiers had been betrayed into bloody hands by the very government in whose defense they were heroically fighting. I know what you will say to this; you will say 'Wait a little longer, and, after all, the best way to have justice done to your people is to get them into the army as fast as you can.' You may be right in this; my argument has been the same; but have we not already waited, and have we not already shown the highest qualities of soldiers, and on this account deserve the protection of the government for which we are fighting? Can any case stronger than that before Charleston ever arise? If the President is ever to demand justice and humanity for black soldiers, is not this the time for him to do it? How many 54ths must be cut to pieces, its mutilated prisoners killed, and its living sold into slavery, to be tortured to death by inches, before Mr. Lincoln shall say, 'Hold, enough!'

"You know the 54th. To you, more than to any one man, belongs the credit of raising that regiment. Think of its noble and brave officers literally hacked to pieces, while many of its rank and file have been sold into slavery worse than death; and pardon me if I hesitate about assisting in raising a fourth regiment until the President shall give the same protection to them as to white soldiers.

With warm and sincere regards,

FREDERICK DOUGLASS."

"Since writing the foregoing letter, which we have now put upon record, we have received assurances from Major Stearns that the government of the United States is already taking measures which will secure the captured colored soldiers at Charleston and elsewhere the same protection against slavery and cruelty that is extended to white soldiers. What ought to have been done at the beginning comes late, but it comes. The poor colored soldiers have purchased interference dearly. It really seems that nothing of justice, liberty, or humanity can come to us except through tears and blood."

## *[A Meeting with His Former Master]*

After a period of more than forty years, I visited and had an interview with Captain Thomas Auld at St. Michaels, Talbot county, Maryland. It will be remembered by those who have followed the thread of my story that St. Michaels was at one time the place of my home and the scene of some of my saddest experiences of slave life, and that I left there, or rather was compelled to leave there, because it was believed that I had written passes for several slaves to enable them to escape from slavery, and that prominent slaveholders in that neighborhood had, for this alleged offense, threatened to shoot me on sight, and to prevent the execution of this threat my master had sent me to Baltimore.

My return, therefore, in peace, to this place and among the same people, was strange enough in itself; but that I should, when there, be formally invited by Captain Thomas Auld, then over eighty years old, to come to the side of his dying bed, evidently with a view to a friendly talk over our past relations, was a fact still more strange, and one which, until its occurrence, I could never have thought possible. To me Captain Auld had sustained the relation of master—a relation which I had held in extremest abhorrence, and which for forty years I had denounced in all bitterness of spirit and fierceness of speech. He had struck down my personality, had subjected me to his will, made property of my body and soul, reduced me to a chattel, hired me out to a noted slave breaker to be worked like a beast and flogged into submission, taken my hard earnings, sent me to prison, offered me for sale, broken up my Sunday-school, forbidden me to teach my fellow-slaves to read on pain of nine and thirty lashes on my bare back and had, without any apparent disturbance of his conscience, sold my body to his brother Hugh and pocketed the price of my flesh and blood. I, on my part, had traveled through the length and breadth of this country and of England, holding up this conduct of his, in common with that of other slaveholders, to the reprobation of all men who would listen to my words. I had by my writings made his name and his deeds familiar to the world in four different languages, yet here we were, after four decades, once more face to face—he on his bed, aged and tremulous, drawing near the sunset of life, and I, his former slave, United States Marshal of the district of Columbia, holding his hand and in friendly conversation with him in a sort of final settlement of past differences preparatory to his stepping into his grave, where all distinctions are at an end, and where the great and the small, the slave and his master, are reduced to the same level. Had I been asked in the days of slavery to visit this man I should have regarded the invitation as one to put fetters on my ankles and handcuffs on my wrists. It would have been an invitation to the auction-block and the slave-whip. I had no business with this man under the old regime but to keep out of his way. But now that slavery was destroyed, and the slave and the master stood upon equal ground, I was not only willing to meet him, but was very glad to do so. The conditions were favorable for remembrance of all his good deeds, and generous extenuation of all his evil ones. He was to me no longer a slaveholder either in fact or in spirit, and I regarded him as I did myself, a victim of the circumstances of birth, education, law, and custom.

Our courses had been determined for us, not by us. We had both been flung, by powers that did not ask our consent, upon a mighty current of life, which we could neither resist nor control. By this current he was a master, and I a slave; but now our lives were verging towards a point where differences disappear, where even the constancy of hate breaks down and where the clouds of pride, passion and selfishness vanish before the brightness of infinite light. At such a time, and in such a place, when a man is about closing his eyes on this world and ready to step into the eternal unknown, no word of reproach or bitterness should reach him or fall from his lips; and on this occasion there was to this rule no transgression on either side.

As this visit to Capt. Auld has been made the subject of mirth by heartless triflers, and by serious-minded men regretted as a weakening of my life-long testimony against slavery, and as the report of it, published in the papers immediately after it occurred, was in some respects defective and colored, it may be proper to state exactly what was said and done at this interview.

It should in the first place be understood that I did not go to St. Michaels upon Capt. Auld's invitation, but upon that of my colored friend, Charles Caldwell; but when once there, Capt. Auld sent Mr. Green, a man in constant attendance upon him during his sickness, to tell me he would be very glad to see me, and wished me to accompany Green to his house, with which request I complied. On reaching the house I was met by Mr. Wm. H. Bruff, a son-in-law of Capt. Auld, and Mrs. Louisa Bruff, his daughter, and was conducted by them immediately to the bed-room of Capt. Auld. We addressed each other simultaneously, he calling me "Marshal Douglass," and I, as I had always called him, "Captain Auld." Hearing myself called by him "Marshal Douglass," I instantly broke up the formal nature of the meeting by saying, "not *Marshal,* but Frederick to you as formerly." We shook hands cordially, and in the act of doing so, he, having been long stricken with palsy, shed tears as men thus afflicted will do when excited by any deep emotion.

The sight of him, the changes which time had wrought in him, his tremulous hands constantly in motion, and all the circumstances of his condition affected me deeply, and for a time choked my voice and made me speechless. We both, however, got the better of our feelings, and conversed freely about the past.

Though broken by age and palsy, the mind of Capt. Auld was remarkably clear and strong. After he had become composed I asked him what he thought of my conduct in running away and going to the north. He hesitated a moment as if to properly formulate his reply, and said: "Frederick, I always knew you were too smart to be a slave, and had I been in your place, I should have done as you did." I said, "Capt. Auld, I am glad to hear you say this. I did not run away from *you,* but from *slavery;* it was not that I loved Caesar less, but Rome more." I told him that I had made a mistake in my narrative, a copy of which I had sent him, in attributing to him ungrateful and cruel treatment of my grandmother; that I had done so on the supposition that in the division of the property of my old master, Mr. Aaron Anthony, my grandmother had fallen to him, and that he had left her in her old age, when she could be no longer of service to him, to pick up her living in solitude with none to help her, or, in other words, had turned her out to die like an old horse. "Ah!" he said, "that was a mistake, I never owned your grandmother; she in the division of the slaves was awarded to my brother-in-law, Andrew Anthony; but," he added quickly, "I brought her down here and took care of her as long as she lived." The fact is, that, after writing my narrative describing the condition of my grandmother, Capt. Auld's attention being thus called to it, he rescued her from her destitution. I told him that this mistake of mine was corrected as soon as I discovered it, and that I had at no time any wish to do him injustice; that I regarded both of us as victims of a system. "Oh, I never liked slavery," he said, "and I meant to emancipate all my slaves when they reached the age of twenty-five years." I told him I had always been curious to know how old I was and that it had been a serious trouble to me, not to know when was my birthday. He said he could not tell me that, but he thought I was born in February, 1818. This date made me one year younger than I had supposed myself from what was told me by Mistress Lucretia, Captain Auld's former wife, when I left Lloyd's for Baltimore in the Spring of 1825; she having then said that I was eight, going on nine. I know that it was in the year 1825 that I went to Baltimore, because it was in that year that Mr. James Beacham built a large frigate at the foot of Alliceana street, for one of the South American Governments. Judging from this, and from certain events which transpired at Col. Lloyd's such as a boy under eight years old, without any knowledge of books, would hardly take cognizance of, I am led to believe that Mrs. Lucretia was nearer right as to my age than her husband.

Before I left his bedside Captain Auld spoke with a cheerful confidence of the great change that awaited him, and felt himself about to depart in peace. Seeing his extreme weakness I did not protract my visit. The whole interview did not last more than twenty minutes, and we parted to meet no more. His death was soon after announced in the papers, and the fact that he had once owned me as a slave was cited as rendering that event noteworthy.

## *[Conclusion to the 1881 Edition]*

As far as this volume can reach that point I have now brought my readers to the end of my story. What may remain of life to me, through what experiences I may pass, what heights I may attain, into what depths I may fall, what good or ill may come to me, or proceed from me in this breathing world where all is change and uncertainty and largely at the mercy of powers over which the individual man has no absolute control; all this, if thought worthy and useful, will probably be told by others when I have passed from the busy stage of life. I am not looking for any great changes in my fortunes or achievements in the future. The most of the space of life is behind me and the sun of my day is nearing the horizon. Notwithstanding all that is contained in this book my day has been a pleasant one. My joys have far exceeded my sorrows and my friends have brought me far more than my enemies have taken from me. I have written out my experience here, not in order to exhibit my wounds and bruises and to awaken and attract sympathy to myself personally, but as a part of the history of a profoundly interesting period in American life and progress. I have meant it to be a small individual contribution to the sum of knowledge of this special period, to be handed down to after-coming generations which may want to know what things were allowed and what prohibited; what moral, social and political relations subsisted between the different varieties of the American people down to the last quarter of the nineteenth century and by what means they were modified and changed. The time is at hand when the last American slave and the last American slaveholder will disappear behind the curtain which separates the living from the dead and when neither master nor slave will be left to tell the story of their respective relations or what happened to either in those relations. My part has been to tell the story of the slave. The story of the master never wanted for narrators. The masters, to tell their story, had at call all the talent and genius that wealth and influence could command. They have had their full day in court. Literature, theology, philosophy, law and learning have come willingly to their service, and, if condemned, they have not been condemned unheard.

It will be seen in these pages that I have lived several lives in one: first, the life of slavery; secondly, the life of a fugitive from slavery; thirdly, the life of comparative freedom; fourthly, the life of conflict and battle; and, fifthly, the life of victory, if not complete, at least assured. To those who have suffered in slavery I can say, I, too, have suffered. To those who have taken some risks and encountered hardships in the flight from bondage I can say, I, too, have endured and risked. To those who have battled for liberty, brotherhood, and citizenship I can say, I, too, have battled. And to those who have lived to enjoy the fruits of victory I can say, I, too, live and rejoice. If I have pushed my example too prominently for the good taste of my Caucasian readers, I beg them to remember that I have written in part for the encouragement of a class whose aspirations need the stimulus of success.

I have aimed to assure them that knowledge can be obtained under difficulties; that poverty may give place to competency; that obscurity is not an absolute bar to distinction, and that a way is open to welfare and happiness to all who will resolutely and wisely pursue that way: that neither slavery, stripes, imprisonment nor proscription need extinguish self-respect, crush manly ambition, or paralyze effort; that no power outside of himself can prevent a man from sustaining an honorable character and a useful relation to his day and generation; that neither institutions nor friends can make a race to stand unless it has strength in its own legs; that there is no power in the world which can be relied upon to help the weak against the strong or the simple against the wise; that races, like individuals, must stand or fall by their own merits; that all the prayers of Christendom cannot stop the force of a single bullet, divest arsenic of poison, or suspend any law of nature. In my communication with the colored people I have endeavored to deliver them from the power of superstition, bigotry, and priest-craft. In theology I have found them strutting about in the old clothes of the masters, just as the masters strut about in the old clothes of the past. The falling power remains among them long since it has ceased to be the religious fashion in our refined and elegant white churches. I have taught that the "fault is not in our stars, but in ourselves, that we are underlings," that "who would be free, themselves must strike the blow." I have urged upon them self-reliance, self-respect, industry, perseverance, and economy, to make the best of both worlds, but to make the best of this world first because it comes first, and that he who does not improve himself by the motives and opportunities afforded by this world gives the best evidence that he would not improve in any other world. Schooled as I have been among the abolitionists of New England, I recognize that the universe is governed by laws which are unchangeable and eternal, that what men sow they will reap, and that there is no way to dodge or circumvent the consequences of any act or deed. My views at this point receive but limited endorsement among my people. They, for the most part, think they have means of procuring special favor and help from the Almighty; and, as their "faith is the substance of things hoped for and the evidence of things not seen," they find much in this expression which is true to faith, but utterly false to fact. But I meant here only to say a word in conclusion. Forty years of my life have been given to the cause of my people, and if I had forty years more they should all be sacredly given to the same great cause. If I have done something for that cause, I am, after all, more a debtor to it than it is debtor to me.

## *[A Rationale for the 1892 Edition]*

Ten years ago when the preceding chapters of this book were written, having then reached in the journey of life the middle of the decade beginning at sixty and ending at seventy, and naturally reminded that I was no longer young, I laid aside my pen with some such sense of relief as might be felt by a weary and overburdened traveler when arrived at the desired end of a long journey, or as an honest debtor wishing to be square with all the world might feel when the last dollar of an old debt was paid off. Not that I wished to be discharged from labor and service in the cause to which I have devoted my life, but from this peculiar kind of labor and service. I hardly need say to those who know me, that writing for the public eye never came quite as easily to me as speaking to the public ear. It is a marvel to me that under the circumstances I learned to write at all. It has been a still greater marvel that in the brief working period in which they lived and wrought, such men as Dickens, Dumas, Carlyle and Sir Walter Scott could have produced the works ascribed to them. But many have been the impediments with which I have had to struggle. I have, too, been embarrassed by the thought of writing so much about myself when there was so much else of which to write. It is far easier to write about others than about one's self. I write freely of myself, not from choice, but because I have, by my cause, been morally forced into thus writing. Time and events have summoned me to stand forth both as a witness and an advocate for a people long dumb, not allowed to speak for themselves, yet much misunderstood and deeply wronged. In the earlier days of my freedom, I was called upon to expose the direful nature of the slave system, by telling my own experience while a slave, and to do what I could thereby to make slavery odious and thus to hasten the day of emancipation. It was no time to mince matters or to stand upon a delicate sense of propriety, in the presence of a crime so gigantic as our slavery was, and the duty to oppose it so imperative. I was called upon to expose even my stripes, and with many misgivings obeyed the summons and tried thus to do my whole duty in this my first public work and what I may say proved to be the best work of my life.

Fifty years have passed since I entered upon that work, and now that it is ended, I find myself summoned again by the popular voice and by what is called the negro problem, to come a second time upon the witness stand and give evidence upon disputed points concerning myself and my emancipated brothers and sisters who, though free, are yet oppressed and are in as much need of an advocate as before they were set free. Though this is not altogether as agreeable to me as was my first mission, it is one that comes with such commanding authority as to compel me to accept it as a present duty. In it I am pelted with all sorts of knotty questions, some of which might be difficult even for Humboldt, Cuvier or Darwin, were they alive, to answer. They are questions which range over the whole field of science, learning and philosophy, and some descend to the depths of impertinent, unmannerly and vulgar curiosity. To be able to answer the higher range of these questions I should be profoundly versed in psychology, anthropology, ethnology, sociology, theology, biology, and all the other ologies, philosophies and sciences. There is no disguising the fact that the American people are much interested and mystified about the mere matter of color as connected with manhood. It seems to them that color has some moral or immoral qualities and especially the latter. They do not feel quite reconciled to the idea that a man of different color from themselves should have all the human rights claimed by themselves. When an unknown man is spoken of in their presence, the first question that arises in the average American mind concerning him and which must be answered is, Of what color is he? and he rises or falls in estimation by the answer given. It is not whether he is a good man or a bad man. That does not seem of primary importance. Hence I have often been bluntly and sometimes very rudely asked, of what color my mother was, and of what color was my father? In what proportion does the blood of the various races mingle in my veins, especially how much white blood and how much black blood entered into my composition? Whether I was not part Indian as well as African and Caucasian? Whether I considered myself more African than Caucasian, or the reverse? Whether I derived my intelligence from my father, or from my mother, from my white, or from my black blood? Whether persons of mixed blood are as strong and healthy as persons of either of the races whose blood they inherit? Whether persons of mixed blood do permanently remain of the mixed complexion or finally take on the complexion of one or the other of the two or more races of which they may be composed? Whether they live as long and raise as large families as other people? Whether they inherit only evil from both parents and good from neither? Whether evil dispositions are more transmissible than good? Why did I marry a person of my father's complexion instead of marrying one of my mother's complexion? How is the race problem to be solved in this country? Will the negro go back to Africa or remain here? Under this shower of purely American questions, more or less personal, I have endeavored to possess my soul in patience and get as much good out of life as was possible with so much to occupy my time; and, though often perplexed, seldom losing my temper, or abating heart or hope for the future of my people. Though I cannot say I have satisfied the curiosity of my countrymen on all the questions raised by them, I have, like all honest men on the witness stand, answered to the best of my knowledge and belief, and I hope I have never answered in such wise as to increase the hardships of any human being of whatever race or color.

When the first part of this book was written, I was, as before intimated, already looking toward the sunset of human life and thinking that my children would probably finish the recital of my life, or that possibly some other persons outside of family ties to whom I am known might think it worth while to tell what he or she might know of the remainder of my story. I considered, as I have said, that my work was done. But friends and publishers concur in the opinion that the unity and completeness of the work require that it shall be finished by the hand by which it was begun.

Many things touched me and employed my thoughts and activities between the years 1881 and 1891. I am willing to speak of them. Like most men who give the world their autobiographies I wish my story to be told as favorably towards myself as it can be with a due regard to truth. I do not wish it to be imagined by any that I am insensible to the singularity of my career, or to the peculiar relation I sustain to the history of my time and country. I know and feel that it is something to have lived at all in this Republic during the latter part of this eventful century, but I know it is more to have had some small share in the great events which have distinguished it from the experience of all other centuries. No man liveth unto himself, or ought to live unto himself. My life has conformed to this Bible saying, for, more than most men, I have been the thin edge of the wedge to open for my people a way in many directions and places never before occupied by them. It has been mine, in some degree, to stand as their defense in moral battle against the shafts of detraction, calumny and persecution, and to labor in removing and overcoming those obstacles which, in the shape of erroneous ideas and customs, have blocked the way to their progress. I have found this to be no hardship, but the natural and congenial vocation of my life. I had hardly become a thinking being when I first learned to hate slavery, and hence I was no sooner free than I joined the noble band of Abolitionists in Massachusetts, headed by William Lloyd Garrison and Wendell Phillips. Afterward, by voice and pen, in season and out of season, it was mine to stand for the freedom of people of all colors, until in our land the last yoke was broken and the last bondsman was set free. In the war for the Union I persuaded the colored man to become a soldier. In the peace that followed, I asked the Government to make him a citizen. In the construction of the rebellious States I urged his enfranchisement.

Much has been written and published during the last ten years purporting to be a history of the anti-slavery movement and of the part taken by the men and women engaged in it, myself among the number. In some of these narrations I have received more consideration and higher estimation than I perhaps deserved. In others I have not escaped underdeserved disparagement, which I may leave to the reader and to the judgment of those who shall come after me to reply to and to set right.

*Selected Writings*

## *[A Comparison of the Treatment of Blacks in the United States and Great Britain]*

In August of 1845, several months after the publication of the *Narrative*, Douglass traveled to Great Britain at the urging of his friends to avoid capture as a fugitive slave. There he delivered many speeches in order to enlist the aid of British abolitionists. In this letter to William Lloyd Garrison, editor of the *Liberator* and a prominent antislavery leader, Douglass explains how he had been received abroad.

Victoria Hotel, Belfast,
January 1, 1846

My Dear Friend Garrison:

I am now about to take leave of the Emerald Isle, for Glasgow, Scotland. I have been here a little more than four months. Up to this time, I have given no direct expression of the views, feelings, and opinions which I have formed, respecting the character and condition of the people in this land. I have refrained thus purposely. I wish to speak advisedly, and in order to do this, I have waited till I trust experience has brought my opinions to an intelligent maturity. I have been thus careful, not because I think what I may say will have much effect in shaping the opinions of the world, but because whatever of influence I may possess, whether little or much, I wish it to go in the right direction, and according to truth. I hardly need say that, in speaking of Ireland, I shall be influenced by prejudices in favor of America. I think my circumstances all forbid that. I have no end to serve, no creed to uphold, no government to defend; and as to nation, I belong to none. I have no protection at home, or resting-place abroad. The land of my birth welcomes me to her shores only as a slave, and spurns with contempt the idea of treating me differently. So that I am an outcast from the society of my childhood, and an outlaw in the land of my birth. "I am a stranger with thee, and a sojourner as all my fathers were." That men should be patriotic is to me perfectly natural; and as a philosophical fact, I am able to give it an *intellectual* recognition. But no further can I go. If ever I had any patriotism, or any capacity for the feeling, it was whipt out of me long since by the lash of the American soul-drivers.

In thinking of America, I sometimes find myself admiring her bright blue sky—her grand old woods—her fertile fields—her beautiful rivers—her mighty lakes, and star-crowned mountains. But my rapture is soon checked, my joy is soon turned to mourning. When I remember that all is cursed with the infernal spirit of slaveholding, robbery and wrong,—when I remember that with the waters of her noblest rivers, the tears of my brethren are borne to the ocean, disregarded and forgotten, and that her most fertile fields drink daily of the warm blood of my outraged sisters, I am filled with unutterable loathing, and led to reproach myself that any thing could fall from my lips in praise of such a land. America will not allow her children to love her. She seems bent on compelling those who would be her warmest friends, to be her worst enemies. May God give her repentance before it is too late, is the ardent prayer of my heart. I will continue to pray, labor and wait, believing that she cannot always be insensible to the dictates of justice, or deaf to the voice of humanity.

My opportunities for learning the character and condition of the people of this land have been very great. I have travelled almost from the hill of "Howth" to the Giant's Causeway, and from the Giant's Causeway to Cape Clear. During these travels, I have met with much in the character and condition of the people to approve, and much to condemn—much that has thrilled me with pleasure—and very much that has filled me with pain. I will not, in this letter, attempt to give any description of those scenes which have given me pain. This I will do hereafter. I have enough, and more than your subscribers will be disposed to read at one time, of the bright side of the picture. I can truly say, I have spent some of the happiest moments of my life since landing in this country. I seem to have undergone a transformation. I live a new life. The warm and generous co-operation extended to me by the friends of my despised race—the prompt and liberal manner with which the press has rendered me its aid—the glorious enthusiasm with which thousands have flocked to hear the cruel wrongs of my down-trodden and long-enslaved fellow-countrymen portrayed—the deep sympathy for the slave, and the strong abhorrence of the slaveholder, everywhere evinced—the cordiality with which members and ministers of various religious bodies, and of various shades of religious opinion, have embraced me, and lent me their aid—the kind hospitality constantly proffered to me by persons of the highest rank in society—the spirit of freedom that seems to animate all with whom I come in contact—and the entire absence of every thing that looked like prejudice against me, on account of the color of my skin—contrasted so strongly with my long and bitter experience in the United States, that I look with wonder and amazement on the transition. In the Southern part of the United States, I was a slave, thought of and spoken of as property. In the language of the LAW, *"held, taken, reputed and adjudged to be a chattel in the hands of my owners and possessors, and their executors, administrators, and assigns, to all intents, constructions, and purposes whatsoever."*—Brev. Digest, 224. In the Northern States, a fugitive slave, liable to be hunted at any moment like a felon, and to be hurled into the terrible jaws of slavery—doomed by an inveterate prejudice against color to insult and outrage on every hand, (Massachusetts out of the question)—denied the privileges and courtesies common to others in the use of the most humble means of conveyance—shut out from the cabins on steamboats—refused admission to respectable hotels—caricatured, scorned, scoffed, mocked and maltreated with impunity by any one, (no matter how black his heart,) so he has a white skin. But now behold the change! Eleven days and a half gone, and I have crossed three thousand miles of the perilous deep. Instead of a democratic government, I am under a monarchical government. Instead of the bright blue sky of America, I am covered with the soft grey fog of the Emerald Isle. I breathe, and lo! the chattel becomes a man. I gaze around in vain for one who will question my equal humanity, claim me as his slave, or offer me an insult. I employ a cab—I am seated beside white people—I reach the hotel—I enter the same door—I am shown into the same parlor—I dine at the same table—and no one is offended. No delicate nose grows deformed in my presence. I find no difficulty here in obtaining admission into any place of worship, instruction or amusement, on equal terms with people as white as any I ever saw in the United States. I meet nothing to remind me of my complexion. I find myself regarded and treated at every turn with the kindness and deference paid to white people. When I go to church, I am met by no upturned nose and scornful lip to tell me, *"We don't allow niggers in here"*!

I remember, about two years ago, there was in Boston, near the southwest corner of Boston Common, a menagerie. I had long desired to see such a collection as I understood were being exhibited there. Never having had an opportunity while a slave, I resolved to seize this, my first, since my escape. I went, and as I approached the entrance to gain admission, I was met and told by the door-keeper, in a harsh and contemptuous tone, "*We don't allow niggers in here.*" I also remember attending a revival meeting in the Rev. Henry Jackson's meeting-house, at New-Bedford, and going up the broad aisle to find a seat. I was met by a good deacon, who told me, in a pious tone, "*We don't allow niggers in here*"*!* Soon after my arrival in New-Bedford from the South, I had a strong desire to attend the Lyceum, but was told, "*They don't allow niggers in here*"*!* While passing from New York to Boston on the steamer Massachusetts, on the night of 9th Dec. 1843, when chilled almost through with the cold, I went into the cabin to get a little warm. I was soon touched upon the shoulder, and told, "*We don't allow niggers in here*"*!* On arriving in Boston from an anti-slavery tour, hungry and tired, I went into an eating-house near my friend Mr. Campbell's, to get some refreshments. I was met by a lad in a white apron, "*We don't allow niggers in here*"*!* A week or two before leaving the United States, I had a meeting appointed at Weymouth, the home of that glorious band of true abolitionists, the Weston family, and others. On attempting to take a seat in the Omnibus to that place, I was told by the driver, (and I never shall forget his fiendish hate,) "*I don't allow niggers in here*"*!* Thank heaven for the respite I now enjoy! I had been in Dublin but a few days, when a gentleman of great respectability kindly offered to conduct me through all the public buildings of that beautiful city; and a little afterwards, I found myself dining with the Lord Mayor of Dublin. What a pity there was not some American democratic Christian at the door of his splendid mansion, to bark out at my approach, *"They don't allow niggers in here"!* The truth is, the people here know nothing of the republican negro hate prevalent in our glorious land. They measure and esteem men according to their moral and intellectual worth, and not according to the color of their skin. Whatever may be said of the aristocracies here, there is none based on the color of a man's skin. This species of aristocracy belongs pre-eminently to "the land of the free, and the home of the brave." I have never found it abroad, in any but Americans. It sticks to them wherever they go. They find it almost as hard to get rid of it as to get rid of their skins.

The second day after my arrival at Liverpool, in company with my friend Buffum, and several other friends, I went to Eaton Hall, the residence of the Marquis of Westminster, one of the most splendid buildings in England. On approaching the door, I found several of our American passengers, who came out with us in the Cambria, waiting at the door for admission, as but one party was allowed in the house at a time. We all had to wait till the company within came out. And of all the faces, expressive of chagrin, those of the Americans were pre-eminent. They looked as sour as vinegar, and bitter as gall, when they found I was to be admitted on equal terms with themselves. When the door was opened, I walked in, on an equal footing with my white fellow-citizens, and from all I could see, I had as much attention paid me by the servants that showed us through the house, as any with a paler skin. As I walked through the building, the statuary did not fall down, the pictures did not leap from their places, the doors did not refuse to open, and the servants did not say, *"We don't allow niggers in here"!*

A happy new year to you, and all the friends of freedom.

Excuse this imperfect scrawl, and believe me to be ever and always yours,

Frederick Douglass.

[Source: *Liberator*, 30 January 1846.]

## *[In Defense of Purchasing Freedom]*

Before Douglass returned to the United States in 1847, some of his friends in England paid more than 700 dollars to buy his freedom. This action generated controversy, because it was perceived by some as an implicit recognition of the right of owners to buy and sell human beings. Douglass' letter to Henry C. Wright, an abolitionist who opposed the purchase, answers the objections that Wright and others had raised.

22, St. Ann's Square, Manchester,
December 22, 1846

Dear Friend:

Your letter of the 12th December reached me at this place, yesterday. Please accept my heartfelt thanks for it. I am sorry that you deemed it necessary to assure me, that it would be the last letter of advice you would ever write me. It looked as if you were about to cast me off for ever! I do not, however, think you meant to convey any such meaning; and if you did, I am sure you will see cause to change your mind, and to receive me again into the fold of those, whom it should ever be your pleasure to advise and instruct.

The subject of your letter is one of deep importance, and upon which, I have thought and felt much; and, being the party of all others most deeply concerned, it is natural to suppose I have an opinion, and ought to be able to give it on all fitting occasions. I deem this a fitting occasion, and shall act accordingly.

You have given me your opinion: I am glad you have done so. You have given it to me direct, in your own emphatic way. You never speak insipidly, smoothly, or mincingly; you have strictly adhered to your custom, in the letter before me. I now take great pleasure in giving you my opinion, as plainly and unreservedly as you have given yours, and I trust with equal good feeling and purity of motive. I take it, that nearly all that can be said against my position is contained in your letter; for if any man in the wide world would be likely to find valid objections to such a transaction as the one under consideration, I regard you as that man. I must, however, tell you, that I have read your letter over, and over again, and have sought in vain to find anything like what I can regard a valid reason *against the purchase of my body, or against my receiving the manumission papers, if they are ever presented to me.*

Let me, in the first place, state the facts and circumstances of the transaction which you so strongly condemn. It is your right to do so, and God forbid that I should ever cherish the slightest desire to restrain you in the exercise of that right. I say to you at once, and in all the fulness of sincerity, speak out; speak freely; keep nothing back; let me know your whole mind. "Hew to the line, though the chips fly in my face." Tell me, and tell me plainly, when you think I am deviating from the strict line of duty and principle; and when I become unwilling to hear, I shall have attained a character which I now despise, and from which I would hope to be preserved. But to the facts.

I am in England, my family are in the United States. My sphere of usefulness is in the United States; my public and domestic duties are there; and there it seems my duty to go. But I am *legally* the property of Thomas

Auld, and if I go to the United States, (no matter to what part, for there is no City of Refuge there, no spot sacred to freedom there,) Thomas Auld, *aided by the American Government,* can seize, bind and fetter, and drag me from my family, feed his cruel revenge upon me, and doom me to unending slavery. In view of this simple statement of facts, a few friends, desirous of seeing me released from the terrible liability, and to relieve my wife and children from the painful trepidation, consequent upon the liability, and to place me on an equal footing of safety with all other anti-slavery lecturers in the United States, and to enhance my usefulness by enlarging the field of my labors in the United States, have nobly and generously paid Hugh Auld, the agent of Thomas Auld, £150—in consideration of which, Hugh Auld (acting as his agent) and the Government of the United States agree, that I shall be free from all further liability.

These, dear friend, are the facts of the whole transaction. The principle here acted on by my friends, and that upon which I shall act in receiving the manumission papers, I deem quite defensible.

First, *as to those who acted as my friends, and their actions.* The actuating motive was, to secure me from a liability full of horrible forebodings to myself and family. With this object, I will do you the justice to say, I believe you fully unite, although some parts of your letters would seem to justify a different belief.

Then, as to the measure adopted to secure this result. Does it violate a fundamental principle, or does it not? This is the question, and to my mind the only question of importance, involved in the discussion. I believe that, on our part, no just or holy principle has been violated.

Before entering upon the argument in support of this view, I will take the liberty (and I know you will pardon it) to say, I think you should have pointed out some principle violated in the transaction, before you proceeded to exhort me to repentance. You have given me any amount of indignation against "Auld" and the United States, in all which I cordially unite, and felt refreshed by reading; but it has no bearing whatever upon the conduct of myself, or friends, in the matter under consideration. It does not prove that I have done wrong, nor does it demonstrate what is right, or the proper course to be pursued. Now that the matter has reached its present point, before entering upon the argument, let me say one other word; it is this—I do not think you have acted quite consistently with your character for promptness, in delaying your advice till the transaction was completed. You knew of the movement at its conception, and have known it through its progress, and have never, to my knowledge, uttered one syllable against it, in conversation or letter, till now that the deed is done. I regret this, not because I think your earlier advice would have altered the result, but because it would have left me more free than I can now be, since the thing is done. Of course, you will not think hard of my alluding to this circumstance. Now, then, to the main question.

The principle which you appear to regard as violated by the transaction in question, may be stated as follows:—*Every man has a natural and inalienable right to himself*. The inference from this is, *"that man cannot hold property in man"—and as man cannot hold property in man, neither can Hugh Auld nor the United States have any right of property in me—and having no right of property in me, they have no right to sell me—and, having no right to sell me, no one has a right to buy me.* I think I have now stated the principle, and the inference from the principle, distinctly and fairly. Now, the question upon which the whole controversy turns is, simply, this: does the transaction, which you condemn, really violate this principle? I own that, to a superficial observer, it would seem to do so.

But I think I am prepared to show, that, so far from being a violation of that principle, it is truly a noble vindication of it. Before going further, let me state here, briefly, what sort of a purchase would have been a violation of this principle, which, in common with yourself, I reverence, and am anxious to preserve inviolate.

1st. It would have been a violation of that principle, had those who purchased me done so, *to make me a slave, instead of a free-man.* And,

2ndly. It would have been a violation of that principle, had those who purchased me done so with a view to compensate the slaveholder, for what he and they regarded as his rightful property.

In neither of these ways was my purchase effected. My liberation was, in their estimation, of more value than £150; the happiness and repose of my family were, in their judgment, more than paltry gold. The £150 was paid to the remorseless plunderer, not because he had any just claim to it, but to induce him to give up his legal claim to something which they deemed of more value than money. It was not to compensate the slaveholder, but to release me from his power; not to establish my *natural right* to freedom, but to release me from all legal liabilities to slavery. And all this, you and I, and the slaveholders, and all who know anything of the transaction, very well understand. The very letter to Hugh Auld, proposing terms of purchase, informed him that those who gave, *denied his right to it.* The error of those, who condemn this transaction, consists in their confounding the crime of buying men *into slavery,* with the meritorious act of buying men out of slavery, and the purchase of legal freedom with abstract right and natural freedom. They say, "If you BUY, you recognize the right to sell. If you receive, you recognize the right of the giver to give." And this has a show of truth, as well as of logic. But a few plain cases will show its entire fallacy.

There is now, in this country, a heavy duty on corn. The government of this country has imposed it; and though I regard it a most unjust and wicked imposition, no man of common sense will charge me with endorsing or recognizing the right of this government to impose this duty, simply because, to prevent myself and family from starving, I buy and eat this corn.

Take another case:—I have had dealings with a man. I have owed him one hundred dollars, and have paid it; I have lost the receipt. He comes upon me the second time for the money. I know, and he knows, he has no right to it; but he is a villain, and has me in his power. The law is with him, and against me. I must pay or be dragged to jail. I choose to pay the bill a second time. To say I sanctioned his right to rob me, because I preferred to pay rather than go to jail, is to utter an absurdity, to which no sane man would give heed. And yet the principle of action, in each of these cases, is the same. The man might indeed say, the claim is unjust—and declare, I will rot in jail, before I will pay it. But this would not, certainly, be demanded by any principle of truth, justice, or humanity; and however much we might be disposed to respect his daring, but little deference could be paid to his wisdom. The fact is, we act upon this principle every day of our lives, and we have an undoubted right to do so. When I came to this country from the United States, I came in the *second* cabin. And why? Not because my natural right to come in the *first* cabin was not as good as that of any other man, but because a wicked and cruel prejudice decided, that the second cabin was the place for me. By coming over in the second, did I sanction or justify this wicked proscription? Not at all. It was the best I could do. I acted from necessity.

One other case, and I have done with this view of the subject. I think you will agree with me, that the case I am now about to put is pertinent, though you may not readily pardon me for making yourself the agent of my illustration. The case respects the passport system on the continent of Europe. That system you utterly condemn. You look upon it as an unjust and wicked interference, a bold and infamous violation of the *natural* and *sacred* right of locomotion. You hold, (and so do I,) that the image of our common God ought to be a passport all over the habitable world. But bloody and tyrannical governments have ordained otherwise; they usurp authority over you, and decide for you, on what conditions you shall travel. They say, you shall have a passport, or you shall be put in prison. Now, the question is, have they a right to prescribe any such terms? and do you, by complying with these terms, sanction their interference? I think you will answer, no; submission to injustice, and sanction of injustice, are different things; and he is a poor reasoner who confounds the two, and makes them one and the same thing. Now, then, for the parallel, and the application of the passport system to my own case.

I wish to go to the United States. I have a natural right to go there, and be free. My natural right is as good as that of Hugh Auld, or James K. Polk; but that plundering government says, I shall not return to the United States in safety—it says, I must allow Hugh Auld to rob me, or my friends, of £150, or be hurled into the infernal jaws of slavery. I must have a "bit of paper, signed and sealed," or my liberty must be taken from me, and I must be torn from my family and friends. The government of Austria said to you, "Dare to come upon my soil, without a passport, declaring you to be an American citizen, (which you say you are not,) you shall at once be arrested, and thrown into prison." What said you to that Government? Did you say that the threat was a villainous one, and an infamous invasion of your right of locomotion? Did you say, "I will come upon your soil; I will go where I please! I dare and defy your government!" Did you say, "I will spurn your passports; I would not stain my hand, and degrade myself, by touching your miserable parchment. You have no right to give it, and I have no right to take it. I trample your laws, and will put your constitutions under my feet! I will not recognize them!" Was this your course? No! dear friend, it was not. Your practice was wiser than your theory. You took the passport, submitted to be examined while travelling, and availed yourself of all the advantages of your "passport"—or, in other words, escaped all the evils which you ought to have done, without it, and would have done, but for the tyrannical usurpation in Europe.

I will not dwell longer upon this view of the subject; and I dismiss it, feeling quite satisfied of the entire correctness of the reasoning, and the principle attempted to be maintained. As to the expediency of the measures, different opinions may well prevail; but in regard to the principle, I feel it difficult to conceive of two opinions. I am free to say, that, had I possessed one hundred and fifty pounds, I would have seen Hugh Auld *kicking,* before I would have given it to him. I would have waited till the emergency came, and only given up the money when nothing else would do. But my friends thought it best to provide against the contingency; they acted on their own responsibility, and I am not disturbed about the result. But, having acted on a true principle, I *do not feel free to disavow their proceedings.*

In conclusion, let me say, I anticipate no such change in my position as you predict. I shall be Frederick Douglass still, and once a slave still. I shall neither be made to forget nor cease to feel the wrongs of my enslaved fellow-countrymen. My knowledge of slavery will be the same, and my hatred of it will be the same. By the way, I have never made my own person and suffering the theme of public discourse, but have always based my appeal upon the wrongs of the three millions now in chains; and these shall still be the burthen of my speeches. You intimate that I may reject the papers, and allow them to remain in the hands of those friends who have effected the purchase, and thus avail myself of the security afforded by them, without sharing any part of the responsibility of the transaction. My objection to this is one of honor. I do not think it would be very honorable on my part, to remain silent during the whole transaction, and giving it more than my silent approval; and then, when the thing is completed, and I am safe, attempt to play the *hero*, by throwing off all responsibility in the matter. It might be said, and said with great propriety, "Mr. Douglass, your indignation is very good, and has but one fault, and that is, *it comes too late!*" It would be a show of bravery when the danger is over. From every view I have been able to take of the subject, I am persuaded to receive the papers, if presented,—not, however, as a proof of my right to be free, for *that is self-evident*, but as a proof that my friends have been legally robbed of £150, in order to secure that which is the birth-right of every man. And I will hold up those papers before the world, in proof of the plundering character of the American government. It shall be the brand of infamy, stamping the nation, in whose name the deed was done, as a great aggregation of hypocrites, thieves and liars,—and their condemnation is just. They declare that all men are created equal, and have a natural and inalienable right to liberty, while they rob me of £150, as a condition of my enjoying this natural and inalienable right. It will be their condemnation, in their own hand-writing, and may be held up to the world as a means of humbling that haughty republic into repentance.

I agree with you, that the contest which I have to wage is against the government of the United States. But the representative of that government is the slaveholder, *Thomas Auld.* He is commander-in-chief of the army and navy. The whole civil and naval force of the nation are at his disposal. He may command all these to his assistance, and bring them all to bear upon me, until I am made entirely subject to his will, or submit to be robbed myself, or allow my friends to be robbed, of seven hundred and fifty dollars. And rather than be subject to his will, I have submitted to be robbed, or allowed my friends to be robbed, of the seven hundred and fifty dollars.

Sincerely yours,
Frederick Douglass

[Source: *Liberator*, 29 January 1847.]

## *[On the Union, Religion, and the Constitution]*

This address, delivered at Market Hall in Syracuse, N.Y. in September of 1847, is a strong denunciation of the Union, the churches, and the Constitution for condoning slavery. Douglass' tone is bitter and satirical as he surveys the institutions and assumptions that uphold slavery.

I like radical measures, whether adopted by Abolitionists or slaveholders. I do not know but I like them better when adopted by the latter. Hence I look with pleasure upon the movements of Mr. Calhoun and his party. I rejoice at any movement in the slave States with reference to this system of Slavery. Any movement there will attract attention to the system—a system, as Junius once said to Lord Granby, "which can only pass without condemnation as it passes without observation." I am anxious to have it seen of all men: hence I am delighted to see any effort to prop up the system on the part of the slaveholders. It serves to bring up the subject before the people; and hasten the day of deliverance. It is meant otherwise. I am sorry that it is so. Yet the wrath of man may be made to praise God. He will confound the wisdom of the crafty, and bring to naught the counsels of the ungodly. The slaveholders are now marshalling their hosts for the propagation and extension of the institution—Abolitionists, on the other hand, are marshalling their forces not only against its propagation and extension, but against its very existence. Two large classes of the community, hitherto unassociated with the Abolitionists, have come up so far towards the right as to become opposed to the farther extension of the crime. I am glad to hear it. I like to gaze upon these two contending armies, for I believe it will hasten the dissolution of the present unholy Union, which has been justly stigmatized as "a covenant with death, an agreement with hell." I welcome the bolt, either from the North or the South, which shall shatter this Union; for under this Union lie the prostrate forms of three millions with whom I am identified. In consideration of their wrongs, of their sufferings, of their groans, I welcome the bolt, either from the celestial or from the infernal regions, which shall sever this Union in twain. Slaveholders are promoting it—Abolitionists are doing so. Let it come, and when it does, our land will rise up from an incubus; her brightness shall reflect against the sky, and shall become the beacon light of liberty in the Western world. She shall then, indeed, become "the land of the free and the home of the brave."

For sixteen years, Wm. Lloyd Garrison and a noble army of the friends of emancipation have been labouring in season and out of season, amid smiles and frowns, sunshine and clouds, striving to establish the conviction through this land, that to hold and traffic in human flesh is a sin against God. They have been somewhat successful; but they have been in no wise so successful as they might have been, had the men and women at the North rallied around them as they had a right to hope from their profession. They have had to contend not only with skilful politicians, with a deeply prejudiced and pro-slavery community, but with eminent Divines, Doctors of Divinity, and Bishops. Instead of encouraging them as friends, they have acted as enemies. For many days did Garrison go the rounds of the city of Boston to ask of the ministers the poor privilege of entering their chapels and lifting up his voice for the dumb. But their doors were bolted, their gates barred, and their pulpits hermetically sealed. It was not till an infidel hall was thrown open, that the voice of dumb millions could be heard in Boston.

I take it that all who have heard at all on this subject, are well convinced that the stronghold of Slavery is in the pulpit. Say what we may of politicians and political parties, the power that holds the keys of the dungeon in which the bondman is confined, is the pulpit. It is that power which is dropping, dropping, constantly dropping on the ear of this people, creating and moulding the moral sentiment of the land. This they have sufficiently under their control that they can change it from the spirit of hatred to that of love to mankind. That they do it not, is evident from the results of their teaching. The men who wield the blood-clotted cow-skin come from our Sabbath Schools in the Southern States. Who act as slave-drivers? The men who go forth from our own congregations here. Why, if the Gospel were truly preached among us, a man would as soon think of going into downright piracy as to offer himself as a slave-driver.

In Farmington, two sons of members of the Society of Friends are coolly proposing to go to the South and engage in the honourable office of slave-driving for a thousand dollars a year. People at the North talk coolly of uncles, cousins, and brothers who are slaveholders, and of their coming to visit them. If the Gospel were truly preached here, you would as soon talk of having an uncle or brother a brothel keeper as a slaveholder; for I hold that every slaveholder, no matter how pure he may be, is a keeper of a house of ill-fame. Every kitchen is a brothel, from that of Dr. Fuller's to that of James K. Polk's (Applause). I presume I am addressing a virtuous audience—I presume I speak to virtuous females—and

I ask you to consider this one feature of Slavery. Think of a million of females absolutely delivered up into the hands of tyrants, to do what they will with them—to dispose of their persons in any way they see fit. And so entirely are they at the disposal of their masters, that if they raise their hands against them, they may be put to death for daring to resist their infernal aggression.

We have been trying to make this thing appear sinful. We have not been able to do so yet. It is not admitted, and I hardly know how to argue against it. I confess that the time for argument seems almost gone by. What do the people want? Affirmation upon affirmation,—denunciation upon denunciation,—rebuke upon rebuke?

We have men in this land now advocating evangelical flogging. I hold in my hand a sermon recently published by Rev. Bishop Meade, of Virginia. Before I read that part in favour of evangelical flogging, let me read a few extracts from another part, relating to the duties of the slave. The sermon, by the way, was published with a view of its being read by *Christian* masters to their slaves. White black birds! (Laughter.)

(*Mr. Douglass here assumed a most grotesque look, and with a canting tone of voice, read as follows.*)

"Having thus shown you the chief duties you owe to your great Master in Heaven, I now come to lay before you the duties you owe to your masters and mistresses on earth. And for this you have one general rule that you ought always to carry in your minds, and that is, to *do all services for them, as if you did it for God himself*. Poor creatures! you little consider when you are idle, and neglectful of your master's business; when you steal, waste, and hurt any of their substance; when you are saucy and impudent; when you are telling them lies and deceiving them; or when you prove stubborn and sullen, and will not do the work you are set about, without stripes and vexation; you do not consider, I say, that what faults you are guilty of towards your masters and mistresses, are faults done against God himself, who hath set your masters and mistresses over you in his own stead, and expects that you will do for them just as you would do for him. And pray, do not think that I want to deceive you, when I tell you that your *masters and mistresses are God's overseers;* and that if you are faulty towards them, God himself will punish you severely for it."

This is some of the Southern religion. Do you not think you would "grow in grace and in the knowledge of the truth." (Applause.)

I come now to evangelical flogging. There is nothing said about flogging—that word is not used. It is called correction; and that word as it is understood at the North, is some sort of medicine. (Laughter.) Slavery has always sought to hide itself under different names. The mass of the people call it "our peculiar institution." There is no harm in that. Others call it (they are the more pious sort), "our Patriarchal institution." (Laughter.) Politicians have called it "our social system"; and people in social life have called it "our domestic institution." Abbot Lawrence has recently discovered a new name for it—he calls it "unenlightened labour." (Laughter.) The Methodists in their last General conference, have invented a new name—"the impediment." (Laughter.) To give you some idea of evangelical flogging, under the name of correction, there are laws of this description,—"any white man killing a slave shall be punished as though he shall have killed a white person, unless such a slave die under *moderate* correction." It commences with a plain proposition.

"Now when correction is given you, you either deserve it, or you do not deserve it." (Laughter.)

That is very plain, almost as safe as that of a certain orator:—"Ladies and Gentlemen, it is my opinion, my deliberate opinion, after a long consideration of the whole matter, that as a general thing, all other things being equal, there are fewer persons to be found in towns sparsely populated, than in larger towns more thickly settled." (Laughter.)

The Bishop goes on to say—

"Whether you really deserve it or not," (one would think that would make a difference), "it is your duty, and Almighty God requires that you bear it patiently. You may perhaps think that this is a hard doctrine," (and it admits of little doubt), "but if you consider it right you must needs think otherwise of it." (It is clear as mud. I suppose he is now going to reason them into the propriety of being flogged evangelically.) "Suppose you deserve correction; you cannot but see that it is just and right you should meet with it. Suppose you do not, or at least so much or so severe; you perhaps have escaped a great many more, and are at last paid for all. Suppose you are quite innocent; is it not possible you may have done some other bad thing which was never discovered, and Almighty God would not let you escape without punishment one time or another? Ought you not in such cases to give glory to Him?" (Glory!) (Much laughter.)

I am glad you have got to the point that you can laugh at the religion of such fellows as this Doctor. There is nothing that will facilitate our cause more than getting the people to laugh at that religion which brings its influence to support traffic in human flesh. It has deceived us so long that it has overawed us.

For a long time when I was a slave, I was led to think from hearing such passages as "servants obey, &c." that if I dared to escape, the wrath of God would follow me. All are willing to acknowledge my right to be free; but after this acknowledgement, the good man goes to the Bible and says "after all I see some difficulty about this thing. You know, after the deluge, there was Shem,

Ham, and Japhet; and you know that Ham was black and had a curse put on him; and I know not but it would be an attempt to thwart the purposes of Jehovah, if these men were set at liberty." It is this kind of religion I wish to have you laugh at—it breaks the charm there is about it. If I could have the men at this meeting who hold such sentiments and could hold up the mirror to let them see themselves as others see them, we should soon make head against this pro-slavery religion.

I dwell mostly upon the religious aspect, because I believe it is the religious people who are to be relied on in this Anti-Slavery movement. Do not misunderstand my railing—do not class me with those who despise religion—do not identify me with the infidel. I love the religion of Christianity—which cometh from above—which is pure, peaceable, gentle, easy to be entreated, full of good fruits, and without hypocrisy. I love that religion which sends its votaries to bind up the wounds of those who have fallen among thieves. By all the love I bear to such a Christianity as this, I hate that of the Priest and Levite, that with long-faced Phariseeism goes up to Jerusalem and worships, and leaves the bruised and wounded to die. I despise that religion that can carry Bibles to the heathen on the other side of the globe and withhold them from the heathen on this side—which can talk about human rights yonder and traffic in human flesh here. I love that which makes its votaries do to others as they would that others should do to them. I hope to see a revival of it—thank God it is revived. I see revivals of it in the absence of the other sort of revivals. I believe it to be confessed now, that there has not been a sensible man converted after the old sort of way, in the last five years. Le Roy Sunderland, the mesmerizer, has explained all this away, so that Knapp and others who have converted men after that sort have failed.

There is another religion. It is that which takes off

fetters instead of binding them on—that breaks every yoke—that lifts up the bowed down. The Anti-Slavery platform is based on this kind of religion. It spreads its table to the lame, the halt, and the blind. It goes down after a long neglected race. It passes, link by link till it finds the lowest link in humanity's chain—humanity's most degraded form in the most abject condition. It reaches down its arm and tells them to stand up. This is Anti-Slavery—this is Christianity. It is reviving gloriously among the various denominations. It is threatening to supersede those old forms of religion having all of the love of God and none of man in it. (Applause.)

I now leave this aspect of the subject and proceed to inquire into that which probably must be the inquiry of every honest mind present. I trust I do not misjudge the character of my audience when I say they are anxious to know in what way they're contributing to uphold Slavery.

The question may be answered in various ways. I leave the outworks of political parties and social arrangements, and come at once to the Constitution, to which I believe all present are devotedly attached—I will not say all, for I believe I know some, who, however they may be disposed to admire some of the beautiful truths set forth in that instrument, recognize its pro-slavery features, and are ready to form a republic in which there shall be neither tyrant nor slave. The Constitution I hold to be radically and essentially slave-holding, in that it gives the physical and numerical power of the nation to keep the slave in his chains, by promising that that power shall in any emergency be brought to bear upon the slave, to crush him in obedience to his master. The language of the Constitution is you shall be a slave or die. We know it is such, and knowing it we are not disposed to have part nor lot with that Constitution. For my part I had rather that my right hand should wither by my side than cast a ballot under the Constitution of the United States.

Then, again, in the clause concerning fugitives—in this you are implicated. Your whole country is one vast hunting ground from Texas to Maine.

Ours is a glorious land; and from across the Atlantic we welcome those who are stricken by the storms of despotism. Yet the damning facts remain, there is not a rood of earth under the stars and the eagle of your flag, where a man of my complexion can stand free. There is no mountain so high, no plain so extensive, no spot so sacred, that it can secure to me the right of liberty. Wherever waves the star-spangled banner there the bondman may be arrested and hurried back to the jaws of Slavery. This is your "land of the free," your "home of the brave." From Lexington, from Ticonderoga, from Bunker Hill, where rises that grand shaft with its capstone in the clouds, asks, in the name of the first blood that spurted in behalf of freedom, to protect the slave from the infernal clutches of his master. That petition would be denied, and he bid go back to the tyrant.

I never knew what freedom was till I got beyond the limits of the American eagle. When I first rested my head on a British Island I felt that the eagle might scream, but from its talons and beak I was free, at least for a time. No slave-holder can clutch me on British soil. There I could gaze the tyrant in the face and with the indignation of a tyrant in my look, wither him before me. But republican, Christian America will aid the tyrant in catching his victim.

I know this kind of talk is not agreeable to what are called patriots. Indeed, some have called me a traitor. That profanely religious Journal "The Olive Branch," edited by the Rev. Mr. Norris, recommended that I be hung as a traitor. Two things are necessary to make a traitor. One is, he shall have a country. (Laughter and applause.) I believe if I had a country, I should be a patriot. I think I have all the feelings necessary—all the moral material, to say nothing about the intellectual. I do not know that I ever felt the emotion, but sometimes thought I had a glimpse of it. When I have been delighted with the little brook that passes by the cottage in which I was born,—with the woods and the fertile fields, I felt a sort of glow which I suspect resembles a little what they call patriotism. I can look with some admiration on your wide lakes, your fertile fields, your enterprise, your industry, your many lovely institutions. I can read with pleasure your Constitution to establish justice, and secure the blessings of liberty to posterity. Those are precious sayings to my mind. But when I remember that the blood of four sisters and one brother, is making fat the soil of Maryland and Virginia,—when I remember that an aged grandmother who has reared twelve children for the Southern market, and these one after another as they arrived at the most interesting age, were torn from her bosom,—when I remember that when she became too much racked for toil, she was turned out by a professed Christian master to grope her way in the darkness of old age, literally to die with none to help her, and the institutions of this country sanctioning and sanctifying this crime, I have no words of eulogy, I have no patriotism. How can I love a country where the blood of my own blood, the flesh of my own flesh, is now toiling under the lash?—America's soil reddened by the stain from woman's shrinking flesh.

No, I make no pretension to patriotism. So long as my voice can be heard on this or the other side of the Atlantic, I will hold up America to the lightning scorn of moral indignation. In doing this, I shall feel myself discharging the duty of a true patriot; for he is a lover of his country who rebukes and does not excuse its sins. It is righteousness that exalteth a nation while sin is a reproach to any people.

But to the idea of what you at the North have to do with Slavery. You furnish the bulwark of protection, and promise to put the slaves in bondage. As the American Anti-Slavery Society says, "if you will go on branding, scourging, sundering family ties, trampling in the dust your down trodden victims, you must do it at your own peril." But if you say, "we of the North will render you no assistance: if you still continue to trample on the slave, you must take the consequences," I tell you the matter will soon be settled.

I have been taunted frequently with the want of valour: so has my race, because we have not risen upon our masters. It is adding insult to injury to say this. You belong to 17,000,000, with arms, with means of locomotion, with telegraphs. We are kept in ignorance three millions to seventeen. You taunt us with not being able to rescue ourselves from your clutch. Shame on you! Stand aside—give us fair play—leave us with the tyrants, and then if we do not take care of ourselves, you may taunt us. I do not mean by this to advocate war and bloodshed. I am not a man of war. The time was when I was. I was then a slave: I had dreams, horrid dreams of freedom through a sea of blood. But when I heard of the Anti-Slavery movement, light broke in upon my dark mind. Bloody visions fled away, and I saw the star of liberty peering above the horizon. Hope then took the place of desperation, and I was led to repose in the arms of Slavery. I said, I would suffer rather than do any act of violence—rather than that the glorious day of liberty might be postponed.

Since the light of God's truth beamed upon my mind, I have become a friend of that religion which teaches us to pray for our enemies—which, instead of shooting balls into their hearts, loves them. I would not hurt a hair of a slaveholder's head. I will tell you what else I would not do. I would not stand around the slave with my bayonet pointed at his breast, in order to keep him in the power of the slaveholder.

I am aware that there are many who think the slaves are very well off, and that they are very well treated, as if it were possible that such a thing could be. A man happy in chains! Even the eagle loves liberty.

*Go, let a cage, with grates of gold,*
*And pearly roof, the eagle hold;*
*Let dainty viands be his fare,*
*And give the captive tenderest care;*
*But say, in luxury's limits pent,*
*Find you the king of birds content?*
*No, oft he'll sound the startling shriek,*
*And dash the grates with angry beak.*
*Precarious freedom's far more dear,*
*Than all the prison's pamp'ring cheer!*
*He longs to see his eyrie's seat,*
*Some cliff on ocean's lonely shore,*
*Whose old bare top the tempests beat,*
*And round whose base the billows roar,*
*When tossed by gales, they yawn like graves,—*
*He longs for joy to skim those waves;*
*Or rise through tempest-shrouded air,*
*And thick and dark, with wild winds swelling,*
*To brave the lightning's lurid glare,*
*And talk with thunders in their dwelling.*

As with the eagle, so with man. No amount of attention or finery, no dainty dishes can be a substitute for liberty. Slaveholders know this, and knowing it, they exclaim,—"The South are surrounded by a dangerous population, degraded, stupid savages, and if they could but entertain the idea that immediate, unconditional death would not be their portion, they would rise at once and enact the St. Domingo tragedy. But they are held in subordination by the consciousness that the whole nation would rise and crush them." Thus they live in constant dread from day to day.

Friends, Slavery must be abolished, and that can only be done by enforcing the great principles of justice. Vainly you talk about voting it down. When you have cast your millions of ballots, you have not reached the evil. It has fastened its root deep into the heart of the nation, and nothing but God's truth and love can cleanse the land. We must change the moral sentiment. Hence we ask you to support the Anti-Slavery Society. It is not an organization to build up political parties, or churches, nor to pull them down, but to stamp the image of Anti-Slavery truth upon the community. Here we may all do something.

*In the world's broad field of battle,*
*In the bivouac of life,*
*Be not like dumb driven cattle—*
*Be a hero in the strife.*

[Source: *National Anti-Slavery Standerd,* 28 October 1847.]

## *[Establishing the* North Star]

Douglass founded his abolitionist paper, the *North Star,* in 1847, despite William Lloyd Garrison's advice not to deflect his energies and talents from his lecture tours. Douglass had faith that his newspaper would succeed, even though many other black papers had failed. While he welcomed the help of whites, he insisted, finally, "the man STRUCK is the man to CRY OUT." Moreover, Douglass wanted to articulate his own voice, not just echo the sentiments of other abolitionists.

We are now about to assume the management of the editorial department of a newspaper, devoted to the cause of Liberty, Humanity and Progress. The position is one which, with the purest motives, we have long desired to occupy. It has long been our anxious wish to see, in this slave-holding, slave-trading, and negro-hating land, a printing press and paper, permanently established, under the complete control and direction of the immediate victims of slavery and oppression.

Animated by this intense desire, we have pursued our object, till on the threshold of obtaining it. Our press and printing materials are bought, and paid for. Our office secured, and is well situated, in the centre of business, in this enterprising city. Our office Agent, an industrious and amiable young man, thoroughly devoted to the interests of humanity, has already entered upon his duties. Printers well recommended have offered their services, and are ready to work as soon as we are prepared for the regular publication of our paper. Kind friends are rallying round us, with words and deeds of encouragement. Subscribers are steadily, if not rapidly coming in, and some of the best minds in the country are generously offering to lend us the powerful aid of their pens. The sincere wish of our heart, so long and so devoutly cherished seems now upon the eve of complete realization.

It is scarcely necessary for us to say that our desire to occupy our present position at the head of an Anti-Slavery Journal, has resulted from no unworthy distrust or ungrateful want of appreciation of the zeal, integrity, or ability of the noble band of white laborers, in this department of our cause; but, from a sincere and settled conviction that such a Journal, if conducted with only moderate skill and ability, would do a most important and indispensable work, which it would be wholly impossible for our white friends to do for us.

It is neither a reflection on the fidelity, nor a disparagement of the ability of our friends and fellow-laborers, to assert what "common sense affirms and only folly denies," that the man who has *suffered the wrong* is the man to *demand redress*,—that the man STRUCK is the man to CRY OUT—and that he who has *endured the cruel pangs of Slavery* is the man to *advocate Liberty*. It is evident we must be our own representatives and advocates, not exclusively, but peculiarly—not distinct from, but in connection with our white friends. In the grand struggle for liberty and equality now waging, it is meet, right and essential that there should arise in our ranks authors and editors, as well as orators, for it is in these capacities that the most permanent good can be rendered to our cause.

Hitherto the immediate victims of slavery and prejudice, owing to various causes, have had little share in this department of effort: they have frequently undertaken, and almost as frequently failed. This latter fact has often been urged by our friends against our engaging in the present enterprise; but, so far from convincing us of the impolicy of our course, it serves to confirm us in the necessity, if not the wisdom of our undertaking. That others have failed, is a reason for OUR earnestly endeavoring to succeed. Our race must be vindicated from the embarrassing imputations resulting from former non-success. We believe that what *ought* to be done, *can* be done. We say this, in no self-confident or boastful spirit, but with a full sense of our weakness and unworthiness, relying upon the Most High for wisdom and strength to support us in our righteous undertaking. We are not wholly unaware of the duties, hardships and responsibilities of our position. We have easily imagined some, and friends have not hesitated to inform us of others. Many doubtless are yet to be revealed by that infallible teacher, experience. A view of them solemnize, but do not appal us. We have counted the cost. Our mind is made up, and we are resolved to go forward.

In aspiring to our present position, the aid of circumstances has been so strikingly apparent as to almost stamp our humble aspirations with the solemn sanctions of a Divine Providence. Nine years ago, as most of our readers are aware, we were held as a slave, shrouded in the midnight ignorance of that infernal system—sunken in the depths of servility and degradation—registered with four footed beasts and creeping things—regarded as property—compelled to toil without wages—with a heart swollen with bitter anguish—and a spirit crushed and broken. By a singular combination of circumstances we finally succeeded in escaping from the grasp of the man who claimed us as his property, and succeeded in safely reaching New Bedford, Mass. In this town we worked three years as a daily laborer on the wharves. Six years ago we became a Lecturer on Slavery. Under the apprehension of being re-taken into bondage, two years ago we embarked for England. During our stay in that country, kind friends, anxious for our safety, ransomed us from slavery, by the payment of a large sum. The same friends, as unexpectedly as generously, placed in our hands the necessary means of purchasing a printing press and printing materials. Finding ourself now in a favorable position for aiming an important blow at slavery and prejudice, we feel urged on in our enterprise by a sense of duty to God and man, firmly believing that our effort will be crowned with entire success.

[Source: *North Star*, 3 December 1847.]

## [North Star: *Statement of Purpose*]

Directed toward blacks who shared an oppressed past, the *North Star* was to be a light that pointed the way to freedom. In addition, Douglass envisioned the paper as a forum for debating other kinds of reforms that might serve "to enlighten, improve, and elevate mankind." Douglass' own abilities were developed as a result of the project, but the paper was in continual financial difficulties.

We solemnly dedicate the *North Star* to the cause of our long oppressed and plundered fellow countrymen. May God bless the offering to your good! It shall fearlessly assert your rights, faithfully proclaim your wrongs, and earnestly demand for you instant and even-handed justice. Giving no quarter to slavery at the South, it will hold no truce with oppressors at the North. While it shall boldly advocate emancipation for our enslaved brethren, it will omit no opportunity to gain for the nominally free, complete enfranchisement. Every effort to injure or degrade you or your cause—originating wheresoever, or with whomsoever—shall find in it a constant, unswerving and inflexible foe.

We shall energetically assail the ramparts of Slavery and Prejudice, be they composed of church or state, and seek the destruction of every refuge of lies, under which tyranny may aim to conceal and protect itself.

Among the multitude of plans proposed and opinions held, with reference to our cause and condition, we shall try to have a mind of our own, harmonizing with all as far as we can, and differing from any and all where we must, but always discriminating between men and measures. We shall cordially approve every measure and effort calculated to advance your sacred cause, and strenuously oppose any which in our opinion may tend to retard its progress. In regard to our position, on questions that have unhappily divided the friends of freedom in this country, we shall stand in our paper where we have ever stood on the platform. Our views written shall accord with our views spoken, earnestly seeking peace with all men, when it can be secured without injuring the integrity of our movement, and never shrinking from conflict or division when summoned to vindicate truth and justice.

While our paper shall be mainly Anti-Slavery, its columns shall be freely opened to the candid and decorous discussion of all measures and topics of a moral and humane character, which may serve to enlighten, improve, and elevate mankind. Temperance, Peace, Capital Punishment, Education,—all subjects claiming the attention of the public mind may be freely and fully discussed here.

While advocating your rights, the *North Star* will strive to throw light on your duties: while it will not fail to make known your virtues, it will not shun to discover your faults. To be faithful to our foes it must be faithful to ourselves, in all things.

Remember that we are one, that our cause is one, and that we must help each other, if we would succeed. We have drunk to the dregs the bitter cup of slavery; we have worn the heavy yoke; we have sighed beneath our bonds, and writhed beneath the bloody lash;—cruel mementoes of our oneness are indelibly marked in our living flesh. We are one with you under the ban of prejudice and proscription—one with you under the slander of inferiority—one with you in social and political disfranchisement. What you suffer, we suffer; what you endure, we endure. We are indissolubly united, and must fall or flourish together.

We feel deeply the solemn responsibility which we have now assumed. We have seriously considered the importance of the enterprise, and have now entered upon it with full purpose of heart. We have nothing to offer in the way of literary ability to induce you to encourage us in our laudable undertaking. You will not expect or require this at our hands. The most that you can reasonably expect, or that we can safely promise, is, a paper of which you need not be ashamed. Twenty-one years of severe bondage at the South, and nine years of active life at the North, while it has afforded us the best possible opportunity for storing our mind with much practical and important information, has left us little time for literary pursuits or attainments. We have yet to receive the advantage of the first day's schooling. In point of education, birth and rank, we are one with yourselves, and of yourselves. What we are, we are not only without help, but against trying opposition. Your knowledge of our history for the last seven years makes it unnecessary for us to say more on this point. What we have been in your cause, we shall continue to be; and not being too old to learn, we may improve in many ways. Patience and Perseverance shall be our motto.

We shall be the advocates of learning, from the very want of it, and shall most readily yield the deference due to men of education among us; but shall always bear in mind to accord most merit to those who have labored hardest, and overcome most, in the praiseworthy pursuit of knowledge, remembering "that the whole need not a physician, but they that are sick," and that "the strong ought to bear the infirmities of the weak."

Brethren, the first number of the paper is before you.

It is dedicated to your cause. Through the kindness of our friends in England, we are in possession of an excellent printing press, types, and all other materials necessary for printing a paper. Shall this gift be blest to our good, or shall it result in our injury? It is for you to say. With your aid, co-operation and assistance, our enterprise will be entirely successful. We pledge ourselves that no effort on our part shall be wanting, and that no subscriber shall lose his subscription—"The *North Star* Shall Live."

[Source: *North Star*, 3 December 1847.]

## *[Black Churches and Segregation]*

Douglass consistently challenged segregated facilities for blacks. He made certain that whenever he was asked to leave a hotel dining room or railroad car, an issue was made of the irrational nature of prejudice. When he perceived blacks contributing to the cause of segregation, he was equally vehement.

One of the greatest evils resulting from separate religious organizations for the exclusive use of colored persons, is the countenance and support which they give to exclusive colored schools. The very existence of the former is an argument in favor of the latter. If there be any good reason for a colored church, the same will hold good in regard to a colored school, and indeed to every other institution founded on complexion. Negro pews in the church; negro boxes in the theatre; negro cars on the railroad; negro berths in the steamboat; negro churches and negro schools in the community, are all the pernicious fruit of a wicked, unnatural, and blasphemous prejudice against our God-given complexion; and as such stand directly in the way of our progress and equality. The axe must be laid at the root of the tree. This whole system of things is false, foul, and infernal, and should receive our most earnest and unceasing reprobation. The evils of separate colored schools are obvious to the common sense of all. Their very tendency is to produce feelings of superiority in the minds of white children, and a sense of inferiority in those of colored children; thus producing pride on the one hand, and servility on the other, and making those who would be the best of friends the worst of enemies. As we have frequently urged on the platform and elsewhere, prejudice is not the creature of birth, but of education. When a boy in the streets of Baltimore, we were never objected to by our white playfellows on account of our color. When the hat was tossed up for a choice of partners in the play, we were selected as readily as any other boy, and were esteemed as highly as any. No one ever objected to our complexion. We could run as fast, jump as far, throw the ball as direct and true, and catch it with as much dexterity and skill as the white boys; and were esteemed for what we could do. And such, in our judgment, would be the case here at the North, but for the many influences tending to a separation of white from colored children. We shall, however, have more to say on this subject at another time; for it is one which ought to receive speedy and thorough attention, not only in this community, but throughout the Union.

Another reason against colored churches originates in the character and qualifications of the men almost universally and necessarily employed as their teachers and pastors. With few exceptions, colored ministers have not the mental qualifications to instruct and improve their congregations; and instead of advancing, they retard the intellectual progress of the people. Some of the most popular colored preachers in this country are men unable to write their own names; and many of them are unable to read without spelling half their words. Colored churches form a field for this class of "would-be ministers;" and their existence is one great reason of the ignorance and mental inactivity, and general want of enterprise among us as a class. We have heard them denounce what they called "letter killeth, but the spirit giveth life: and that all we should care about is to get to heaven when we die." Of course the effect of such teachers and teaching is to establish the conviction, that "ignorance is bliss, and it is folly to be wise." A virtue is made of ignorance, and sound is preferred to sense. In point of elevation and improvement, wicked as are the white churches, and corrupt as are their white ministers, colored persons would have gained much more by remaining in them, than they have done by coming out from them; and they might ere this, in the northern States, at least have obtained equal rights in every department of the church, had they remained in them and contended for their rights. The example set by a few colored men in New England, with respect to the unjust and odious distinctions formerly practised there in the use of railroad cars, is worthy of imitation in the churches. We have frequently gone into cars intended only for white passengers, and allowed ourself to be beaten and dragged out by the servants and conductors, as a means of distinctly asserting the equal rights of colored persons in the use of those cars. And what has been the result of such conduct on our part! Why this—the whole system of compelling colored persons to ride in separate cars from others has been totally abolished. The railroad companies became ashamed of their proscription, and abandoned it. Colored men are now treated with the utmost kindness and equality on the same roads where five years ago, they were insulted and degraded. We should like to see the same course pursued toward white churches. Colored members should go in and take seats, without regard to their complexion, and allow themselves to be dragged out by the ministers, elders, and deacons. Such a course would very soon settle the question, and in the right way. It would compel the church to develop her character in such a manner as either to secure the rights of her colored members, or to secure her own destruction. We shall practice on this principle, and in every instance give white religious worshippers the trouble of removing us from among them, or the pain of enduring our dark appearance.

Another evil of colored churches is their expensiveness. Colored people are scattered over the country in small numbers, and are generally poor; and to be compelled to build churches for themselves, and hire their own minister, is by no means a trifling hardship. The minister and his family must be supported, though the members have scarcely the means of living, to say nothing of the means of educating and improving the minds of their children. We have known of churches composed of a dozen good colored women and as many men; the former gaining their living over the washtub, and the latter obtaining theirs by daily toil; at the same time supporting a minister and his family at an expense of from two to three hundred dollars a year.

[Source: *North Star*, 10 March 1848.]

## *[American Colorphobia]*

Here Douglass examines the nature of white prejudice against color. He argues that the source of this prejudice is not to be found in ancient history or in nature but in the beginnings of the African slave trade. The abolition of slavery would, then, liberate blacks from chains and whites from racism.

Prejudice against color! Pray tell us *what* color? Black? brown? copper color? yellow? tawny? or olive? Native Americans of all these colors everywhere experience hourly indignities at the hands of persons claiming to be white. Now, is all this for *color's* sake? If so, which of these colors excites such commotion in those sallow-skinned Americans who call themselves white? Is it black? When did they begin to be so horrified at black? Was it before black stocks came into fashion? Black coats? black hats? black walking canes? black reticules? black umbrellas? black-walnut tables? black ebony picture frames and sculptural decorations? black eyes, hair and whiskers? bright black shoes, and glossy black horses? How this American colorphobia would have lashed itself into a foam at the sight of the celebrated *black* goddess Diana, of Ephesus! How it would have gnashed upon the old statue and hacked away at it out of sheer spite at its color! What exemplary havoc it would have made of the most celebrated statues of antiquity. Forsooth they were *black*! Their color would have been their doom. These half-white Americans owe the genius of sculpture a great grudge. She has so often crossed their path in the hated color, it would fare hard with her if she were to fall into their clutches. By the way, it would be well for Marshall and other European sculptors to keep a keen lookout upon all Americans visiting their collections. American colorphobia would be untrue to itself if it did not pitch battle with every black statue and bust that came in its way in going the rounds. A black Apollo, whatever the symmetry of his proportions, the majesty of his attitude, or the divinity of his air, would meet with great good fortune if it escaped mutilation at its hands, or at least defilement from its spittle. If all foreign artists, whose collections are visited by Americans, would fence off a corner of their galleries for a "negro pew," and straightway colonize in thither every specimen of ancient and modern art that is chiselled or cast in *black*, it would be wise precaution. The only tolerable substitute for such colonization would be plenty of *whitewash*, which would avail little as a peace-offering to brother Jonathan unless *freshly* put on: in that case a thick coat of it might sufficiently placate his outraged sense of propriety to rescue the finest models of art from American Lynch-law: but it would not be best to presume too far, for colorphobia has no lucid intervals, *the fit is on all the time*. The anti-black feeling, being "a law of nature," must have vent; and unless it be provided, wherever it goes, with a sort of portable Liberia to scrape the offensive color into it twitches and jerks in convulsions directly. But stop—this anti-black passion is, we are told, "a law of nature," and not to be trifled with! "Prejudice against color" "a law of nature!" Forsooth! What a sinner against *nature* old Homer was! He goes off in ecstasies in his description, of the *black* Ethiopians, praises their beauty, calls them the favorites of the gods, and represents all the ancient divinities as selecting them from all the nations of the world as their intimate companions, the objects of their peculiar complacency.

If Homer had only been indoctrinated into this "law of nature," he would have insulted his deities by representing them as making negroes their chosen associates. What impious trifling with this sacred "law," was perpetrated by the old Greeks, who represented Minerva their favorite goddess of Wisdom as an *African* princess. Herodotus pronounces the Ethiopians the most majestic and beautiful of men. The great father of history was fated to live and die in the dark, as to this great "law of nature!" Why do so many Greek and Latin authors adorn with eulogy the beauty and graces of the black Memnon who served at the siege of Troy, styling him, in their eulogiums, the son of Aurora? Ignoramuses! They knew nothing of this great "law of nature." How little reverence for this sublime "law" had Solon, Pythagoras, Plato, and those other master spirits of ancient Greece, who, in their pilgrimage after knowledge, went to Ethiopia and Egypt, and sat at the feet of black philosophers, to drink in wisdom. Alas for the multitudes who flocked from all parts of the world to the instructions of that negro, Euclid, who three hundred years before Christ, was at the head of the most celebrated mathematical school in the world. However learned in the mathematics, they were plainly numbskulls in the "law of nature!"

How little had Antiochus the Great the fear of this "law of nature" before his eyes, when he welcomed to his court, with the most signal honors, the black African Hannibal; and what an impious perverter of this same law was the great conqueror of Hannibal, since he made the *black* poet Terence one of his most intimate associates and confidants. What heathenish darkness brooded over the early ages of Christianity respecting this "law of nature." What a sin of ignorance! The most celebrated fathers of the church, Origen, Cyprian, Tertullian, Augustine, Clemens, Alexandrinus, and Cyril—why were not these black African bishops colonized into a "negro pew," when attending the ecclesiastical councils of their day? Alas, though the sun of righteousness had risen on primitive Christians, this great "law of nature" had not! This leads us reverently to ask the age of this law. A law of nature, being a part of nature, must be as old as nature: but perhaps human nature was created by piecemeal, and this part was overlooked in the early editions, but supplied in a later revisal. Well, what is the date of the revised edition? We will save our readers the trouble of fumbling for it, by just saying that this "law of nature" was never heard of till long after the commencement of the African slave trade; and that the feeling called "prejudice against color," has never existed in Great Britain, France, Spain, Portugal, the Italian States, Prussia, Austria, Russia, or in any part of the world where colored persons have not been held as slaves. Indeed, in many countries, where multitudes of Africans and their descendants have been long held slaves, no prejudice against color has ever existed. This is the case in Turkey, Brazil, and Persia. In Brazil there are more than two millions of slaves. Yet some of the highest offices of state are filled by black men. Some of the most distinguished officers in the Brazilian army are blacks and mulattoes. Colored lawyers and physicians are found in all parts of the country. Besides this, hundreds of the Roman Catholic clergy are black and colored men, these minister to congregations made up indiscriminately of blacks and whites.

[Source: *North Star*, 5 May 1848.]

## *[Women's Rights]*

The Seneca Falls Convention in 1848 is often described as the beginning of the women's rights movement in the United States. Douglass actively participated in the conference and warmly endorsed its efforts to secure the legal, social, educational, and political rights women had been denied. Women played an important role in the abolition movement, and Douglass was quick to acknowledge their contribution and decry the prejudice that limited their rights.

One of the most interesting events of the past week, was the holding of what is technically styled a Woman's Rights Convention at Seneca Falls. The speaking, addresses, and resolutions of this extraordinary meeting was almost wholly conducted by women; and although they evidently felt themselves in a novel position, it is but simple justice to say that their whole proceedings were characterized by marked ability and dignity. No one present, we think, however much he might be disposed to differ from the views advanced by the leading speakers on that occasion, will fail to give them credit for brilliant talents and excellent dispositions. In this meeting, as in other deliberative assemblies, there were frequent differences of opinion and animated discussion; but in no case was there the slightest absence of good feeling and decorum. Several interesting documents setting forth the rights as well as the grievances of women were read. Among these was a Declaration of Sentiments, to be regarded as the basis of a grand movement for attaining the civil, social, political, and religious rights of women. We should not do justice to our own convictions, or to the excellent persons connected with this infant movement, if we did not in this connection offer a few remarks on the general subject which the Convention met to consider and the objects they seek to attain.

In doing so, we are not insensible that the bare mention of this truly important subject in any other than terms of contemptuous ridicule and scornful disfavor, is likely to excite against us the fury of bigotry and the folly of prejudice. A discussion of the rights of animals would be regarded with far more complacency by many of what are called the *wise* and the *good* of our land, than would a discussion of the rights of women. It is, in their estimation, to be guilty of evil thoughts, to think that woman is entitled to equal rights with man. Many who have at last made the discovery that the negroes have some rights as well as other members of the human family, have yet to be convinced that women are entitled to any. Eight years ago a number of persons of this description actually abandoned the anti-slavery cause, lest by giving their influence in that direction they might possibly be giving countenance to the dangerous heresy that woman, in respect to rights, stands on an equal footing with man. In the judgment of such persons the American slave system, with all its concomitant horrors, is less to be deplored than this *wicked* idea. It is perhaps needless to say, that we cherish little sympathy for such sentiments or respect for such prejudices. Standing as we do upon the watch-tower of human freedom, we cannot be deterred from an expression of our approbation of any movement, however humble, to improve and elevate the character of any members of the human family. While it is impossible for us to go into this subject at length, and dispose of the various objections which are often urged against such a doctrine as that of female equality, we are free to say that in respect to political rights, we hold woman to be justly entitled to all we claim for man. We go farther, and express our conviction that all political rights which it is expedient for man to exercise, it is equally so for woman. All that distinguishes man as an intelligent and accountable being, is equally true of woman, and if that government only is just which governs by the free consent of the governed, there can be no reason in the world for denying to woman the exercise of the elective franchise, or a hand in making and administering the laws of the land. Our doctrine is that "Right is of no sex." We therefore bid the women engaged in this movement our humble God-speed.

[Source: *North Star,* 28 July 1848.]

## *[Letter to His Former Master]*

Written on September 3, 1848, this letter marked the tenth anniversary of Douglass' escape from slavery. Because he describes what has happened to him since he ran away, the letter serves as a useful summary of his life as well as a vindication of his escape.

Sir—

The long and intimate, though by no means friendly relation which unhappily subsisted between you and myself, leads me to hope that you will easily account for the great liberty which I now take in addressing you in this open and public manner. The same fact may possibly remove any disagreeable surprise which you may experience on again finding your name coupled with mine, in any other way than in an advertisement, accurately describing my person, and offering a large sum for my arrest. In thus dragging you again before the public, I am aware that I shall subject myself to no inconsiderable amount of censure. I shall probably be charged with an unwarrantable, if not a wanton and reckless disregard of the rights and proprieties of private life. There are those North as well as South who entertain a much higher respect for rights which are merely conventional, than they do for rights which are personal and essential. Not a few there are in our country, who, while they have no scruples against robbing the laborer of the hard earned results of his patient industry, will be shocked by the extremely indelicate manner of bringing your name before the public. Believing this to be the case, and wishing to meet every reasonable or plausible objection to my conduct, I will frankly state the ground upon which I justify myself in this instance, as well as on former occasions when I have thought proper to mention your name in public. All will agree that a man guilty of theft, robbery, or murder, has forfeited the right to concealment and private life; that the community have a right to subject such persons to the most complete exposure. However much they may desire retirement, and aim to conceal themselves and their movements from the popular gaze, the public have a right to ferret them out, and bring their conduct before the proper tribunals of the country for investigation. Sir, you will undoubtedly make the proper application of these generally admitted principles, and will easily see the light in which you are regarded by me. I will not therefore manifest ill temper, by calling you hard names. I know you to be a man of some intelligence, and can readily determine the precise estimate which I entertain of your character. I may therefore indulge in language which may seem to others indirect and ambiguous, and yet be quite well understood by yourself.

I have selected this day on which to address you, because it is the anniversary of my emancipation; and knowing of no better way, I am led to this as the best mode of celebrating that truly important event. Just ten years ago this beautiful September morning, yon bright sun beheld me a slave—a poor, degraded chattel—trembling at the sound of your voice, lamenting that I was a man, and wishing myself a brute. The hopes which I had treasured up for weeks of a safe and successful escape from your grasp, were powerfully confronted at this last hour by dark clouds of doubt and fear, making my person shake and my bosom to heave with the heavy contest between hope and fear. I have no words to describe to you the deep agony of soul which I experienced on that never to be forgotten morning—(for I left by daylight). I was making a leap in the dark. The probabilities, so far as I could by reason determine them, were stoutly against the undertaking. The preliminaries and precautions I had adopted previously, all worked badly. I was like one going to war without weapons—ten chances of defeat to one of victory. One in whom I had confided, and one who had promised me assistance, appalled by fear at the trial hour, deserted me, thus leaving the responsibility of success or failure solely with myself. You, sir, can never know my feelings. As I look back to them, I can scarcely realize that I have passed through a scene so trying. Trying however as they were, and gloomy as was the prospect, thanks be to the Most High, who is ever the God of the oppressed, at the moment which was to determine my whole earthly career. His grace was sufficient, my mind was made up. I embraced the golden opportunity, took the morning tide at the flood, and a free man, young, active and strong, is the result.

I have often thought I should like to explain to you the grounds upon which I have justified myself in running away from you. I am almost ashamed to do so now, for by this time you may have discovered them yourself. I will, however, glance at them. When yet but a child about six years old, I imbibed the determination to run away. The very first mental effort that I now remember on my part, was an attempt to solve the mystery, Why am I a slave? and with this question my youthful mind was troubled for many days, pressing upon me more heavily at times than others. When I saw the slave-driver whip a slave woman, cut the blood out of her neck, and heard her piteous cries, I went away into the corner of the fence, wept and pondered over the mystery. I had, through some medium, I know not what, got some idea of God, the Creator of all mankind, the black and the white, and that he had made the blacks to serve the whites as slaves. How he could do this and be *good,* I could not tell. I was not satisfied with this theory, which made God responsible for slavery, for it pained me greatly, and I have wept over it long and often. At one time, your first wife, Mrs. Lucretia, heard me singing and saw me shedding tears, and asked of me the matter, but I was afraid to tell her. I was puzzled with this question, till one night, while sitting in the kitchen, I heard some of the old slaves talking of their parents having been stolen from Africa by white men, and were sold here as slaves. The whole mystery was solved at once. Very soon after this my aunt Jinny and uncle Noah ran away, and the great noise made about it by your father-in-law, made me for the first time acquainted with the fact, that there were free States as well as slave States. From that time, I resolved that I would some day run away. The morality of the act, I dispose as follows: I am myself; you are yourself; we are two distinct persons, equal persons. What you are, I am. You are a man, and so am I. God created both, and made us separate beings. I am not by nature bound to you, or you to me. Nature does not make your existence depend upon me, or mine to depend upon yours. I cannot walk upon your legs, or you upon mine. I cannot breathe for you, or you for me; I must breathe for myself, and you for yourself. We are distinct persons, and are each equally provided with faculties necessary to our individual existence. In leaving you, I took nothing but what belonged to me, and in no way lessened your means for obtaining an *honest* living. Your faculties remained yours, and mine became useful to their rightful owner. I therefore see no wrong in any part of the transaction. It is true, I went off secretly, but that was more your fault than mine. Had I let you into the secret, you would have defeated the enterprise entirely; but for this, I should have been really glad to have made you acquainted with my intentions to leave.

You may perhaps want to know how I like my present condition. I am free to say, I greatly prefer it to that which I occupied in Maryland. I am, however, by no means prejudiced against the State as such. Its geography, climate, fertility and products, are such as to make it a very desirable abode for any man; and but for the existence of slavery there, it is not impossible that I might again take up my abode in that State. It is not that I love Maryland less, but freedom more. You will be surprised to learn that people at the North labor under the strange delusion that if the slaves were emancipated at the South, they would flock to the North. So far from this being the case, in that event, you would see many old and familiar faces back again to the South. The fact is, there are few here who would not return to the South in the event of emancipation. We want to live in the land of our birth, and to lay our bones by the side of our fathers'; and nothing short of an intense love of personal freedom keeps us from the South. For the sake of this, most of us would live on a crust of bread and a cup of cold water.

Since I left you, I have had a rich experience. I have occupied stations which I never dreamed of when a slave. Three out of the ten years since I left you, I spent as a common laborer on the wharves of New Bedford, Massachusetts. It was there I earned my first free dollar. It was mine. I could spend it as I pleased. I could buy hams or herring with it, without asking any odds of any body. That was a precious dollar to me. You remember when I used to make seven or eight, or even nine dollars a week in Baltimore, you would take every cent of it from me every Saturday night, saying that I belonged to you, and my earnings also. I never liked this conduct on your part—to say the best, I thought it a little mean. I would not have served you so. But let that pass. I was a little awkward about counting money in New England fashion when I first landed in New Bedford. I like to have betrayed myself several times. I caught myself saying phip, for fourpence; and at one time a man actually charged me with being a runaway, whereupon I was silly enough to become one by running away from him, for I was greatly afraid he might adopt measures to get me again into slavery, a condition I then dreaded more than death.

I soon, however, learned to count money, as well as to make it, and got on swimmingly. I married soon after leaving you: in fact, I was engaged to be married before I left you; and instead of finding my companion a burden, she was truly a helpmeet. She went to live at service, and I to work on the wharf, and though we toiled hard the first winter, we never lived more happily. After remaining in New Bedford for three years, I met with Wm. Lloyd Garrison, a person of whom you have *possibly* heard, as he is pretty generally known among slaveholders. He put it into my head that I might make myself serviceable to the cause of the slave by devoting a portion of my time to telling my own sorrows, and those of other slaves which had come under my observation. This was the commencement of a higher state of existence than any to which I had ever aspired. I was thrown into society the most pure, enlightened and benevolent that the country affords. Among these I have never forgotten you, but have invariably made you the topic of conversation—thus giving you all the notoriety I could do. I need not tell you that the opinion formed of you in these circles, is far from being favorable. They have little respect for your honesty, and less for your religion.

But I was going on to relate to you something of my

interesting experience. I had not long enjoyed the excellent society to which I have referred, before the light of its excellence exerted a beneficial influence on my mind and heart. Much of my early dislike of white persons was removed, and their manners, habits and customs, so entirely unlike what I had been used to in the kitchen-quarters on the plantations of the South, fairly charmed me, and gave me a strong disrelish for the coarse and degrading customs of my former condition. I therefore made an effort so to improve my mind and deportment, as to be somewhat fitted to the station to which I seemed almost providentially called. The transition from degradation to respectability was indeed great, and to get from one to the other without carrying some marks of one's former condition, is truly a difficult matter. I would not have you think that I am now entirely clear of all plantation peculiarities, but my friends here, while they entertain the strongest dislike to them, regard me with that charity to which my past life somewhat entitles me, so that my condition in this respect is exceedingly pleasant. So far as my domestic affairs are concerned, I can boast of as comfortable a dwelling as your own. I have an industrious and neat companion, and four dear children—the oldest a girl of nine years, and three fine boys, the oldest eight, the next six, and the youngest four years old. The three oldest are now going regularly to school—two can read and write, and the other can spell with tolerable correctness words of two syllables: Dear fellows! they are all in comfortable beds, and are sound asleep, perfectly secure under my own roof. There are no slaveholders here to rend my heart by snatching them from my arms, or blast a mother's dearest hopes by tearing them from her bosom. These dear children are ours—not to work up into rice, sugar and tobacco, but to watch over, regard, and protect, and to rear them up in the nurture and admonition of the gospel—to train them up in the paths of wisdom and virtue, and, as far as we can to make them useful to the world and to themselves. Oh! sir, a slaveholder never appears to me so completely an agent of hell, as when I think of and look upon my dear children. It is then that my feelings rise above my control. I meant to have said more with respect to my own prosperity and happiness, but thoughts and feelings which this recital has quickened unfits me to proceed further in that direction. The grim horrors of slavery rise in all their ghastly terror before me, the wails of millions pierce my heart, and chill my blood. I remember the chain, the gag, the bloody whip, the death-like gloom overshadowing the broken spirit of the fettered bondman, the appalling liability of his being torn away from wife and children, and sold like a beast in the market. Say not that that this is a picture of fancy. You well know that I wear stripes on my back inflicted by your direction; and that you, while we were brothers in the same church, caused this right hand, with which I am now penning this letter, to be closely tied to my left, and my person dragged at the pistol's mouth, fifteen miles, from the Bay side to Easton to be sold like a beast in the market, for the alleged crime of intending to escape from your possession. All this and more you remember, and know to be perfectly true, not only of yourself, but of nearly all of the slaveholders around you.

At this moment, you are probably the guilty holder of at least three of my own dear sisters, and my only brother in bondage. These you regard as your property. They are recorded on your ledger, or perhaps have been sold to human flesh mongers, with a view to filling your own ever-hungry purse. Sir, I desire to know how and where these dear sisters are. Have you sold them? or are they still in your possession? What has become of them? are they living or dead? And my dear old grandmother, whom you turned out like an old horse, to die in the woods—is she still alive? Write and let me know all about them. If my grandmother be still alive, she is of no service to you, for by this time she must be nearly eighty years old—too old to be cared for by one to whom she has ceased to be of service, send her to me at Rochester, or bring her to Philadelphia, and it shall be the crowning happiness of my life to take care of her in her old age. Oh! she was to me a mother, and a father, so far as hard toil for my comfort could make her such. Send me my grandmother! that I may watch over and take care of her in her old age. And my sisters, let me know all about them. I would write to them, and learn all I want to know of them, without disturbing you in any way, but that, through your unrighteous conduct, they have been entirely deprived of the power to read and write. You have kept them in utter ignorance, and have therefore robbed them of the sweet enjoyments of writing or receiving letters from absent friends and relatives. Your wickedness and cruelty committed in this respect on your fellow-creatures, are greater than all the stripes you have laid upon my back, or theirs. It is an outrage upon the soul—a war upon the immortal spirit, and one for which you must give account at the bar of our common Father and Creator.

The responsibility which you have assumed in this regard is truly awful—and how you could stagger under it these many years is marvellous. Your mind must have become darkened, your heart hardened, your conscience seared and petrified, or you would have long since thrown off the accursed load and sought relief at the hands of a sin-forgiving God. How, let me ask, would you look upon me, were I some dark night in company with a band of hardened villains, to enter the precincts of your elegant dwelling and seize the person of your own lovely daughter Amanda, and carry her off from your family, friends and all the loved ones of her youth—make her my slave—compel her to work, and I take her wages—place her name on my ledger as property—disregard her personal rights—fetter the powers of her immortal soul by denying her the right and privilege of learning to read and write—feed her coarsely—clothe her scantily, and whip her on the naked back occasionally; more and still more horrible, leave her unprotected—a degraded victim to the brutal lust of fiendish overseers, who would pollute, blight, and blast her fair soul—rob her of all dignity—destroy her virtue, and annihilate all in her person the graces that adorn the character of virtuous womanhood? I ask how would you regard me, if such were my conduct? Oh! the vocabulary of the damned would not afford a word sufficiently infernal, to express your idea of my God-provoking wickedness. Yet sir, your treatment of my beloved sisters is in all essential points, precisely like the case I have now supposed. Damning as would be such a deed on my part, it would be no more so than that which you have committed against me and my sisters.

I will now bring this letter to a close, you shall hear from me again unless you let me hear from you. I intend to make use of you as a weapon with which to assail the system of slavery—as a means of concentrating public attention on the system, and deepening their horror of trafficking in the souls and bodies of men. I shall make use of you as a means of exposing the character of the American church and clergy—and as a means of bringing this guilty nation with yourself to repentance. In doing this I entertain no malice towards you personally. There is no roof under which you would be more safe than mine, and there is nothing in my house which you might need for your comfort, which I would not readily grant. Indeed, I should esteem it a privilege, to set you an example as to how mankind ought to treat each other.

I am your fellow man, but not your slave,

Frederick Douglass

[Source: *Liberator*, 22 September 1848.]

## [The Evils of War]

Douglass' views on violence and war were influenced by Garrisonian abolitionists, who argued that moral suasion and nonresistance were the only true means to effect reform. Though never a pacifist (particularly by the 1850s), Douglass had a keen sense of the costs of war and he believed that wars were rarely waged for righteous causes.

Did you ever think of the evils of War? Did you ever realize that it was one of the greatest curses of mankind? Did you ever see that the practice of war filled the world with Blood, with Slavery, with Barbarism and every species of Misery; Yet this is the case; and, reader, are you not a military man, or guilty in some way of promoting War? If so, complain not of want, suffering, ignorance, or degradation. Oppressed Laboring man or Factory girl, don't murmur at your hard lot; if your politics, religion or social influence upholds war, the reproach falls upon your own head. You foolishly empty your own pockets and cause your own sufferings. Benevolent man, Philanthropist—do you favor armies, navies, and military governments? Wonder not, then at the depravity of man and the slow progress of truth and righteousness. Your self-contradiction and inconsistency in sustaining the custom of war, swells the current of wickedness more than your good efforts can that of righteousness.

*What has War done?*—Evil, evil! It has done nothing but evil! It has destroyed human life, property, virtue and happiness. Nothing else has it aimed to do. Drunkenness, profanity and licentiousness have been its legitimate products. Widows, orphans, paupers, beggars it has multiplied. Dr. Dick estimates that *fourteen thousand millions* of human beings have been slaughtered by war—inhabitants enough to people 18 worlds like the Earth! Think of this. What greater curse could wickedness invent? Plague, Pestilence and Famine have followed in its track; but these of themselves have not begun to equal war in their number of victims. Had Hyenas, Tigers, Panthers and Serpents been the world's only inhabitants, they would not have equaled Man in the destruction of life. What a field of human bones! What a sea of human blood!

*What has War cost?*—The mere money cost of war has been enough to pauperize the world. According to reliable estimate the present unpaid War Debt of Europe and the United States, incurred within the last 160 years, is about *Seven Thousand Million Dollars!* The annual interest of this debt, including the expenses of the Army and Navy, is nearly *Four Hundred Million Dollars.* The specie circulation of the world does not equal this amount, and, according to Humboldt, the mines of South America and Mexico have not yielded this sum since the discovery of the New World by Columbus! 50 per cent of the annual expenditures of European governments goes for military purposes. No wonder the people are crushed beneath such a load, on top of the expenses of royalty, nobility and aristocracy. No wonder the people are taxed for all they eat, drink and wear, for sunshine, air and water—taxed for being born, taxed for breathing, taxed for dying.

In the United States, the Executive, Legislative and Judicial departments of government are not poorly paid at all. But for every 21 cents they receive $1 is paid for purposes of war. 80 per cent, of the government expenses are for war! Within the borders of Massachusetts scarcely a cent has been expended for schools, colleges and charitable asylums where dollars have been lavished upon war-ships, the Navy-Yard and the Arsenal. In addition to all this, the annual cost, in time and money of training the militia of the United States is calculated to be *Fifty Million Dollars.* Why shouldn't there be poverty and hard times in this country?

[Source: *North Star*, 22 December 1848.]

## *[On Being Seen Walking with Two White Women]*

White women played a significant part in antislavery activities. It was, therefore, inevitable that Douglass would have contact with them. This satirical (but serious) account of Douglass' being seen with two white women on the streets of New York in 1849 suggests how much anxiety such encounters caused whites. Douglass met with a similar response in 1884 when, after the death of his first wife, he married a white woman.

The fifth of May will long be remembered as the most trying day ever experienced by the unfortunate victims of colorphobia in the city of New York. The disease was never more malignant or general than on that day. The streets were literally crowded with persons of all classes afflicted with this terrible malady. Whole omnibus loads were attacked at the same moment, and their hideous and unearthly howls were truly distressing, excruciating. It will be impossible to describe, or give the reader any correct idea either of the extent of the disease or the agony it seemed to occasion. Like most epidemics, its chief havoc was among the baser sort. The suffering here was fearful and intense. If the genteel suffered from the plague, they managed to suppress and control their feelings better than what are called the "lower orders." But, even here, there could be no successful concealment. The strange plague defied all concealment, and would show itself in spite of veils, white pocket handkerchiefs, parasols, hats, bonnets and umbrellas. In the refined the presence of the plague might be seen by a distortion of the countenance, a red and furious look about the cheek, a singular turn up of the nose, and a *"lower me!"* expression of the eyes.

Among the low and vulgar the symptoms were different;—the hand clinched, head shaking, teeth grating, hysteric yells and horrid imprecation, marked the presence of the disease and the agony of the miserable creatures who were its unfortunate victims. Persons who, at a distance of thirty or forty yards, appeared the very pictures of health, were found, on a nearer approach, most horribly cut and marred.

But the effect upon the outward man was not half so strange and dreadful as that upon the mind. Here all was utter ruin. Gough's description of "delirium tremens" would not be much out of place in describing one haunted and afflicted with colorphobia. Monsters, goblins, demons, snakes, lizards and scorpions—all that was foul, strange and loathsome—seized upon their bewildered imaginations. Pointing with outstretched arm towards us, its victims would exclaim, as if startled by some terrible sight—"Look! look!" "Where?" "Ah, what?" "Why?" "Why, don't you see?" "See what?" "Why, that BLACK! black! *black!*" Then, with eyes turned up in horror, they would exclaim in the most unearthly manner, and start off in a furious gallop—running all around us, and gazing at us, as if they would read our very hearts. The whole scene was deeply afflicting and terrible.

But to the cause of this wide-spread plague, or rather the manifestation of it. We think it can all be made plain to the dullest comprehension. There had arrived in New York, a few days previous, two *English* Ladies, from London—friends of Frederick Douglass—and had taken apartments at the Franklin House, Broadway; and were not only called upon at that Hotel by Mr. Douglass, but really allowed themselves to take his arm, and to walk many times up and down Broadway, in broad-day light, when that great thoroughfare was crowded with pure American ladies and gentlemen. Such an open, glaring outrage upon *pure American* tastes had never before been perpetrated. Two ladies, elegantly attired, educated, and of the most approved manners, faultless in appearance and position, actually walking, and leaning upon the arm of a person, with a skin not colored like their own! Oh! monstrous! Was it not enough to cause the very stones to leap up with indignation from the pavement! and to "stir them up to mutiny and rage"? More and worse still, these ladies appeared wholly indifferent to, and oblivious of, all the indignation and fury going on about them; but walked, talked and acted as though nothing unusual was passing. In a word, they seemed to forget that they were in the greatest Commercial Emporium of this, the mightest Nation in the world, and to act as though they had been in the paltry city of London!! instead of New York. What could they have been thinking about? How strange that they had not made themselves acquainted with the institutions and customs of the great Nation, upon whose sacred soil they were *allowed* to land? How singular that their friends had not warned them against such a monstrous outrage upon the established customs of this, the *"freest"* country in the world? They certainly must have been deceived. It is impossible "that nature so could err." "Charms, conjuration—mighty magic," must have bewildered and misled them. They would have been kindly received and hospitably entertained by some of the most respectable and refined families in the city of New York; but, with a strange hallucination, they preferred to identify themselves with the most despised and injured portion of all the people of America—and thus to make themselves of no reputation, and cut themselves off from all sympathy and attention of the highly favored and accomplished sons and daughters of America. Before quitting this subject, we wish to call attention to certain singular inconsistencies connected with the development of the feeling, called (erroneously) prejudice against color. The first is this. The poor creatures who seemed most disturbed by the fact that these ladies walked through the streets of New York in company with a colored man, felt in no wise shocked at seeing ladies seated in their gilded carriages, with colored persons seated near them, driving their horses and otherwise assisting such ladies. All this was perfectly right. They were in the capacity of servants. Hence New York toadyism is rather pleased than disgusted. It is not with colored servants that New York loafers are displeased; but with colored *gentlemen*. It is with the colored man as a gentleman that they feel the most intense displeasure. They cannot bear it, and they must pour out their pent-up wrath, whenever an opportunity is afforded for doing so.

In this same Franklin Hotel, in which we could not be allowed to dine on account of our color, we saw a large number of colored waiters in the nearest proximity to white gentlemen and ladies, without offence.

We, however, tire of this subject. This prejudice is so unjust, unnatural and irrational, that ridicule and indignation seem to be the only weapons with which to assail it.

Our friends informed us that when they landed, they were assured that they had reached the shores of a free country, and were congratulated upon that fact. But they had scarcely reached the hotel, when they were informed that a friend of theirs, who was not deemed unfit to be associated with in London, and who would have been kindly received at the best hotels in that city, and in Paris, would not be allowed to take dinner with them at the Franklin Hotel, in the city of New York. In this free country one is not permitted to choose and enjoy the society of his friends, without being subjected to innumerable insults and annoyances.

We shall not, however, despair on this point. A marked improvement has already taken place in the manner of treating colored travelers, and the change is going on still. Nothing, however, facilitates this more than such examples of fidelity to principle, and indifference to a corrupt and brutal public opinion, as is presented in the conduct of these two English ladies, and others. This prejudice must be removed; and the way for abolitionists and colored persons to remove it, is to act as though it did not exist, and to associate with their fellow creatures irrespective of all complexional differences. We have marked out this path for ourselves, and we mean to pursue it at all hazards.

[Source: *North Star*, 25 May 1849.]

## *[The Heroic Slave]*

This melodramatic novella, though weak in plot and characterization, is Douglass' imaginative account of the life of the slave Madison Washington, who led a mutiny aboard the slave ship *Creole* in 1841. For a historical perspective, see Howard Jones, "The Peculiar Institution and National Honor: The Case of the *Creole* Slave Revolt," *Civil War History*, 21 (March 1975), 28-50.

### PART I

Oh! child of grief, why weepest thou?
  Why droops thy sad and mournful brow?
Why is thy look so like despair?
  What deep, sad sorrow lingers there?

The State of Virginia is famous in American annals for the multitudinous array of her statesmen and heroes. She has been dignified by some the mother of statesmen. History has not been sparing in recording their names, or in blazoning their deeds. Her high position in this respect, has given her an enviable distinction among her sister States. With Virginia for his birth-place, even a man of ordinary parts, on account of the general partiality for her sons, easily rises to eminent stations. Men, not great enough to attract special attention in their native States, have, like a certain distinguished citizen in the State of New York, sighed and repined that they were not born in Virginia. Yet not all the great ones of the Old Dominion have, by the fact of their birth-place, escaped undeserved obscurity. By some strange neglect, *one* of the truest, manliest, and bravest of her children,—one who, in after years, will, I think, command the pen of genius to set his merits forth, holds now no higher place in the records of that grand old Commonwealth than is held by a horse or an ox. Let those account for it who can, but there stands the fact, that a man who loved liberty as well as did Patrick Henry,—who deserved it as much as Thomas Jefferson,—and who fought for it with a valor as high, an arm as strong, and against odds as great, as he who led all the armies of the American colonies through the great war for freedom and independence, lives now only in the chattel records of his native State.

Glimpses of this great character are all that can now be presented. He is brought to view only by a few transient incidents, and these afford but partial satisfaction. Like a guiding star on a stormy night, he is seen through the parted clouds and the howling tempests; or, like the gray peak of a menacing rock on a perilous coast, he is seen by the quivering flash of angry lightning, and he again disappears covered with mystery.

Curiously, earnestly, anxiously we peer into the dark, and wish even for the blinding flash, or the light of northern skies to reveal him. But alas! he is still enveloped in darkness, and we return from the pursuit like a wearied and disheartened mother, (after a tedious and unsuccessful search for a lost child,) who returns weighed down with disappointment and sorrow. Speaking of marks, traces, possibles, and probabilities, we come before our readers.

In the spring of 1835, on a Sabbath morning, within hearing of the solemn peals of the church bells at a distant village, a Northern traveller through the State of Virginia drew up his horse to drink at a sparkling brook, near the edge of a dark pine forest. While his weary and thirsty steed drew in the grateful water, the rider caught the sound of a human voice, apparently engaged in earnest conversation.

Following the direction of the sound, he descried, among the tall pines, the man whose voice had arrested his attention. "To whom can he be speaking?" thought the traveller. "He seems to be alone." The circumstance interested him much, and he became intensely curious to know what thoughts and feelings, or, it might be, high aspirations, guided those rich and mellow accents. Tieing his horse at a short distance from the brook, he stealthily drew near the solitary speaker; and, concealing himself by the side of a huge fallen tree, he distinctly heard the following soliloquy:—

"What, then, is life to me? it is aimless and worthless, and worse than worthless. Those birds, perched on yon swinging boughs, in friendly conclave, sounding forth their merry notes in seeming worship of the rising sun, though liable to the sportsman's fowling-piece, are still my superiors. They *live free,* though they may die slaves. They fly where they list by day, and retire in freedom at night. But what is freedom to me, or I to it? I am a *slave,*—born a slave, an abject slave,—even before I made part of this breathing world, the scourge was platted for my back; the fetters were forged for my limbs. How mean a thing am I. That accursed and crawling snake, that miserable reptile, that has just glided into its slimy home, is freer and better off than I. He escaped my blow, and is safe. But here am I, a man,—yes, *a man!*—with thoughts and wishes, with powers and faculties as far as angel's flight above that hated reptile,—yet he is my superior, and scorns to own me as his master, or to stop to take my blows. When he saw my uplifted arm, he darted beyond my reach, and turned to give me battle. I dare not do as much as that. I neither run nor fight, but do meanly stand, answering each heavy blow of a cruel master with doleful wails and piteous cries. I am galled with irons; but even these are more tolerable than the consciousness, the *galling* consciousness of cowardice and indecision. Can it be that I *dare* not run away? *Perish the thought,* I *dare* do any thing which may be done by another. When that young man struggled with the waves *for life*, and others stood back appalled in helpless horror, did I not plunge in, forgetful of life, to save his? The raging bull from whom all others fled, pale with fright, did I not keep at bay with a single pitchfork? Could a coward do that? *No,—no,*—I wrong myself,—I am no coward. *Liberty* I will have, or die in the attempt to gain it. This working that others may live in idleness! This cringing submission to insolence and curses! This living under the constant dread and apprehension of being sold and transferred, like a mere brute, is *too* much for me. I will stand it no longer. What others have done, I will do. These trusty legs, or these sinewy arms shall place me among the free. Tom escaped; so can I. The North Star will not be less kind to me than to him. I will follow it. I will at least make the trial. I have nothing to lose. If I am caught, I shall only be a slave. If I am shot, I shall only lose a life which is a burden and a curse. If I get clear, (as something tells me I shall,) liberty, the inalienable birth-right of every man, precious and priceless, will be mine. My resolution is fixed. *I shall be free.*"

At these words the traveller raised his head cautiously and noiselessly, and caught, from his hiding-place, a full view of the unsuspecting speaker. Madison (for that was the name of our hero) was standing erect, a smile of satisfaction rippled upon his expressive countenance, like that which plays upon the face of one who has but just solved a difficult problem, or vanquished a malignant foe; for at that moment he was free, at least in spirit. The future gleamed brightly before him, and his fetters lay broken at his feet. His air was triumphant.

Madison was of manly form. Tall, symmetrical, round, and strong. In his movements he seemed to combine, with the strength of the lion, a lion's elasticity. His torn sleeves disclosed arms like polished iron. His face was "black, but comely." His eye, lit with emotion, kept guard under a brow as dark and as glossy as the raven's wing. His whole appearance betokened Herculean strength; yet there was nothing savage or forbidding in his aspect. A child might play in his arms, or dance on his shoulders. A giant's strength, but not a giant's heart was in him. His broad mouth and nose spoke only of good nature and kindness. But his voice, that unfailing index of the soul, though full and melodious, had that in it which could terrify as well as charm. He was just the man you would choose when hardships were to be endured, or danger to be encountered,—intelligent and brave. He had the head to conceive, and the hand to execute. In a word, he was one to be sought as a friend, but to be dreaded as an enemy.

As our traveller gazed upon him, he almost trembled at the thought of his dangerous intrusion. Still he could not quit the place. He had long desired to sound the mysterious depths of the thoughts and feelings of a slave. He was not, therefore, disposed to allow so providential an opportunity to pass unimproved. He resolved to hear more; so he listened again for those mellow and mournful accents which, he says, made such an impression upon him as can never be erased. He did not have to wait long. There came another gush from the same full fountain; now bitter, and now sweet. Scathing denunciations of the cruelty and injustice of slavery; heart-touching narrations of his own personal suffering, intermingled with prayers to the God of the oppressed for help and deliverance, were followed by presentations of the dangers and difficulties of escape, and formed the burden of his eloquent utterances; but his high resolution clung to him,—for he ended each speech by an emphatic declaration of his purpose to be free. It seemed that the very repetition of this, imparted a glow to his countenance. The hope of freedom seemed to sweeten, for a season, the bitter cup of slavery, and to make it, for a time, tolerable; for when in the very whirlwind of anguish,—when his heart's cord seemed screwed up to snapping tension, hope sprung up and soothed his troubled spirit. Fitfully he would exclaim, "How can I leave her? Poor thing! what can she do when I am gone? Oh! oh! 't is impossible that I can leave poor Susan!"

A brief pause intervened. Our traveller raised his head, and saw again the sorrow-smitten slave. His eye was fixed upon the ground. The strong man staggered under a heavy load. Recovering himself, he argued thus aloud: "All is uncertain here. To-morrow's sun may not rise before I am sold, and separated from her I love. What, then, could I do for her? I should be in more hopeless slavery, and she no nearer to liberty,—whereas if I were free,—my arms my own,—I might devise the means to rescue her."

This said, Madison cast around a searching glance, as if the thought of being overheard had flashed across his mind. He said no more, but, with measured steps, walked away, and was lost to the eye of our traveller amidst the wildering woods.

Long after Madison had left the ground, Mr. Listwell (our traveller) remained in motionless silence, meditating on the extraordinary revelations to which he had listened. He seemed fastened to the spot, and stood half hoping, half fearing the return of the sable preacher to his solitary temple. The speech of Madison rung through the chambers of his soul, and vibrated through his entire frame. "Here is indeed a man," thought he, "of rare endowments,—a child of God,—guilty of no crime but the color of his skin,—hiding away from the face of humanity, and pouring out his thoughts and feelings, his hopes and resolutions to the lonely woods; to him those distant church bells have no grateful music. He shuns the church, the altar, and the great congregation of christian worshippers, and wanders away to the gloomy forest, to utter in the vacant air complaints and griefs, which the religion of his times and his country can neither console nor relieve. Goaded almost to madness by the sense of the injustice done him, he resorts hither to give vent to his pent up feelings, and to debate with himself the feasibility of plans, plans of his own invention, for his own deliverance. From this hour I am an abolitionist. I have seen enough and heard enough, and I shall go to my home in Ohio resolved to atone for my past indifference to this ill-starred race, by making such exertions as I shall be able to do, for the speedy emancipation of every slave in the land.

## PART II

> "The gaudy, blabbling and remorseful day
> Is crept into the bosom of the sea;
> And now loud-howling wolves arouse the jades
> That drag the tragic melancholy night;
> Who with their drowsy, slow, and flagging wings
> Clip dead men's graves, and from their misty jaws
> Breathe foul contagions, darkness in the air."
> Shakspeare

Five years after the foregoing singular occurrence, in the winter of 1840, Mr. and Mrs. Listwell sat together by the fireside of their own happy home, in the State of Ohio. The children were all gone to bed. A single lamp burnt brightly on the centre-table. All was still and comfortable within; but the night was cold and dark; a heavy wind sighed and moaned sorrowfully around the house and barn, occasionally bringing against the clattering windows a stray leaf from the large oak trees that embowered their dwelling. It was a night for strange noises and for strange fancies. A whole wilderness of thought might pass through one's mind during such an evening. The smouldering embers, partaking of the spirit of the restless night, became fruitful of varied and fantastic pictures, and revived many bygone scenes and old impressions. The happy pair seemed to sit in silent fascination, gazing on the fire. Suddenly this *reverie* was interrupted by a heavy growl. Ordinarily such an occurrence would have scarcely provoked a single word, or excited the least apprehension. But there are certain seasons when the slightest sound sends a jar through all the subtle chambers of the mind; and such a season was this. The happy pair started up, as if some sudden danger had come upon them. The growl was from their trusty watch-dog.

"What can it mean? certainly no one can be out on such a night as this," said Mrs. Listwell.

"The wind has deceived the dog, my dear; he has mistaken the noise of falling branches, brought down by the wind, for that of the footsteps of persons coming to the house. I have several times to-night thought that I heard the sound of footsteps. I am sure, however, that it was but the wind. Friends would not be likely to come out at such an hour, or such a night; and thieves are too lazy and self-indulgent to expose themselves to this biting frost; but should there be any one about, our brave old Monte, who is on the lookout, will not be slow in sounding the alarm."

Saying this they quietly left the window, whither they had gone to learn the cause of the menacing growl, and re-seated themselves by the fire, as if reluctant to leave the slowly expiring embers, although the hour was late.

A few minutes only intervened after resuming their seats, when again their sober meditations were disturbed. Their faithful dog now growled and barked furiously, as if assailed by an advancing foe. Simultaneously the good couple arose, and stood in mute expectation. The contest without seemed fierce and violent. It was, however, soon over,—the barking ceased, for, with true canine instinct, Monte quickly discovered that a friend, not an enemy of the family, was coming to the house, and instead of rushing to repel the supposed intruder, he was now at the door, whimpering and dancing for the admission of himself and his newly made friend.

Mr. Listwell knew by this movement that all was well; he advanced and opened the door, and saw by the light that streamed out into the darkness, a tall man advancing slowly towards the house, with a stick in one hand, and a small bundle in the other. "It is a traveller," thought he, "who has missed his way, and is coming to inquire the road. I am glad we did not go to bed earlier,—I have felt all the evening as if somebody would be here to-night."

The man had now halted a short distance from the door, and looked prepared alike for flight or battle. "Come in, sir, don't be alarmed, you have probably lost your way."

Slightly hesitating, the traveller walked in; not, however, without regarding his host with a scrutinizing glance. "No, sir," said he "I have come to ask you a greater favor."

Instantly Mr. Listwell exclaimed, (as the recollection of the Virginia forest scene flashed upon him,) "Oh, sir, I know not your name, but I have seen your face, and heard your voice before. I am glad to see you. *I know all.* You are flying for your liberty,—be seated,—be seated,—banish all fear. You are safe under my roof."

This recognition, so unexpected, rather disconcerted and disquieted the noble fugitive. The timidity and suspicion of persons escaping from slavery are easily awakened, and often what is intended to dispel the one, and to allay the other, has precisely the opposite effect. It was so in this case. Quickly observing the unhappy impression made by his words and action, Mr. Listwell assumed a more quiet and inquiring aspect, and finally succeeded in removing the apprehensions which his very natural and generous salutation had aroused.

Thus assured, the stranger said, "Sir, you have rightly guessed, I am, indeed, a fugitive from slavery. My name is Madison,—Madison Washington my mother used to call me. I am on my way to Canada, where I learn that persons of my color are protected in all the rights of men; and my object in calling upon you was, to beg the privilege of resting my weary limbs for the night in your barn. It was my purpose to have continued my journey till morning; but the piercing cold, and the frowning darkness compelled me to seek shelter; and, seeing a light through the lattice of your window, I was encouraged to come here to beg the privilege named. You will do me a great favor by affording me shelter for the night."

"A resting-place, indeed, sir, you shall have; not, however, in my barn, but in the best room of my house. Consider yourself, if you please, under the roof of a friend; for such I am to you, and to all your deeply injured race."

While this introductory conversation was going on, the kind lady had revived the fire, and was diligently preparing supper; for she, not less than her husband, felt for the sorrows of the oppressed and hunted ones of earth, and was always glad of an opportunity to do them a service. A bountiful repast was quickly prepared, and the hungry and toil-worn bondman was cordially invited to partake thereof. Gratefully he acknowledged the favor of his benevolent benefactress; but appeared scarcely to understand what such hospitality could mean. It was the first time in his life that he had met so humane and friendly a greeting at the hands of persons whose color was unlike his own; yet it was impossible for him to doubt the charitableness of his new friends, or the genuineness of the welcome so freely given; and he therefore, with many thanks, took his seat at the table with Mr. and Mrs. Listwell, who, desirous to make him feel at home, took a cup of tea themselves, while urging upon Madison the best that the house could afford.

Supper over, all doubts and apprehensions banished, the three drew around the blazing fire, and a conversation commenced which lasted till long after midnight.

"Now," said Madison to Mr. Listwell, "I was a little surprised and alarmed when I came in, by what you said; do tell me, sir, *why* you thought you had seen my face before, and by what you knew me to be a fugitive from slavery; for I am sure that I never was before in this neighborhood, and I certainly sought to conceal what I supposed to be the manner of a fugitive slave."

Mr. Listwell at once frankly disclosed the secret; describing the place where he first saw him; rehearsing the language which he (Madison) had used; referring to the effect which his manner and speech had made upon him; declaring the resolution he there formed to be an abolitionist; telling how often he had spoken of the circumstance, and the deep concern he had ever since felt to know what had become of him; and whether he had carried out the purpose to make his escape, as in the woods he declared he would do.

"Ever since that morning," said Mr. Listwell, "you have seldom been absent from my mind, and though now I did not dare to hope that I should ever see you again, I have often wished that such might be my fortune; for, from that hour, your face seemed to be daguerreotyped on my memory."

Madison looked quite astonished, and felt amazed at the narration to which he had listened. After recovering himself he said, "I well remember that morning, and the bitter anguish that wrung my heart; I will state the occasion of it. I had, on the previous Saturday, suffered a cruel lashing; had been tied up to the limb of a tree, with my feet chained together, and a heavy iron bar placed between my ankles. Thus suspended, I received on my naked back forty stripes, and was kept in this distressing position three or four hours, and was then let down, only to have my torture increased; for my bleeding back, gashed by the cow-skin, was washed by the overseer with old brine, partly to augment my suffering, and partly, as he said, to prevent inflammation. My crime was that I had stayed longer at the mill, the day previous, than it was thought I ought to have done, which, I assured my master and the overseer, was no fault of mine; but no excuses were allowed. 'Hold your tongue, you impudent rascal,' met my every explanation. Slave-holders are so imperious when their passions are excited, as to construe every word of the slave into insolence. I could do nothing but submit to the agonizing infliction. Smarting still from the wounds, as well as from the consciousness of being whipt for no cause, I took advantage of the absence of my master, who had gone to church, to spend the time in the woods, and brood over my wretched lot. Oh, sir, I remember it well,—and can never forget it."

"But this was five years ago; where have you been since?"

"I will try to tell you," said Madison. "Just four weeks after that Sabbath morning, I gathered up the few rags of clothing I had, and started, as I supposed, for the North and for freedom. I must not stop to describe my feelings on taking this step. It seemed like taking a leap into the dark. The thought of leaving my poor wife and two little children caused me indescribable anguish; but consoling myself with the reflection that once free, I could, possibly, devise ways and means to gain their freedom also, I nerved myself up to make the attempt. I started, but ill-luck attended me; for after being out a whole week, strange to say, I still found myself on my master's grounds; the third night after being out, a season of clouds and rain set in, wholly preventing me from seeing the North Star, which I had trusted as my guide, not dreaming that clouds might intervene between us.

"This circumstance was fatal to my project, for in losing my star, I lost my way; so when I supposed I was far towards the North, and had almost gained my freedom, I discovered myself at the very point from which I had started. It was a severe trial, for I arrived at home in great destitution; my feet were sore, and in travelling in the dark, I had dashed my foot against a stump, and started a nail, and lamed myself. I was wet and cold; one week had exhausted all my stores; and when I landed on my master's plantation, with all my work to do over again,—hungry, tired, lame, and bewildered,—I almost cursed the day that I was born. In this extremity I approached the quarters. I did so stealthily, although in my desperation I hardly cared whether I was discovered or not. Peeping through the rents of the quarters, I saw my fellow-slaves seated by a warm fire, merrily passing away the time, as though their hearts knew no sorrow. Although I envied their seeming contentment, all wretched as I was, I despised the cowardly acquiescence in their own degradation which it implied, and felt a kind of pride and glory in my own desperate lot. I dared not enter the quarters,—for where there is seeming contentment with slavery, there is certain treachery to freedom. I proceeded towards the great house, in the hope of catching a glimpse of my poor wife, whom I knew might be trusted with my secrets even on the scaffold. Just as I reached the fence which divided the field from the garden, I saw a woman in the yard, who in the darkness I took to be my wife; but a nearer approach told me it was not she. I was about to speak; had I done so, I would not have been here this night; for an alarm would have been sounded, and the hunters been put on my track. Here were hunger, cold, thirst, disappointment, and chagrin, confronted only by the dim hope of liberty. I tremble to think of that dreadful hour. To face the deadly cannon's mouth in warm blood unterrified, is, I think, a small achievement, compared with a conflict like this with gaunt starvation. The gnawings of hunger conquers by degrees, till all that a man has he would give in exchange for a single crust of bread. Thank God, I was not quite reduced to this extremity.

"Happily for me, before the fatal moment of utter despair, my good wife made her appearance in the yard. It was she; I knew her step. All was well now. I was, however, afraid to speak, lest I should frighten her. Yet speak I did; and, to my great joy, my voice was known. Our meeting can be more easily imagined than described. For a time hunger, thirst, weariness, and lameness were forgotten. But it was soon necessary for her to return to the house. She being a house-servant, her absence from the kitchen, if discovered, might have excited suspicion. Our parting was like tearing the flesh from my bones; yet it was the part of wisdom for her to go. She left me with the purpose of meeting me at midnight in the very forest where you last saw me. She knew the place well, as one of my melancholy resorts, and could easily find it, though the night was dark.

"I hastened away, therefore, and concealed myself, to

await the arrival of my good angel. As I lay there among the leaves, I was strongly tempted to return again to the house of my master and give myself up; but remembering my solemn pledge on that memorable Sunday morning, I was able to linger out the two long hours between ten and midnight. I may well call them long hours. I have endured much hardship; I have encountered many perils; but the anxiety of those two hours, was the bitterest I ever experienced. True to her word, my wife came laden with provisions, and we sat down on the side of a log, at that dark and lonesome hour of the night. I cannot say we talked; our feelings were too great for that; yet we came to an understanding that I should make the woods my home, for if I gave myself up, I should be whipped and sold away; and if I started for the North, I should leave a wife doubly dear to me. We mutually determined, therefore, that I should remain in the vicinity. In the dismal swamps I lived, sir, five long years,—a cave for my home during the day. I wandered about at night with the wolf and the bear,—sustained by the promise that my good Susan would meet me in the pine woods at least once a week. This promise was redeemed, I assure you, to the letter, greatly to my relief. I had partly become contented with my mode of life, and had made up my mind to spend my days there; but the wilderness that sheltered me thus long took fire, and refused longer to be my hiding-place.

"I will not harrow up your feelings by portraying the terrific scene of this awful conflagration. There is nothing to which I can liken it. It was horribly and indescribably grand. The whole world seemed on fire, and it appeared to me that the day of judgment had come; that the burning bowels of the earth had burst forth, and that the end of all things was at hand. Bears and wolves, scorched from their mysterious hiding-places in the earth, and all the wild inhabitants of the untrodden forest, filled with a common dismay, ran forth, yelling, howling, bewildered amidst the smoke and flame. The very heavens seemed to rain down fire through the towering trees; it was by the merest chance that I escaped the devouring element. Running before it, and stopping occasionally to take breath, I looked back to behold its frightful ravages, and to drink in its savage magnificence. It was awful, thrilling, solemn, beyond compare. When aided by the fitful wind, the merciless tempest of fire swept on, sparkling, creaking, cracking, curling, roaring, out-doing in its dreadful splendor a thousand thunderstorms at once. From tree to tree it leaped, swallowing them up in its lurid, baleful glare; and leaving them leafless, limbless, charred, and lifeless behind. The scene was overwhelming, stunning,—nothing was spared—cattle, tame and wild, herds of swine and of deer wild beasts of every name and kind,—huge night-birds bats, and owls, that had retired to their homes in lofty tree-tops to rest, perished in that fiery storm. The long-winged buzzard and croaking raven mingled their dismal cries with those of the countless myriads of small birds that rose up to the skies, and were lost to the sight in clouds of smoke and flame. Oh, I shudder when I think of it! Many a poor wandering fugitive, who, like myself, had sought among wild beasts the mercy denied by our fellow men, saw, in helpless consternation, his dwelling-place and city of refuge reduced to ashes forever. It was this grand conflagration that drove me hither; I ran alike from fire and from slavery"

After a slight pause, (for both speaker and hearers were deeply moved by the above recital,) Mr. Listwell, addressing Madison, said, "If it does not weary you too much, do tell us something of your journeyings since this disastrous burning,—we are deeply interested in everything which can throw light on the hardships of persons escaping from slavery; we could hear you talk all night; are there no incidents that you could relate of your travels hither? or are they such that you do not like to mention them."

"For the most part, sir, my course has been uninterrupted; and, considering the circumstances, at times even pleasant. I have suffered little for want of food; but I need not tell you how I got it. Your moral code may differ from mine, as your customs and usages are different. The fact is, sir, during my flight, I felt myself robbed by society of all my just rights; that I was in an enemy's land, who sought both my life and my liberty. They had transformed me into a brute; made merchandise of my body, and, for all the purposes of my flight, turned day into night,—and guided by my own necessities, and in contempt of their conventionalities, I did not scruple to take bread where I could get it."

"And just there you were right," said Mr. Listwell; "I once had doubts on this point myself, but a conversation with Gerrit Smith, (a man, by the way, that I wish you could see, for he is a devoted friend of your race, and I know he would receive you gladly,) put an end to all my doubts on this point. But do not let me interrupt you."

"I had but one narrow escape during my whole journey," said Madison.

"Do let us hear of it," said Mr. Listwell.

"Two weeks ago," continued Madison, "after travelling all night, I was overtaken by daybreak, in what seemed to me an almost interminable wood. I deemed it unsafe to go farther, and, as usual, I looked around for a suitable tree in which to spend the day. I liked one with a bushy top, and found one just to my mind. Up I climbed, and hiding myself as well as I could, I, with this strap, (pulling one out of his old coat-pocket,) lashed myself to a bough, and flattered myself that I should get a *good night's* sleep that day; but in this I was soon disappointed. I had scarcely got fastened to my natural hammock, when I heard the voices of a number of persons, apparently approaching the part of the woods where I was. Upon my word, sir, I dreaded more these human voices than I should have done those of wild beasts. I was at a loss to know what to do. If I descended, I should probably be discovered by the men; and if they had dogs I should, doubtless, be *'treed.'* It was an anxious moment, but hardships and dangers have been the accompaniments of my life; and have, perhaps, imparted to me a certain hardness of character, which, to some extent, adapts me to them. In my present predicament, I decided to hold my place in the tree-top, and abide the consequences. But here I must disappoint you; for the men, who were all colored, halted at least a hundred yards from me, and began with their axes, in right good earnest, to attack the trees. The sound of their laughing axes was like the report of as many well-charged pistols. By and by there came down at least a dozen trees with a terrible crash. They leaped upon the fallen trees with an air of victory. I could see no dog with them, and felt myself comparatively safe, though I could not forget the possibility that some freak or fancy might bring the axe a little nearer my dwelling than comported with my safety.

"There was no sleep for me that day, and I wished for night. You may imagine that the thought of having the tree attacked under me was far from agreeable, and that it very easily kept me on the look-out. The day was not without diversion. The men at work seemed to be a gay set; and they would often make the woods resound with that uncontrolled laughter for which we, as a race, are remarkable. I held my place in the tree till sunset,—saw the men put on their jackets to be off. I observed that all left the ground except one, whom I saw sitting on the side of a stump, with his head bowed, and his eyes apparently fixed on the ground. I became interested in him. After sitting in the position to which I have alluded ten or fifteen minutes, he left the stump, walked directly towards the tree in which I was secreted, and halted almost under the same. He stood for a moment and looked around, deliberately and reverently took off his hat, by which I saw that he was a man in the evening of life, slightly bald and quite gray. After laying down his hat carefully, he knelt and prayed aloud, and such a prayer, the most fervent, earnest, and solemn, to which I think I ever listened. After reverently addressing the Almighty, as the all-wise, all-good, and the common Father of all mankind, he besought God for grace, for strength, to bear up under, and to endure, as a good soldier, all the hardships and trials which beset the journey of life, and to enable him to live in a manner which accorded with the gospel of Christ. His soul now broke out in humble supplication for deliverance from bondage. 'O thou,' said he, 'that hearest the raven's cry, take pity on poor me! O deliver me! O deliver me! in mercy, O God, deliver me from the chains and manifold hardships of slavery! With thee, O Father, all things are possible. Thou canst stand and measure the earth. Thou hast beheld and drove asunder the nations,—all power is in thy hand,—thou didst say of old, "I have seen the affliction of my people, and am come to deliver them,"—Oh look down upon our afflictions, and have mercy upon us.' But I cannot repeat his prayer, nor can I give you an idea of its deep pathos. I had given but little attention to religion, and had but little faith in it; yet, as the old man prayed, I felt almost like coming down and kneel by his side, and mingle my broken complaint with his.

"He had already gained my confidence; as how could it be otherwise? I knew enough of religion to know that the man who prays in secret is far more likely to be sincere than he who loves to pray standing in the street, or in the great congregation. When he arose from his knees, like another Zacheus, I came down from the tree. He seemed a little alarmed at first, but I told him my story, and the good man embraced me in his arms, and assured me of his sympathy.

"I was now about out of provisions, and thought I might safely ask him to help me replenish my store. He said he had no money; but if he had, he would freely give it me. I told him I had *one dollar;* it was all the money I had in the world. I gave it to him, and asked him to purchase some crackers and cheese, and to kindly bring me the balance; that I would remain in or near that place, and would come to him on his return, if he would whistle. He was gone only about an hour. Meanwhile, from some cause or other, I know not what, (but as you shall see very wisely,) I changed my place. On his return I started to meet him; but it seemed as if the shadow of approaching danger fell upon my spirit, and checked my progress. In a very few minutes, closely on the heels of the old man, I distinctly saw *fourteen men*, with something like guns in their hands."

"Oh! the old wretch!" exclaimed Mrs. Listwell "he had betrayed you, had he?"

"I think not," said Madison, "I cannot believe that the old man was to blame He probably went into a store, asked for the articles for which I sent, and presented the bill I gave him; and it is so unusual for slaves in the country to have money, that fact, doubtless, excited suspicion, and gave rise to inquiry. I can easily believe that the truthfulness of the old man's character compelled him to disclose the facts; and thus were these blood-thirsty men put on my track. Of course I did not present myself; but hugged my hiding-place securely. If discovered and attacked, I resolved to sell my life as dearly as possible.

"After searching about the woods silently for a time, the whole company gathered around the old man; one charged him with lying, and called him an old villain; said he was a thief; charged him with stealing money; said if he did not instantly tell where he got it, they would take the shirt from his old back, and give him thirty-nine lashes.

"'I did *not* steal the money,' said the old man, 'it was given me, as I told you at the store; and if the man who gave it me is not here, it is not my fault.'

"'Hush! you lying old rascal; we'll make you smart for it. You shall not leave this spot until you have told where you got that money.'

"They now took hold of him, and began to strip him; while others went to get sticks with which to beat him. I felt, at the moment, like rushing out in the midst of them; but considering that the old man would be whipped the more for having aided a fugitive slave, and that, perhaps, in the *melée* he might be killed outright, I disobeyed this impulse. They tied him to a tree, and began to whip him. My own flesh crept at every blow, and I seem to hear the old man's piteous cries even now. They laid thirty-nine lashes on his bare back, and were going to repeat that number, when one of the company besought his comrades to desist. 'You'll kill the d—d old scoundrel! You've already whipt a dollar's worth out of him, even if he stole it!' 'O yes,' said another, 'let him down. He'll never tell us another lie, I'll warrant ye!' With this, one of the company untied the old man, and bid him go about his business.

The old man left, but the company remained as mucn as an hour, scouring the woods. Round and round they went, turning up the underbrush, and peering about like so many bloodhounds. Two or three times they came within six feet of where I lay. I tell you I held my stick with a firmer grasp than I did in coming up to your house tonight. I expected to level one of them at least. Fortunately, however, I eluded their pursuit, and they left me alone in the woods.

"My last dollar was now gone, and you may well suppose I felt the loss of it; but the thought of being once again free to pursue my journey, prevented that depression which a sense of destitution causes; so swinging my little bundle on my back, I caught a glimpse of the *Great Bear* (which ever points the way to my beloved star,) and I started again on my journey. What I lost in money I made up at a hen-roost that same night, upon which I fortunately came."

"But you didn't eat your food raw? How did you cook it?" said Mrs. Listwell.

"O no, Madam," said Madison, turning to his little bundle;—"I had the means of cooking." Here he took out of his bundle an old-fashioned tinder-box, and taking up a piece of a file, which he brought with him, he struck it with a heavy flint, and brought out at least a dozen sparks at once. "I have had this old box," said he, "more than five years. It is the *only* property saved from the fire in the dismal swamp. It has done me good service. It has given me the means of broiling many a chicken!"

It seemed quite a relief to Mrs. Listwell to know that Madison had, at least, lived upon cooked food. Women have a perfect horror of eating uncooked food.

By this time thoughts of what was best to be done about getting Madison to Canada, began to trouble Mr. Listwell; for the laws of Ohio were very stringent against any one who should aid, or who were found aiding a slave to escape through that State. A citizen, for the simple act of taking a fugitive slave in his carriage, had just been stripped of all his property, and thrown penniless upon the world. Notwithstanding this, Mr. Listwell was determined to see Madison safely on his way to Canada. "Give yourself no uneasiness, said he to Madison, for if it cost my farm, I shall see you safely out of the States, and on your way to a land of liberty. Thank God that there is *such* a land so near us! You will spend to-morrow with us, and to-morrow night I will take you in my carriage to the Lake. Once upon that, and you are safe."

"Thank you! thank you," said the fugitive; "I will commit myself to your care."

For the *first* time during *five* years, Madison enjoyed the luxury of resting his limbs on a comfortable bed, and inside a human habitation. Looking at the white sheets, he said to Mr. Listwell, "What, sir! you don't mean that I shall sleep in that bed?"

"Oh yes, oh yes."

After Mr. Listwell left the room, Madison said he really hesitated whether or not he should lie on the floor; for that was *far* more comfortable and inviting than any bed to which he had been used.

We pass over the thoughts and feelings, the hopes and fears, the plans and purposes, that revolved in the mind of Madison during the day that he was secreted at the house of Mr. Listwell. The reader will be content to know that nothing occurred to endanger his liberty, or to excite alarm. Many were the little attentions bestowed upon him in his quiet retreat and hiding-place. In the evening, Mr. Listwell, after treating Madison to a new suit of winter clothes, and replenishing his exhausted purse with five dollars, all in silver, brought out his two-horse wagon, well provided with buffaloes, and silently started off with him to Cleveland. They arrived there without interruption, a few minutes before sunrise the next morning. Fortunately the steamer Admiral lay at the wharf, and was to start for Canada at nine o'clock. Here the last anticipated danger was surmounted. It was feared that just at this point the hunters of men might be on the look-out, and, possibly, pounce upon their victim. Mr. Listwell saw the captain of the boat; cautiously sounded him on the matter of carrying liberty-loving passengers, before he introduced his precious charge. This done, Madison was conducted on board. With usual generosity this true subject of the emancipating queen welcomed Madison, and assured him that he should be safely landed in Canada, free of charge. Madison now felt himself no more a piece of merchandise, but a passenger, and, like any other passenger, going about his business, carrying with him what belonged to him, and nothing which rightfully belonged to anybody else.

Wrapped in his new winter suit, snug and comfortable, a pocket full of silver, safe from his pursuers, embarked for a free country, Madison gave every sign of sincere gratitude, and bade his kind benefactor farewell, with such a grip of the hand as bespoke a heart full of honest manliness, and a soul that knew how to appreciate kindness. It need scarcely be said that Mr. Listwell was deeply moved by the gratitude and friendship he had excited in a nature so noble as that of the fugitive. He went to his home that day with a joy and gratification which knew no bounds. He had done something "to deliver the spoiled out of the hands of the spoiler," he had given bread to the hungry, and clothes to the naked; he had befriended a man to whom the laws of his country forbade all friendship,—and in proportion to the odds against his righteous deed, was the delightful satisfaction that gladdened his heart. On reaching home, he exclaimed, "*He is safe,—he is safe,—he is safe,*"—and the cup of his joy was shared by his excellent lady. The following letter was received from Madison a few days after.

"WINDSOR, CANADA WEST, DEC. 16, 1840.

My dear Friend,—for such you truly are:—

Madison is out of the woods at last; I nestle in the mane of the British lion, protected by his mighty paw from the talons and the beak of the American eagle. I AM FREE, and breathe an atmosphere too pure for *slaves*, slave-hunters, or slave-holders. My heart is full. As many thanks to you, sir, and to your kind lady, as there are pebbles on the shores of Lake Erie; and may the blessing of God rest upon you both. You will never be forgotten by your profoundly grateful friend,

MADISON WASHINGTON."

## PART III

——His head was with his heart,
And that was far away!

*Childe Harold*

Just upon the edge of the great road from Petersburg, Virginia, to Richmond, and only about fifteen miles from the latter place, there stands a somewhat ancient and famous public tavern, quite notorious in its better days, as being the grand resort for most of the leading gamblers, horse-racers, cock-fighters, and slave-traders from all the country round about. This old rookery, the nucleus of all sorts of birds, mostly those of ill omen, has, like everything else peculiar to Virginia, lost much of its ancient consequence and splendor; yet it keeps up some appearance of gaiety and high life, and is still frequented, even by respectable travellers, who are unacquainted with its past history and present condition. Its fine old portico looks well at a distance, and gives the building an air of grandeur. A nearer view, however, does little to sustain this pretension. The house is large, and its style imposing, but time and dissipation, unfailing in their results, have made ineffaceable marks upon it, and it must, in the common course of events, soon be numbered with the things that were. The gloomy mantle of ruin is, already, outspread to envelop it, and its remains, even but now remind one of a human skull, after the flesh has mingled with the earth. Old hats and rags fill the places in the upper windows once occupied by large panes of glass, and the moulding boards along the roofing have dropped off from their places, leaving holes and crevices in the rented wall for bats and swallows to build their nests in. The platform of the portico, which fronts the highway is a rickety affair, its planks are loose, and in some places entirely gone, leaving effective mantraps in their stead for nocturnal ramblers. The wooden pillars, which once supported it, but which now hang as encumbrances, are all rotten, and tremble with the touch. A part of the stable, a fine old structure in its day, which has given comfortable shelter to hundreds of the noblest steeds of "the Old Dominion" at once, was blown down many years ago, and never has been, and probably never will be, rebuilt. The doors of the barn are in wretched condition; they will shut with a little human strength to help their worn out hinges, but not otherwise. The side of the great building seen from the road is much discolored in sundry places by slops poured from the upper windows, rendering it unsightly and offensive in other respects. Three or four great dogs, looking as dull and gloomy as the mansion itself, lie stretched out along the door-sills under the portico; and double the number of loafers, some of them completely rum-ripe, and others ripening, dispose themselves like so many sentinels about the front of the house. These latter understand the science of scraping acquaintance to perfection. They know every-body, and almost every-body knows them. Of course, as their title implies, they have no regular employment. They are (to use an expressive phrase) *hangers on*, or still better, they are what sailors would denominate *holders-on to the slack, in every-body's mess, and in nobody's watch.* They are, however, as good as the newspaper for the events of the day, and they sell their knowledge almost as cheap. Money they seldom have; yet they always have capital the most reliable. They make their way with a succeeding traveller by intelligence gained from a preceding one. All the great names of Virginia they know by heart, and have seen their owners often. The history of the house is folded in their lips, and they rattle off stories in connection with it, equal to the guides at Dryburgh Abbey. He must be a shrewd man, and well skilled in the art of evasion, who gets out of the hands of these fellows without being at the expense of a treat.

It was at this old tavern, while on a second visit to the State of Virginia in 1841, that Mr. Listwell, unacquainted with the fame of the place, turned aside, about sunset, to pass the night. Riding up to the house, he had scarcely dismounted, when one of the half dozen barroom fraternity met and addressed him in a manner exceedingly bland and accommodating.

"Fine evening, sir."

"Very fine," said Mr. Listwell. "This is a tavern, I believe?"

"Oh yes, sir, yes; although you may think it looks a little the worse for wear, it was once as good a house as any in Virginy. I make no doubt if ye spend the night here, you'll think it a good house yet; for there aint a more accommodating man in the country than you'll find the landlord."

*Listwell.* "The most I want is a good bed for myself, and a full manger for my horse. If I get these, I shall be quite satisfied."

*Loafer.* "Well, I alloys like to hear a gentleman talk for his horse; and just becase the horse can't talk for itself. A man that don't care about his beast, and don't look arter it when he's travelling, aint much in my eye anyhow. Now, sir, I likes a horse, and I'll guarantee your horse will be taken good care on here. That old stable, for all you see it looks so shabby now, once sheltered the great *Eclipse,* when he run here agin *Batchelor* and *Jumping Jemmy.* Them was fast horses, but he beat 'em both."

*Listwell.* "Indeed."

*Loafer.* "Well, I rather reckon you've travelled a right smart distance to-day, from the look of your horse?"

*Listwell.* "Forty miles only."

*Loafer.* "Well! I'll be darned if that aint a pretty good *only.* Mister, that beast of yours is a singed cat, I warrant you. I never see'd a creature like that that was'nt good on the road. You've come about forty miles, then?"

*Listwell.* "Yes, yes, and a pretty good pace at that."

*Loafter.* "You're somewhat in a hurry, then, I make no doubt? I reckon I could guess if I would, what you're going to Richmond for? It would'nt be much of a guess either; for it's rumored hereabouts, that there's to be the greatest sale of niggers at Richmond to-morrow that has taken place there in a long time; and I'll be bound you're a going there to have a hand in it."

*Listwell.* "Why, you must think, then, that there's money to be made at that business?"

*Loafer.* "Well, 'pon my honor, sir, I never made any that way myself; but it stands to reason that it's a money making business; for almost all other business in Virginia is dropped to engage in this. One thing is sartain, I never see'd a nigger-buyer yet that had'nt a plenty of money, and he was'nt as free with it as water. I has known one on 'em to treat as high as twenty times in a night; and, ginerally speaking, they's men of edication, and knows all about the government. The fact is, sir, I alloys like to hear 'em talk, bekase I alloys can learn something from them."

*Listwell.* "What may I call your name, sir?"

*Loafer.* "Well, now, they calls me Wilkes. I'm known all around by the gentlemen that comes here. They all knows old Wilkes."

*Listwell.* "Well, Wilkes, you seem to be acquainted here, and I see you have a strong liking for a horse. Be so good as to speak a kind word for mine to the hostler to-night, and you'll not lose anything by it."

*Loafer.* "Well, sir, I see you don't say much, but you've got an insight into things. It's alloys wise to get the good will of them that's acquainted about a tavern; for a man don't know when he goes into a house what may happen, or how much he may need a friend. Here the loafer gave Mr. Listwell a significant grin, which expressed a sort of triumphant pleasure at having, as he supposed, by his tact succeeded in placing so fine appearing a gentleman under obligations to him.

The pleasure, however, was mutual; for there was something so insinuating in the glance of this loquacious customer, that Mr. Listwell was very glad to get quit of him, and to do so more successfully, he ordered his supper to be brought to him in his private room, private to the eye, but not to the ear. This room was directly over the bar, and the plastering being off, nothing but pine boards and naked laths separated him from the disagreeable company below,—he could easily hear what was said in the bar-room, and was rather glad of the advantage it afforded, for, as you shall see, it furnished him important hints as to the manner and deportment he should assume during his stay at that tavern.

Mr. Listwell says he had got into his room but a few moments, when he heard the officious Wilkes below, in a tone of disappointment, exclaim, "Whar's that gentleman?" Wilkes was evidently expecting to meet with his friend at the bar-room, on his return, and had no doubt of his doing the handsome thing. "He has gone to his room," answered the landlord, "and has ordered his supper to be brought to him."

Here some one shouted out, "Who is he, Wilkes? Where's he going?"

"Well, now, I'll be hanged if I know; but I'm willing to make any man a bet of this old hat agin a five dollar bill, that that gent is as full of money as a dog is of fleas. He's going down to Richmond to buy niggers, I make no doubt. He's no fool, I warrant ye."

"Well, he acts d——d strange," said another, "anyhow. I likes to see a man, when he comes up to a tavern, to come straight into the bar-room, and show that he's a man among men. Nobody was going to bite him."

"Now, I don't blame him a bit for not coming in here. That man knows his business, and means to take care on his money," answered Wilkes.

"Wilkes, you're a fool. You only say that, becase you hope to get a few coppers out on him."

"You only measure my corn by your half-bushel, I won't say that you're only mad becase I got the chance of speaking to him first."

"O Wilkes! you're known here. You'll praise up any body that will give you a copper; besides, 't is my opinion that that fellow who took his long slab-sides up stairs, for all the world just like a half-scared woman, afraid to look honest men in the face, is a *Northerner*, and as mean as dishwater."

"Now what will you bet of that," said Wilkes.

The speaker said, "I make no bets with you, 'kase you can get that fellow up stairs there to say anything."

"Well," said Wilkes, "I am willing to bet any man in the company that *that* gentleman is a *nigger*-buyer. He did'nt tell me so right down, but I reckon I knows enough about men to give a pretty clean guess as to what they are arter."

The dispute as to *who* Mr. Listwell was, what his business, where he was going, etc., was kept up with much animation for some time, and more than once threatened a serious disturbance of the peace. Wilkes had his friends as well as his opponents. After this sharp debate, the company amused themselves by drinking whiskey, and telling stories. The latter consisting of quarrels, fights, *rencontres*, and duels, in which distinguished persons of that neighborhood, and frequenters of that house, had been actors. Some of these stories were frightful enough, and were told, too, with a relish which bespoke the pleasure of the parties with the horrid scenes they portrayed. It would not be proper here to give the reader any idea of the vulgarity and dark profanity which rolled, as "a sweet morsel," under these corrupt tongues. A more brutal set of creatures, perhaps, never congregated.

Disgusted, and a little alarmed withal, Mr. Listwell, who was not accustomed to such entertainment, at length retired, but not to sleep. He was *too* much wrought upon by what he had heard to rest quietly, and what snatches of sleep he got, were interrupted by dreams which were anything than pleasant. At eleven o'clock, there seemed to be several hundreds of persons crowding into the house. A loud and confused clamour, cursing and cracking of whips, and the noise of chains startled him from his bed; for a moment he would have given the half of his farm in Ohio to have been at home. This uproar was kept up with undulating course, till near morning. There was loud laughing,—loud singing,—loud cursing,—and yet there seemed to be weeping and mourning in the midst of all. Mr. Listwell said he had heard enough during the forepart of the night to convince him that a buyer of men and women stood the best chance of being respected. And he, therefore, thought it best to say nothing which might undo the favorable opinion that had been formed of him in the bar-room by at least one of the fraternity that swarmed about it. While he would not avow himself a purchaser of slaves, he deemed it not prudent to disavow it. He felt that he might, properly, refuse to cast such a pearl before parties which, to him, were worse than swine. To reveal himself, and to impart a knowledge of his real character and sentiments would, to say the least, be imparting intelligence with the certainty of seeing it and himself both abused. Mr. Listwell confesses, that this reasoning did not altogether satisfy his conscience, for, hating slavery as he did, and regarding it to be the immediate duty of every man to cry out against it, "without compromise and without concealment," it was hard for him to admit to himself the possibility of circumstances wherein a man might, properly, hold his tongue on the subject. Having as little of the spirit of a martyr as Erasmus, he concluded, like the latter, that it was wiser to trust the mercy of God for his soul, than the humanity of slave-traders for his body. Bodily fear, not conscientious scruples, prevailed.

In this spirit he rose early in the morning, manifesting no surprise at what he had heard during the night. His quondam friend was soon at his elbow, boring him with all sorts of questions. All, however, directed to find out his character, business, residence, purposes, and destination. With the most perfect appearance of good nature and carelessness, Mr. Listwell evaded these meddlesome inquiries, and turned conversation to general topics, leaving himself and all that specially pertained to him, out of discussion. Disengaging himself from their troublesome companionship, he made his way towards an old bowling-alley, which was connected with the house, and which, like all the rest, was in very bad repair.

On reaching the alley Mr. Listwell saw, for the first time in his life, a slave-gang on their way to market. A sad sight truly. Here were one hundred and thirty human beings,—children of a common Creator—guilty of no crime—men and women, with hearts, minds, and deathless spirits, chained and fettered, and bound for the market, in a christian country,—in a country boasting of its liberty, independence, and high civilization! Humanity converted into merchandise, and linked in iron bands, with no regard to decency or humanity! All sizes, ages, and sexes, mothers, fathers, daughters, brothers, sisters,—all huddled together, on their way to market to be sold and separated from home, and from each other *forever.* And all to fill the pockets of men too lazy to work for an honest living, and who gain their fortune by plundering the helpless, and trafficking in the souls and sinews of men. As he gazed upon this revolting and heart-rending scene, our informant said he almost doubted the existence of a God of justice! And he stood wondering that the earth did not open and swallow up such wickedness.

In the midst of these reflections, and while running his eye up and down the fettered ranks, he met the glance of one whose face he thought he had seen before. To be resolved, he moved towards the spot. It was MADISON WASHINGTON! Here was a scene for the pencil! Had Mr. Listwell been confronted by one risen from the dead, he could not have been more appalled. He was completely stunned. A thunderbolt could not have struck him more dumb. He stood, for a few moments, as motionless as one petrified; collecting himself, he at length exclaimed, *"Madison! is that you?"*

The noble fugitive, but little less astonished than himself, answered cheerily, "O yes, sir, they've got me again."

Thoughtless of consequences for the moment, Mr. Listwell ran up to his old friend, placing his hands upon his shoulders, and looked him in the face! Speechless they stood gazing at each other as if to be doubly resolved that there was no mistake about the matter, till Madison motioned his friend away, intimating a fear lest the keepers should find him there, and suspect him of tampering with the slaves.

"They will soon be out to look after us. You can come when they go to breakfast, and I will tell you all."

Pleased with this arrangement, Mr. Listwell passed out of the alley; but only just in time to save himself, for, while near the door, he observed three men making their way to the alley. The thought occurred to him to await their arrival, as the best means of diverting the ever ready suspicions of the guilty.

While the scene between Mr. Listwell and his friend Madison was going on, the other slaves stood as mute spectators,—at a loss to know what all this could mean. As he left, he heard the man chained to Madison ask, "Who is that gentleman?"

"He is a friend of mine. I cannot tell you now. Suffice it to say he is a friend. You shall hear more of him before long, but mark me! whatever shall pass between that gentleman and me, in your hearing, I pray you will say nothing about it. We are all chained here together,—ours is a common lot; and that gentleman is not less *your* friend than *mine*." At these words, all mysterious as they were, the unhappy company gave signs of satisfaction and hope. It seems that Madison, by that mesmeric power which is the invariable accompaniment of genius, had already won the confidence of the gang, and was a sort of general-in-chief among them.

By this time the keepers arrived. A horrid trio, well fitted for their demoniacal work. Their uncombed hair came down over foreheads *"villainously low,"* and with eyes, mouths, and noses to match. "Hallo! hallo!" they growled out as they entered. "Are you all there!"

"All here," said Madison.

"Well, well, that's right! your journey will soon be over. You'll be in Richmond by eleven to-day, and then you'll have an easy time on it."

"I say, gal, what in the devil are you crying about?" said one of them. I'll give you something to cry about, if you don't mind." This was said to a girl, apparently not more than twelve years old, who had been weeping bitterly. She had, probably, left behind her a loving mother, affectionate sisters, brothers, and friends, and her tears were but the natural expression of her sorrow, and the only solace. But the dealers in human flesh have *no* respect for such sorrow. They look upon it as a protest against their cruel injustice, and they are prompt to punish it.

This is a puzzle not easily solved. *How* came he here? what can I do for him? may I not even now be in some way compromised in this affair? were thoughts that troubled Mr. Listwell, and made him eager for the promised opportunity of speaking to Madison.

The bell now sounded for breakfast, and keepers and drivers, with pistols and bowie-knives gleaming from their belts, hurried in, as if to get the best places. Taking the chance now afforded, Mr. Listwell hastened back to the bowling-alley. Reaching Madison, he said, "Now *do* tell me all about the matter. Do you know me?"

"Oh, yes," said Madison, "I know you well, and shall never forget you nor that cold and dreary night you gave me shelter. I must be short," he continued, "for they'll soon be out again. This, then, is the story in brief. On reaching Canada, and getting over the excitement of making my escape, sir, my thoughts turned to my poor wife, who had well deserved my love by her virtuous fidelity and undying affection for me. I could not bear the thought of leaving her in the cruel jaws of slavery, without making an effort to rescue her. First, I tried to get money to buy her; but oh! the process was *too slow.* I despaired of accomplishing it. She was in all my thoughts by day, and my dreams by night. At times I could almost hear her voice, saying, 'O Madison! Madison! will you then leave me here? can you leave me here to die? No! no! you will come! you will come!' I was wretched. I lost my appetite. I could neither work, eat, nor sleep, till I resolved to hazard my own liberty, to gain that of my wife! But I must be short. Six weeks ago I reached my old master's place. I laid about the neighborhood nearly a week, watching my chance, and, finally, I ventured upon the desperate attempt to reach my poor wife's room by means of a ladder. I reached the window, but the noise in raising it frightened my wife, and she screamed and fainted. I took her in my arms, and was descending the ladder, when the dogs began to bark furiously, and before I could get to the woods the white folks were roused. The cool night air soon restored my wife, and she readily recognized me. We made the best of our way to the woods, but it was now *too* late,—the dogs were after us as though they would have torn us to pieces. It was all over with me now! My old master and his two sons ran out with loaded rifles, and before we were out of gunshot, our ears were assailed with *'Stop! stop! or be shot down.'* Nevertheless we ran on. Seeing that we gave no heed to their calls, they fired, and my poor wife fell by my side dead, while I received but a slight flesh wound. I now became desperate, and stood my ground, and awaited their attack over her dead body. They rushed upon me, with their rifles in hand. I parried their blows, and fought them 'till I was knocked down and overpowered."

"Oh! it was madness to have returned," said Mr. Listwell.

"Sir, I could not be free with the galling thought that my poor wife was still a slave. With her in slavery, my body, not my spirit, was free. I was taken to the house,—chained to a ring-bolt,—my wounds dressed. I was kept there three days. All the slaves, for miles around, were brought to see me. Many slave-holders came with their slaves, using me as proof of the completeness of their power, and of the impossibility of slaves getting away. I was taunted, jeered at, and berated by them, in a manner that pierced me to the soul. Thank God, I was able to smother my rage, and to bear it all with seeming composure. After my wounds were nearly healed, I was taken to a tree and stripped, and I received sixty lashes on my naked back. A few days after, I was sold to a slave-trader, and placed in this gang for the New Orleans market."

"Do you think your master would sell you to me?"

"O no, sir! I was sold on condition of my being taken South. Their motive is revenge."

"Then, then," said Mr. Listwell, "I fear I can do nothing for you. Put your trust in God, and bear your sad lot with the manly fortitude which becomes a man. I shall see you at Richmond, but don't recognize me." Saying this, Mr. Listwell handed Madison ten dollars; said a few words to the other slaves; received their hearty "God bless you," and made his way to the house.

Fearful of exciting suspicion by too long delay, our friend went to the breakfast table, with the air of one who half reproved the greediness of those who rushed in at the sound of the bell. A cup of coffee was all that he could manage. His feelings were too bitter and excited, and his heart was too full with the fate of poor Madison (whom he loved as well as admired) to relish his breakfast; and although he sat long after the company had left the table, he really did little more than change the position of his knife and fork. The strangeness of meeting again one whom he had met on two several occasions before, under extraordinary circumstances, was well calculated to suggest the idea that a supernatural power, a wakeful providence, or an inexorable fate, had linked their destiny together; and that no efforts of his could disentangle him from the mysterious web of circumstances which enfolded him.

On leaving the table, Mr. Listwell nerved himself up and walked firmly into the bar-room. He was at once greeted again by that talkative chatter-box, Mr. Wilkes.

"Them's a likely set of niggers in the alley there," said Wilkes.

"Yes, they're fine looking fellows, one of them I should like to purchase, and for him I would be willing to give a handsome sum."

Turning to one of his comrades, and with a grin of victory, Wilkes said, "Aha, Bill, did you hear that? I told you I know'd that gentleman wanted to buy niggers, and would bid as high as any purchaser in the market."

"Come, come," said Listwell, "don't be too loud in your praise, you are old enough to know that prices rise when purchasers are plenty."

"That's a fact," said Wilkes, "I see you knows the ropes—and there's not a man in old Virginy whom I'd rather help to make a good bargain than you, sir."

"Mr. Listwell here threw a dollar at Wilkes, (which the latter caught with a dexterous hand,) saying, "Take that for your kind good will." Wilkes held up the dollar to his right eye, with a grin of victory, and turned to the morose grumbler in the corner who had questioned the liberality of a man of whom he knew nothing.

Mr. Listwell now stood as well with the company as any other occupant of the bar-rom.

We pass over the hurry and bustle, the brutal vociferations of the slave-drivers in getting their unhappy gang in motion for Richmond; and we need not narrate every application of the lash to those who faltered in the journey. Mr. Listwell followed the train at a long distance, with a sad heart; and on reaching Richmond left his horse at a hotel, and made his way to the wharf in the direction of which he saw the slave-coffle driven. He was just in time to see the whole company embark for New Orleans. The thought struck him that, while mixing with the multitude, he might do his friend Madison one last service, and he stept into a hardware store and purchased three strong *files.* These he took with him, and standing near the small boat, which lay in waiting to bear the company by parcels to the side of the brig that lay in the stream, he managed, as Madison passed him, to slip the files into his pocket, and at once darted back among the crowd.

All the company now on board, the imperious voice of the captain sounded, and instantly a dozen hardy seamen were in the rigging, hurrying aloft to unfurl the broad canvas of our Baltimore built American Slaver. The sailors hung about the ropes, like so many black cats, now in the round-tops, now in the cross-trees, now on the yard-arms; all was bluster and activity. Soon the broad fore topsail, the royal and top gallant sail were spread to the breeze. Round went the heavy windlass, clank, clank went the fall-bit,—the anchors weighed,—jibs, mainsails, and topsails hauled to the wind, and the long, low, black slaver, with her cargo of human flesh, careened and moved forward to the sea.

Mr. Listwell stood on the shore, and watched the slaver till the last speck of her upper sails faded from sight, and announced the limit of human vision. "Farewell! farewell! brave and true man! God grant that brighter skies may smile upon your future than have yet looked down upon your thorny pathway."

Saying this to himself, our friend lost no time in completing his business, and in making his way homewards, gladly shaking off from his feet the dust of Old Virginia.

## PART IV

Oh, where's the slave so lowly
Condemn'd to chains unholy,
Who could he burst
His bonds at first
Would pine beneath them slowly?

*Moore*

——Know ye not
Who would be free, *themselves* must strike the blow.

*Childe Harold*

What a world of inconsistency, as well as of wickedness, is suggested by the smooth and gliding phrase, AMERICAN SLAVE TRADE; and how strange and perverse is that moral sentiment which loathes, execrates, and brands as piracy and as deserving of death the carrying away into captivity men, women, and children from the *African coast;* but which is neither shocked nor disturbed by a similar traffic, carried on with the same motives and purposes, and characterized by even *more* odious peculiarities on the coast of our MODEL REPUBLIC. We execrate and hang the wretch guilty of this crime on the coast of Guinea, while we respect and applaud the guilty participators in this murderous business on the enlightened shores of the Chesapeake. The inconsistency is so flagrant and glaring, that it would seem to cast a doubt on the doctrine of the innate moral sense of mankind.

Just two months after the sailing of the Virginia slave brig, which the reader has seen move off to sea so proudly with her human cargo for the New Orleans market, there chanced to meet, in the Marine Coffeehouse at Richmond, a company of *ocean birds,* when the following conversation, which throws some light on the subsequent history, not only of Madison Washington, but of the hundred and thirty human beings with whom we last saw him chained.

"I say, shipmate, you had rather rough weather on your late passage to Orleans?" said Jack Williams, a regular old salt, tauntingly, to a trim, compact, manly looking person, who proved to be the first mate of the slave brig in question.

"Foul play, as well as foul weather," replied the firmly knit personage, evidently but little inclined to enter upon a subject which terminated so ingloriously to the captain and officers of the American slaver.

"Well, betwixt you and me," said Williams, that whole affair on board of the Creole was miserably and disgracefully managed. Those black rascals got the upper hand of ye altogether; and, in my opinion, the whole disaster was the result of ignorance of the real character of *darkies* in general. With half a dozen *resolute* white men, (I say it not boastingly,) I could have had the rascals in irons in ten minutes, not because I'm so strong, but I know how to manage 'em. With my back against the *caboose,* I could, myself, have flogged a dozen of them; and had I been on board, by every monster of the deep, every black devil of 'em all would have had his neck stretched from the yard-arm. Ye made a mistake in yer manner of fighting 'em. All that is needed in dealing with a set of rebellious *darkies* , is to show that yer not afraid of 'em. For my own part, I would not honor a dozen niggers by pointing a gun at one of 'em,—a good stout whip, or a stiff rope's end, is better than all the guns at Old Point to quell a *nigger* insurrection. Why, sir, to take a gun to a *nigger* is the best way you can select to tell him you are afraid of him, and the best way of inviting his attack."

This speech made quite a sensation among the company, and a part of them indicated solicitude for the answer which might be made to it. Our first mate replied, "Mr. Williams, all that you've now said sounds very well *here* on shore, where, perhaps, you have studied negro character. I do not profess to understand the subject as well as yourself; but it strikes me, you apply the same rule in dissimilar cases. It is quite easy to talk of flogging niggers here on land, where you have the sympathy of the community, and the whole physical force of the government, State and national, at your command; and where, if a negro shall lift his hand against a white man, the whole community, with one accord, are ready to unite in shooting him down. I say, in such circumstances, it's easy to talk of flogging negroes and of negro cowardice; but, sir, I deny that the negro is, naturally, a coward, or that your theory of managing slaves will stand the test of *salt* water. It may do very well for an overseer, a contemptible hireling, to take advantage of fears already in existence, and which his presence has no power to inspire; to swagger about whip in hand, and discourse on the timidity and cowardice of negroes; for they have a smooth sea and a fair wind. It is one thing to manage a company of slaves on a Virginia plantation, and quite another thing to quell an insurrection on the lonely billows of the Atlantic, where every breeze speaks of courage and liberty. For the negro to act cowardly on shore, may be to act wisely; and I've some doubts whether *you,* Mr. Williams, would find it very convenient were you a slave in Algiers, to raise your hand against the bayonets of a whole government."

"By George, shipmate," said Williams, you're coming rather *too* near. Either I've fallen very low in your estimation, or your notions of negro courage have got up a button-hole too high. Now I more than ever wish I'd been on board of that luckless craft. I'd have given ye practical evidence of the truth of my theory. I don't doubt there's some difference in being at sea. But a nigger's a nigger, on sea or land; and is a coward, find him where you will; a drop of blood from one on 'em will skeer a hundred. A knock on the nose, or a kick on the shin, will tame the wildest *'darkey'* you can fetch me. I say again, and will stand by it, I could, with half a dozen good men, put the whole nineteen on 'em in irons, and have carried them safe to New Orleans too. Mind, I don't blame you, but I do say, and every gentleman here will bear me out in it, that the fault was somewhere, or them niggers would never have got off as they have done. For my part I feel ashamed to have the idea go abroad, that a ship load of slaves can't be safely taken from Richmond to New Orleans. I should like, merely to redeem the character of Virginia sailors, to take charge of a ship load on 'em to-morrow."

Williams went on in this strain, occasionally casting an imploring glance at the company for applause for his wit, and sympathy for his contempt of negro courage. He had, evidently, however, waked up the wrong passenger; for besides being in the right, his opponent carried that in his eye which marked him a man not to be trifled with.

"Well, sir," said the sturdy mate, "you can select your own method for distinguishing yourself;—the path of ambition in this direction is quite open to you in Virginia, and I've no doubt that you will be highly appreciated and compensated for all your valiant achievements in that line; but for myself, while I do not profess to be a giant, I have resolved never to set my foot on the deck of a slave ship, either as officer, or common sailor again; I have got enough of it."

"Indeed! indeed!" exclaimed Williams, derisively.

"Yes, *indeed,*" echoed the mate; "but don't misunderstand me. It is not the high value that I set upon my life that makes me say what I have said; yet I'm resolved never to endanger my life again in a cause which my conscience does not approve. I dare say *here* what many men *feel,* but *dare not speak,* that this whole slave-trading business is a disgrace and scandal to Old Virginia."

"Hold! hold on! shipmate," said Williams, "I hardly thought you'd have shown your colors so soon,—I'll be hanged if you're not as good an abolitionist as Garrison himself."

The mate now rose from his chair, manifesting some excitement. "What do you mean, sir," said he, in a commanding tone. *"That man does not live who shall offer me an insult with impunity."*

The effect of these words was marked; and the company clustered around. Williams, in an apologetic tone, said, "Shipmate! keep your temper. I mean't no insult. We all know that Tom Grant is no coward, and what I said about your being an abolitionist was simply this: you *might* have put down them black mutineers and murderers, but your conscience held you back."

"In that, too," said Grant, "you were mistaken. I did all that any man with equal strength and presence of mind could have done. The fact is, Mr. Williams, you underrate the courage as well as the skill of these negroes, and further, you do not seem to have been correctly informed about the case in hand at all."

"All I know about it is," said Williams," that on the ninth day after you left Richmond, a dozen or two of the niggers ye had on board, came on deck and took the ship from you;—had her steered into a British port, where, by the by, every woolly head of them went ashore and was free. Now I take this to be a discreditable piece of business, and one demanding explanation."

"There are a great many discreditable things in the world," said Grant. For a ship to go down under a calm sky is, upon the first flush of it, disgraceful either to sailors or caulkers. But when we learn, that by some mysterious disturbance in nature, the waters parted beneath, and swallowed the ship up, we lose our indignation and disgust in lamentation of the disaster, and in awe of the Power which controls the elements."

"Very true, very true," said Williams, "I should be very glad to have an explanation which would relieve the affair of its present discreditable features. I have desired to see you ever since you got home, and to learn from you a full statement of the facts in the case. To me the whole thing seems unaccountable. I cannot see how a dozen or two of ignorant negroes, not one of whom had ever been to sea before, and all of them were closely ironed between decks, should be able to get their fetters off, rush out of the hatchway in open daylight, kill two white men, the one the captain and the other their master, and then carry the ship into a British port, where every '*darkey*' of them was set free. There must have been great carelessness, or cowardice somewhere!"

The company which had listened in silence during most of this discussion, now became much excited. One said, I agree with Williams; and several said the thing looks black enough. After the temporary tumultous exclamations had subsided,—

"I see," said Grant, "how you regard this case, and how difficult it will be for me to render our ship's company blameless in your eyes. Nevertheless, I will state the fact precisely as they came under my own observation. Mr. Williams speaks of 'ignorant negroes,' and, as a general rule, they are ignorant; but had he been on board the *Creole* as I was, he would have seen cause to admit that there are exceptions to this general rule. The leader of the mutiny in question was just as shrewd a fellow as ever I met in my life, and was as well fitted to lead in a dangerous enterprise as any one white man in ten thousand. The name of this man, strange to say, (ominous of greatness,) was MADISON WASHINGTON. In the short time he had been on board, he had secured the confidence of every officer. The negroes fairly worshipped him. His manner and bearing were such, that no one could suspect him of a murderous purpose

The only feeling with which we regarded him was, that he was a powerful, good-disposed negro. He seldom spake to any one, and when he did speak, it was with the utmost propriety. His words were well chosen, and his pronunciation equal to that of any schoolmaster. It was a mystery to us *where* he got his knowledge of language; but as little was said to him, none of us knew the extent of his intelligence and ability till it was too late. It seems he brought three files with him on board, and must have gone to work upon his fetters the first night out; and he must have worked well at that; for one the day of the rising, he got the irons *off eighteen* besides himself.

"The attack began just about twilight in the evening. Apprehending a squall, I had commanded the second mate to order all hands on deck, to take in sail. A few minutes before this I had seen Madison's head above the hatchway, looking out upon the white-capped waves at the leeward. I think I never saw him look more good-natured. I stood just about midship, on the larboard side. The captain was pacing the quarter-deck on the starboard side, in company with Mr. Jameson, the owner of most of the slaves on board. Both were armed. I had just told the men to lay aloft, and was looking to see my orders obeyed, when I heard the discharge of a pistol on the starboard side; and turning suddenly around, the very deck seemed covered with fiends from the pit. The nineteen negroes were all on deck, with their broken fetters in their hands, rushing in all directions. I put my hand quickly in my pocket to draw out my jack-knife; but before I could draw it, I was knocked senseless to the deck. When I came to myself, (which I did in a few minutes, I suppose, for it was yet quite light,) there was not a white man on deck. The sailors were all aloft in the rigging, and dared not come down. Captain Clarke and Mr. Jameson, lay stretched on the quarter-deck,—both dying,—while Madison himself stood at the helm unhurt.

"I was completely weakened by the loss of blood, and had not recovered from the stunning blow which felled me to the deck; but it was a little too much for me, even in my prostrate condition, to see our good brig commanded by a *black murderer.* So I called out to the men to come down and take the ship, or die in the attempt. Suiting the action to the word, I started aft. You murderous villain, said I, to the imp at the helm, and rushed upon him to deal him a blow, when he pushed me back with his strong, black arm, as though I had been a boy of twelve. I looked around for the men. They were still in the rigging. Not one had come down. I started towards Madison again. The rascal now told me to stand back. 'Sir,' said he, 'your life is in my hands. I could have killed you a dozen times over during this last half hour, and could kill you now. You call me a *black murderer.* I am not a murderer. God is my witness that LIBERTY, not *malice,* is the motive for this night's work. I have done no more to those dead men yonder, than they would have done to me in like circumstances. We have struck for our freedom, and if a true man's heart be in you, you will honor us for the deed. We have done that which you applaud your fathers for doing, and if we are murderers, *so were they.*'

"I felt little disposition to reply to this impudent speech. By heaven, it disarmed me. The fellow loomed up before me. I forgot his blackness in the dignity of his manner, and the eloquence of his speech. It seemed as if the souls of both the great dead (whose names he bore) had entered him. To the sailors in the rigging he said: 'Men! the battle is over,—your captain is dead. I have complete command of this vessel. All resistance to my authority will be in vain. My men have won their liberty, with no other weapons but their own BROKEN FETTERS.

We are nineteen in number. We do not thirst for your blood, we demand only our rightful freedom. Do not flatter yourselves that I am ignorant of chart or compass. I know both. We are now only about sixty miles from Nassau. Come down, and do your duty. Land us in Nassau, and not a hair of your heads shall be hurt.'

"I shouted, *Stay where you are, men,*—when a sturdy black fellow ran at me with a handspike, and would have split my head open, but for the interference of Madison, who darted between me and the blow. 'I know what you are up to,' said the latter to me. 'You want to navigate this brig into a slave port, where you would have us all hanged; but you'll miss it; before this brig shall touch a slave-cursed shore while I am on board, I will myself put a match to the magazine, and blow her, and be blown with her, into a thousand fragments. Now I have saved your life twice within these last twenty minutes,—for, when you lay helpless on deck, my men were about to kill you. I held them in check. And if you now (seeing I am your friend and not your enemy) persist in your resistance to my authority, I give you fair warning, YOU SHALL DIE.'

"Saying this to me, he cast a glance into the rigging where the terror-stricken sailors were clinging, like so many frightened monkeys, and commanded them to come down, in a tone from which there was no appeal; for four men stood by with muskets in hand, ready at the word of command to shoot them down.

"I now became satisfied that resistance was out of the question; that my best policy was to put the brig into Nassau, and secure the assistance of the American consul at that port. I felt sure that the authorities would enable us to secure the murderers, and bring them to trial.

"By this time the apprehended squall had burst upon us. The wind howled furiously,—the ocean was white with foam, which, on account of the darkness, we could see only by the quick flashes of lightning that darted occasionally from the angry sky. All was alarm and confusion. Hideous cries came up from the slave women. Above the roaring billows a succession of heavy thunder rolled along, swelling the terrific din. Owing to the great darkness, and a sudden shift of the wind, we found ourselves in the trough of the sea. When shipping a heavy sea over the starboard bow, the bodies of the captain and Mr. Jameson were washed overboard. For awhile we had dearer interests to look after than slave property. A more savage thunder-gust never swept the ocean. Our brig rolled and creaked as if every bolt would be started, and every thread of oakum would be pressed out of the seams. To the pumps! to the pumps! I cried, but not a sailor would quit his grasp. Fortunately this squall soon passed over, or we must have been food for sharks.

"During all the storm, Madison stood firmly at the helm,—his keen eye fixed upon the binnacle. He was not indifferent to the dreadful hurricane; yet he met it with the equanimity of an old sailor. He was silent but not agitated. The first words he uttered after the storm had slightly subsided, were characteristic of the man. 'Mr. mate, you cannot write the bloody laws of slavery on those restless billows. The ocean, if not the land, is free.' I confess, gentlemen, I felt myself in the presence of a superior man; one who, had he been a white man, I would have followed willingly and gladly in any honorable enterprise. Our difference of color was the only ground for difference of action. It was not that his principles were wrong in the abstract; for they are the principles of 1776. But I could not bring myself to recognize their application to one whom I deemed my inferior.

"But to my story. What happened now is soon told.

Two hours after the frightful tempest had spent itself, we were plump at the wharf in Nassau. I sent two of our men immediately to our consul with a statement of facts, requesting his interference in our behalf. What he did, or whither he did anything, I don't know; but, by order of the authorities, a company of *black* soldiers came on board, for the purpose, as they said, of protecting the property. These impudent rascals, when I called on them to assist me in keeping the slaves on board, sheltered themselves adroitly under their instructions only to protect property,—and said they did not recognize *persons* as *property*. I told them that by the laws of Virginia and the laws of the United States, the slaves on board were as much property as the barrels of flour in the hold. At this the stupid blockheads showed their *ivory*, rolled up their white eyes in horror, as if the idea of putting men on a footing with merchandise were revolting to their humanity. When these instructions were understood among the negroes, it was impossible for us to keep them on board. They deliberately gathered up their baggage before our eyes, and, against our remonstrances, poured through the gangway,—formed themselves into a procession on the wharf,—bid farewell to all on board, and, uttering the wildest shouts of exultation, they marched, amidst the deafening cheers of a multitude of symphathizing spectators, under the triumphant leadership of their heroic chief and deliverer, MADISON WASHINGTON."

[Source: Julia Griffiths, ed., *Autographs for Freedom* (Boston: John P. Jewett, 1853), pp. 174-239.]

## *[Free Blacks Must Learn Trades]*

If blacks were to be self-supporting and free of charity as well as pity, Douglass urged that they learn mechanical trades to equip them to find work. Without such skills, economic dependence for blacks would result in another form of slavery as each wave of new immigrants took up jobs formerly held by blacks.

These are the obvious alternatives sternly presented to the free colored people of the United States. It is idle, yea even ruinous, to disguise the matter for a single hour longer; every day begins and ends with the impressive lesson that free negroes must learn trades, or die.

The old avocations, by which colored men obtained a livelihood, are rapidly, unceasingly and inevitably passing into other hands; every hour sees the black man elbowed out of employment by some newly arrived emigrant, whose hunger and whose color are thought to give him a better title to the place; and so we believe it will continue to be until the last prop is levelled beneath us.

As a black man, we say if we cannot stand up, let us fall down. We desire to be a man among men while we do live; and when we cannot, we wish to die. It is evident, painfully evident to every reflecting mind, that the means of living, for colored men, are becoming more and more precarious and limited. Employments and callings, formerly monopolized by us, are so no longer.

White men are becoming house-servants, cooks and stewards on vessels—at hotels.—They are becoming porters, stevedores, wood-sawyers, hod-carriers, brick-makers, white-washers and barbers, so that the blacks can scarcely find the means of subsistence—a few years ago, and a *white* barber would have been a curiosity—now their poles stand on every street. Formerly blacks were almost the exclusive coachmen in wealthy families: this is so no longer; white men are now employed, and for aught we see, they fill their servile station with an obsequiousness as profound as that of the blacks. The readiness and ease with which they adapt themselves to these conditions ought not to be lost sight of by the colored people. The meaning is very important, and we should learn it. We are taught our insecurity by it. Without the means of living, life is a curse, and leaves us at the mercy of the oppressor to become his debased slaves. Now, colored men, what do you mean to do, for you must do something? The American Colonization Society tells you to go to Liberia. Mr. Bibbs tells you to go to Canada. Others tell you to go to school. We tell you to go to work; and to work you must go or die. Men are not valued in this country, or in any country, for what they *are;* they are valued for what they can *do.* It is in vain that we talk about being men, if we do not the work of men. We must become valuable to society in other departments of industry than those servile ones from which we are rapidly being excluded. We must show that we can *do* as well as *be;* and to this end we must learn trades. When we can build as well as live in houses; when we can *make* as well as *wear* shoes; when we can produce as well as consume wheat, corn and rye—then we shall become valuable to society. Society is a hard-hearted affair.—With it the helpless may expect no higher dignity than that of paupers. The individual must lay society under obligation to him, or society will honor him only as a stranger and sojourner. *How* shall this be done? In this manner: use every means, strain every nerve to master some important merchanical art. At present, the facilities for doing this are few—institutions of learning are more readily opened to you than the work-shop; but the Lord helps them who will help themselves, and we have no doubt that new facilities will be presented as we press forward.

If the alternative were presented to us of learning a trade or of getting an education, we would learn the trade, for the reason, that with the trade we could get the education, while with the education we could not get the trade. What we, as a people, need most, is the means for our own elevation.—An educated colored man, in the United States, unless he has within him the heart of a hero, and is willing to engage in a lifelong battle for his rights, as a man, finds few inducements to remain in this country. He is isolated in the land of his birth—debarred by his color from congenial association with whites; he is equally cast out by the ignorance of the *blacks*. The remedy for this must comprehend the elevation of the masses; and this can only be done by putting the mechanic arts within the reach of colored men.

We have now stated pretty strongly the case of our colored countrymen; perhaps some will say, *too* strongly; but we know whereof we affirm.

In view of this state of things, we appeal to the abolitionists, What boss anti-slavery mechanic will take a black boy into his wheelwright's shop, his blacksmith's shop, his joiner's shop, his cabinet shop? Here is something *practical;* where are the whites and where are the blacks that will respond to it? Where are the anti-slavery milliners and seamstresses that will take colored girls and teach them trades, by which they can obtain an honorable living? The fact that we have made good cooks, good waiters, good barbers, and white-washers, induces the belief that we may excel in higher branches of industry. *One thing is certain: we must find new methods of obtaining a livelihood, for the old ones are failing us very fast.*

We, therefore, call upon the intelligent and thinking ones amongst us, to urge upon the colored people within their reach, in all seriousness, the duty and the necessity of giving their children useful and lucrative trades, by which they may commence the battle of life with weapons commensurate with the exigencies of the conflict.

[Source: *Frederick Douglass' Paper,* 4 March 1853.]

## *[Three Kinds of Abolitionists]*

Here Douglass sets out the differences he sees among three antislavery positions: that of the Republican party, the Garrisonian Abolitionists, and the Radical Abolitionists. After describing the limitations of the first two groups, he aligns himself with the Radical Abolitionists.

All men desire Liberty. They desire to possess this inalienable birthright themselves, if they are not concerned about others being the recipients of its countless blessings. They instinctively shrink from the idea of having their Intellectual, their Moral, and their Physical organism, subjugated to the entire control of Tyranny, clothed in the vesture of assumed superiority. This love of their own identity is inseparably connected with their desire and hope of immortality. And even those who attack the citadel of man's personality, and seek to reduce him to a thing, are jealous of any invasion of their own Rights, and will resist to the death any encroachment upon the sacred domain of their own personal liberty. They are Abolitionists, as they seek to abolish any system of Oppression *which has them* for its victims, even though they trample their own principles in the dust, when the Rights of others are invaded. This is neither just nor generous. No man should crave the possession of that which he assiduously endeavors to withhold from another.

Again, we maintain that no man has a Right to make any concession to Tyranny, which he would refuse to make if *he* were the victim.—He has no Right to make any compromise of contract in reference to the "Institution" of slavery, as it is falsely called, which he would be unwilling to make, were he, himself the slave. He should place himself, as it were, in the position of the slave, and advocate those principles and measures, which, judging from his stand-point, he would deem just and advisable.

Now, we hold that there is but one class of men and women in the land, who stand upon the slave's platform, and advocate the principles and measures which he would advocate, had he the opportunity. Abolitionism in this country is a sort of heterogeneous compound. It is composed, too, of certain elements, some of which are totally dissimilar. They have no affinity, in some respects, the one for the other; and the lack of homogeneousness must, in some way, be supplied, before a perfect fusion, or commingling of the elements can be effected.

We have the Free Soil, or Republican Party, as the representative of Principles and Measures which are themselves totally distinct, and diverse from those which are advocated with so much zeal and ability by those who rejoice in the cognomen of Garrison Abolitionists. Then we have the Radical Abolitionists, who profess to believe the Principles and Measures adverted to, unsound, unjust, impracticable, and, of course, wholly intenable.

What, then are the distinctive features of these respective organizations? Wherein do they differ? What do they propose to accomplish? Let us briefly examine them. This is the Age of Inquiry, of deep, sober, rational Investigation. All systems, and opinions, and creeds, and Institutions, which cannot withstand the ordeal of the most rigid Investigation, cannot, at this crisis, find a lodgment in the popular heart; they cannot receive the approving smiles of the popular conscience.

First, then we have the Free Soil, or Republican Party. This is a powerful Party, so far as numbers and influence is concerned, and is sweeping over the country with restless efficacy. What are *its* characteristics? The Principle which imparts vitality to the Republican organization is, simply, the *Non-Extension of Slavery.* Its motto is, "No Slavery Outside the Slave States." It proposes to restrict Slavery, and keep it within what is called its *constitutional limits.* It does not propose to interfere with Slavery where it already exists, but seeks to prevent the spread of the infectious malady. It virtually concedes to slaveholders, the constitutional right of plundering their helpless victims and plundering them as long as they are able, *provided they do so in a certain locality.* In a word, it proceeds upon the gratuitous assumption of the legality and constitutionality of Slavery, and, at the same time, seeks to relieve the Federal Government from all responsibility for its existence or continuance. It thunders in the ear of the Government, the declaration that "Slavery is Sectional; Liberty, National." Not one of its leading advocates, so far as we have any knowledge, has ever intimated a desire in public, to abolish Slavery, by Legislation; thus to strike off the fetters of the three millions and a half of men, women, and children, *who are the present victims of the insatiate rapacity of American Despotism.* To intimate such an intention would place them in advance of the party with which they are identified. They, indeed, hate Slavery, and affirm, that by surrounding the slave States with a girdle of Freedom, Slavery will eventually die, for lack of room and air in which to breathe. This, we believe, is a fair and impartial statement of the position of the Free Soil, or Republican Party. If we have erred in stating its true position, we have done so unintentionally, and stand ready to be corrected.

Secondly, we have another body of Anti-Slavery men in the country, who style themselves Garrison Abolitionists. These, too, are powerful, if not in numbers, in the array of talent, wealth, and energy, at their command.—

The motto of the Garrison party, is "no union with salveholders." They affirm the Constitution of the United States to be pro-Slavery in its character, and therefore denounce it, as "an agreement with Death and a covenant with Hell." They are opposed to *political action, for the Abolition of Slavery,* and refuse to vote for the officers of the Government, because of the alleged pro-Slavery character of the Constitution, by which it professes to be guided in its administration. Its disunion sentiments were thus distinctly stated at an annual meeting of the Pennsylvania Anti-Slavery Society, convened in the city of Philadelphia, Oct. 25th, '52:

"*Resolved.* That, independent of all questions as to the meaning of particular clauses of the Constitution, and whether it be admitted or denied that it contains certain guarantees for the benefit of slavery, the effort to establish a union between States that are slaveholding and States that are free must in the nature of things be abortive, since the legislation demanded by the former is diametrically opposed to that required by the latter; and therefore we reiterate the doctrine of the American Anti-Slavery Society, 'No Union with Slaveholders.'"

At the same meeting W. Lloyd Garrison thus stated the position of those who occupy the Platform of the American Anti-Slavery Society. Said he:

"The position of this Society upon the Constitution is well known. We hold that it contains certain wicked compromises of the rights of the Slave. It gives the Slaveholders a political representation for their slaves, thus bribing them to hold and multiply their human chattels. I cannot swear to give such power to Slaveholders. Does our Declaration of Sentiment require me to do it? On the contrary, the principles and spirit forbid such an oath.—So of the obligation to put down a slave insurrection and return fugitive slaves. To be faithful to the principles of that Declaration, I must stand outside of the government organized upon pledges to do such acts. So if I find that the church of which I am a member, is pro-slavery, as I recognize its Christian character by that membership, I must stand outside the church."

So much then, for the position of the Garrison Abolitionists. They are *in* the country, but at the same time, they profess to stand outside of the Government. But this is not all. The Free Soil or Republican Party says, "Let *Slavery* take care of its own interests." The Garrison Party, through one of the most eloquent exponents of its theory, virtually tells the Slave to take care of *himself*. This may seem to be an unjust and ungenerous assertion. But what says one of the most able advocates of the disunion movement. Hear him:

> "All the slave asks of us, is to stand out of the way, withdraw our pledge to keep the peace on the plantation; withdraw our pledge to return him, withdraw that representation which the Constitution gives in proportion to the number of slaves, and without any agitation here, without any individual virtue, which the times have eaten out of us, God will vindicate the oppressed, by the laws of justice which he has founded, Trample under foot your own unjust pledges, break in pieces your compact with hell by which you become the abettors of oppression. Stand alone, and let no cement of the Union bind the slave, and he will right himself."

The idea of the slave righting himself, presupposes his ability to do so, unaided by Northern interference. O no! the slave *cannot* "right himself" any more than an infant can grapple with a giant. He must receive the effective aid of those who, at the North, are, despite their denial, the members of the confederacy, and, as such, "verily guilty concerning their brother."

But we have another Anti-Slavery or Abolition Party, the Liberty Party, or Radical Abolitionists. Who are they? What do they propose to effect?

They deny that Slavery can be legalized, and, therefore, affirm that all slaveholding enactments are illegal. They also deny that the Constitution of the United States is a pro-slavery instrument, and affirm that it is, legitimately, susceptible only, of an Anti-Slavery interpretation. They regard it as having been established for the express purpose of establishing justice, &c., and of securing the blessings of Liberty to all the people of the Confederacy, not merely one class of People, but the whole, *we*, the people, as well as *you*, or *they*, the People. Radical Abolitionism asserts, that if the various provisions of the Constitution, (right of trial by Jury, *habeas corpus*, and others,) were faithfully executed, it would instantly free every Slave in the land. All they ask, is, that the present Constitution, imperfect as it is, shall receive a righteous, a correct interpretation, that its manifold provisions be executed, and Slavery will find no refuge under it.

Radical Abolitionism lays the axe at the root of the tree. It proposes not only to hew down the Upas Tree, but to tear it up root and branch. It believes that the Federal Government has the power to abolish Slavery everywhere in the United States, and that such is the duty of the Government. They are opposed to a dissolution of the Union, *unless a Southern Confederacy could be organized in which there would be no abolitionists, white or black, and a Northern Confederacy, in which there would be no apologists for Slavery.* By withdrawing from the Slave States, we withdraw from nearly four millions of Abolitionists, black and white. And on the other hand, we retain in our midst some of the most influential supporters of the traffic in human flesh. These are some of the leading views entertained by Radical Abolitionists. We believe them to be just, tenable, and practicable; and thus believing, can conscientiously give our adhesion and our support to no other.—Of their ultimate triumph, we have not the shadow of a doubt. We know they are regarded as impracticable. But those who assume their impracticability, pronounced, a few years ago, the same judgment upon the views they now cherish so ardently, and promulgated with so much zeal and ability. They even deprecated the idea of any agitation, whatever, upon the subject. And we do not despair of yet congratulating them upon their admission into the ranks of Radical Abolitionists. We shall, therefore, contribute our mite toward effecting this desirable consummation.

[Source: *Frederick Douglass' Paper,* 16 November 1855.]

## *[Resolutions Against Capital Punishment]*

Douglass' interest in reform led him to oppose capital punishment. The following resolutions were written on behalf of a convicted murderer whose death sentence Douglass and others sought to have changed to life in prison.

Resolved, That life is the great primary and most precious and comprehensive of all human rights—that whether it be coupled with virtue, honor, or happiness, or with sin, disgrace and misery, the continued possession of it is rightfully not a matter of volition; that it is neither deliberately nor voluntarily assumed, nor to be deliberately or voluntarily destroyed, either by individuals separately, or combined in what is called Government; that it is a right derived solely and directly from God—the source of all goodness and the centre of all authority—and is most manifestly designed by Him to be held, esteemed, and reverenced among men as the most sacred, solemn and inviolable of all his gifts to man.

Resolved, That the love of man as manifested in his actions to his fellows, whether in his public or private relations, has ever been the surest test of the presence of God in the soul; that the degree in which the sacredness of human life has been exemplified in all ages of the world, has been the truest index of the measure of human progress; that in proportion as the tide of barbarism has receded, a higher regard has been manifested for the God-given right to life, its inviolability has been strengthened in proportion to the development of the intellect and moral sentiments, and that conscience, reason and revelation unite their testimony against the continuance of a custom, barbarous in its origin, antichristian in its continuance, vindictive in its character, and demoralizing in its tendencies.

Resolved, That any settled custom, precept, example or law, the observance of which necessarily tends to cheapen human life, or in any measure serves to diminish and weaken man's respect for it, is a custom, precept, example and law utterly inconsistent with the law of eternal goodness written on the constitution of man by his Maker, and is diametrically opposed to the safety, welfare and happiness of mankind; and that however ancient and honorable such laws and customs may be in the eyes of prejudice, superstition and bigotry, they ought to be discountenanced, abolished, and supplanted by a higher civilization and a holier and more merciful Christianity.

Resolved, That in the opinion of this meeting, when a criminal is firmly secured in the iron grasp of the government, and on that account can no longer endanger the peace and safety of society; that when he is wasted and emaciated by heavy chains and horrid thoughts, and long confinement in a gloomy cell—when, as is often the case, he is completely transformed, both in temper and spirit—the execution of the death penalty on such an one is an act of cold blooded and barbarous enormity, and is as cowardly as it is cruel, and that instead of repressing and preventing the horrid crime of murder, it really serves by shocking and blunting the finer and better feelings of human nature, to undermine respect for human life, and leads directly to the perpetration of the crime which it would extinguish.

Resolved, That the time to advance opinions and principles is when those opinions and principles are upon trial, and threatened with outrage; and that while we have respectfully remained silent till the ends of justice have been served in fixing the guilt of the criminal, we now come in the sacred office of humanity and benevolence, to appeal for mercy at the hands of his Excellency, Governor King, on behalf of young Ira Stout, and to ask that his punishment shall be commuted from being capitally executed to imprisonment for life.

Resolved, That punishment as such, is a form of revenge, wreaking upon the criminal the pain he has inflicted on another, wrong in principle and pernicious in practice; arises out of the lowest propensities of human nature, and is opposed to the highest civilization; that it has no sanction in the spirit and teachings of Christ, which everywhere abound in loving kindness and forgiveness.

Resolved, That rather than visit the crime upon the head of the criminal, thus descending to his level, we ought to place him in a position to develop his higher nature; and instead of descending to a spirit of revenge, and degrading ourselves on the one hand, and the criminal on the other, we should urge a thorough reform in our criminal laws—basing them on the truly Christian principle of love and good will towards man, and to reject forever the cold blooded and barbarous principle of retaliation.

Resolved, That a copy of the foregoing resolutions, and the proceedings of this meeting, be transmitted to his Excellency, Governor King, as an expression of the sense of this meeting, and that the same be subscribed by the Chairman and Secretary thereof.

Frederick Douglass, Chairman.
J. Bower, Secretary.

[Source: *Liberator*, 22 October 1858.]

## *[Contradictions in American Civilization]*

Like his contemporaries, Douglass appreciated the progress, newness, and hope that America represented in the nineteenth century—but he also perceived that the country's moral development did not match its material achievements.

The pride of the American people, the thing which they most frequently cite as a proof of their superiority over other nations, is the high degree of civilization which they have attained—a civilization as rapid in its progress as it is peculiar in its features, and strikingly different from that of other countries. It may be truly called *American civilization.* If a stranger should look at some of our largest cities, the centers of commerce, business life, and industry of all description, and should be told, as he might be by persons very far from claiming the honor of being counted among 'the oldest inhabitants,' that they distinctly remember the time when the place so full of life and bustle was covered with the primeval forests, he could hardly credit the story, and would be inclined to think that they had been called into existence by the command of some magician; but upon looking deeper into the machinery and the network of this truly astonishing spectacle, he would perceive that America had availed herself of the unparalleled inventive development of the nineteenth century, doing the work in a day by two men which forty years ago would have required a week or a month to be performed by twenty men. By availing herself of the capital of other nations, she has surpassed all other nations in the rapid increase of her railroads.—With foreign capital, foreign skill, and the Irish laborer, she has been able to reduce to cultivation enormous tracts of land, to level the forest, to remove the rocks, to tunnel mountains, to span the broadest and deepest chasms, and overcome ten thousand other difficulties in rendering her borders accessible, each to all, and all to each. The contact into which men are brought by those means of communication, is one of the most powerful promoters of general and uniform culture; and in vain would one look here for the isolated, secluded places which a traveler will frequently meet with even in the middle of the most cultivated countries of Europe, where a small population is found entirely isolated, cut off from the rest of the world, speaking their own peculiar dialect, preserving their own manners, and perpetuating a style of dress of unknown origin, forming a little world by themselves, whose frontiers they hardly ever cross, and whose mental horizon does not reach farther than the extent of the acres they cultivate. Here, on the contrary, everywhere, in the middle of deserts, on nearly inaccessible mountains we hear our own language almost uncorruptedly spoken, and meet with people hardly different from ourselves in manners, notions and knowledge. Even foreigners soon show the influence of that general leveling civilization. The clumsy appearance, the awkward and queer behavior of the German and Irish peasant, are soon modified and made to give way to the force of American manners, and to take upon them an American appearance. The miserable clay huts, sometimes without chimney or windows, in which they may be found in their native countries, are supplanted by snug frame houses and shanties like those of the American farmer. But it is not only in respect to the material acquisitions that the Americans claim the front rank in civilization, for while they generously admit that in the fine arts they cannot yet compete with the old world, they do not forget to claim superior excellence over the nations of Europe in respect to social and political institutions, as well as in almost all branches of knowledge and science. It is their pride that owing to the system of public schools, there are hardly any Americans found within the free States who do not know how to read and to write.

Now, it must be submitted that if civilization naturally tends to improve the material and intellectual as well as the moral state of a nation, it would seem as if the Americans really had excellent reasons for claiming, as they do, to be the first nation on the face of the earth. Unfortunately, however, for this claim, American civilization abounds in strange and puzzling contradictions. It is true we have unequalled means of communication, and may fly with almost the speed of an eagle from the shores of the Atlantic to those of the Pacific, but it is also true that we do it at the peril of our lives. One of the first features which mark the distinction between a civilized, and a rude nation, is the value attached to human life, and the protection given it by the former, while the bold risking of it, the cold braving of death, is considered one of the chief virtues among savage tribes. Respect for human life, and vigilant protection of it, is a feature of civilization sadly absent in this counry. In slow, conservative Europe, by railroad or by steamer, a journey is not thought much more of as being dangerous than a walk on a promenade. When in the course of several years an accident happens by which there is a loss of life, the whole country is seized with horror and consternation; while here their frequency is so great as to project one over another, and it is with difficulty in speaking of the last accident not to confound it with some other that just occurred. The same insecurity is found concerning the protection of health. All sorts of quackery run with a loose rein here. In Europe, the government provides for the people in this respect by not allowing any physician to practice unless he has undergone the strictest examination; but such restraint would not agree with the principle of liberty peculiar to this Republic. Any quack, any runaway barber or apothecary's clerk may cure, kill or poison as he pleases. No apothecary here, as in Romeo and Juliet, hesitates to sell poison. What was penal in this respect even before Shakespeare wrote, is now free and unrestricted.

This peculiarly American carelessness in the protection of life appears still more strikingly in the almost undisturbed freedom allowed to Rowdyism. In fact, Rowdyism is itself a plant of genuine American growth; for however wild, coarse and rude the mob may be in other countries, they do stand in fear of the law. Outbreaks of such brutality and ferocity as that witnessed lately in Baltimore, when a gang of those outcasts of humanity wantonly, and without the slightest provocation, attacked a whole party of unoffending and peaceful passengers of a steamer, would be nearly impossible anywhere in Europe. Even in poor, uncultivated Turkey, such a thing could not happen; and it may be doubted if such an outrage finds its equals in the darkest times of the Middle Ages. Here, however, such outrages are by no means exceptions.—It is but a few months since a similar occurrence took place within sight of New York City, on Staten Island ferry, where an unoffending man was suddenly attacked and beaten by a group of rowdies, without any attempt being made by the bystanders or the officers of the boat to interfere or arrest the ruffians. It is not a year yet since a citizen of Baltimore was shot on the threshold of his house, and not two years since a colored man was shot for mere sport in New York. And now the papers are discussing an outrage perpetrated at Hartford on the reception of Gov. Seymour, which is an exhibition of the superlative contempt for human life in America, even in the best parts of it. Here the perpetrator of the murder was not a rowdy by profession, but a genuine citizen, a member of the armed force for the maintenance of law and order, yet he deliberately kills a citizen to make way for the carriage of another fellow-citizen! Has the reign of King Bomba an outrage more savage to boast of? But even this fades into nothingness compared with the numberless instances of lynch law, tarring and feathering, so characteristic of American civilization, and which are pointed to by the conservative classes in monarchical Europe as the natural and inevitable accompaniments of popular sovereignty.

The fact that such outrages and crimes are almost always committed by the outcasts of humanity, and are generally condemned and denounced by the higher and better classes of society, does not make them less chargeable to American civilization; for when we compare them with other enormities, the chief distinction is, that the one class is perpetrated in the name and under the sanction of law, and the other is not. And shocking and brutal as are the first, the latter are more pernicious in their consequences, since they corrupt by example the whole body of society. It was the wealth and respectability of our country which formerly mobbed the Abolitionists, which burned Pennsylvania Hall, which passed the Fugitive Slave Law, which gave us the Nebraska Bill, and which gave us the Dred Scott decision, dooming a whole race to insult, outrage and outlawry. Where else under the whole heavens can be found States solemnly passing laws compelling a part of their people to choose between enslavement or banishment? Where but in America can be found in the nineteenth century a church built up out of the proceeds of the sale of human flesh? Wnere but in America are men excluded from public halls, degraded in churches, insulted on the side-walk, proscribed in theatres, kicked out of omnibuses, dragged from the cars, hooted at in the street, denied admission to schools and colleges, for no better reason than that such persons differ in complexion from the majority?

All these facts certainly ought not to shake our faith in civilization, whose wholesome and ennobling effects are known by the examples of other countries; but certainly they do demonstrate that the American people have yet attained only the outside, the mere surface of civilization and refinement; that while boasting to be first, they are little more than last in the true elements of high civilization; that in fact every phase of it, aside from mere material improvement, is still in its infancy. Part of this defect may be properly ascribed to the astonishing rapidity of its growth. Everywhere else, civilization was the result of an internal process, slow in its progress, taking deep roots, modifying, shaping and governing life in all its ramifications. Here it came like a whirlwind, sweeping over the land unequally, leveling mountains, cutting down forests, covering all that it touches with an outside polish, without the power to penetrate under the surface. A sort of sham civilization, which resembled the savages of whom Humboldt tells, who painted themselves coats, pants and vests on their bare skins, that they might appear in European style.

[Source: *Douglass' Monthly,* October 1859.]

## *[Lincoln's New Presidency]*

Only days before Lincoln's inauguration, Douglass expressed cautious optimism that the new president would uphold the principles of liberty while attempting to preserve the Union. Douglass was keenly aware that Lincoln's character would be severely tested in Washington, and he hoped, though he was not certain, that Lincoln would avoid being compromised.

Of one satisfaction, one ray of hope amid the darkness of the passing hour, and the reign of doubt and distraction, we may now safely begin to assure ourselves. Before we can again speak to our respected readers through this channel, the long desired 4th of March will have come, Lincoln will be inaugurated at Washington and his policy declared. Whatever that policy may be towards the seceded and confederated States; whatever it may be towards Slavery, the ruling cause of our nation's troubles, it will at least be a great relief to know it, to rejoice in and defend it, if right, and to make war upon it if wrong. To know what it is, is now the main thing. If he is going to abandon the principles upon which he was elected, compliment the South for being wrong, and censure himself and friends for being right, court treason and curse loyalty, desert his friends and cleave to his enemies, turn his back on the cause of Freedom and give new guarantees to the system of Slavery—whatever policy, whether of peace or war, or neither, it will be a vast gain at least to know what it is. Much of the present trouble is owing to the doubt and suspense caused by the shuffling, do-nothing policy of Mr. Buchanan.—No man has been able to tell an hour before hand what to expect from that source. However well disposed he may have been, the slaveholding thieves and traitors about him have had him under their thumb from the beginning unti now. Every man who wishes well to the country will rejoice at his outgoing, and feel that though he leaves the body politic weakened, and the nation's Constitution shattered, his out going, like the subsidence of some pestilence walking in darkness, is a cause for devout thanksgiving. A month longer in power, and perhaps, the epitaph of the American Republic might, if it may not now, be written, and its death consigned to the mouldy tombs of once great, but now extinct, nations.

While not at all too confident of the incorruptible purity of the new President, (for we remember the atmosphere of Washington, and the subtle devices of the enemies of Liberty, among whom he has now gone,) still we hope something from him. His stately silence during these last tumultuous and stormy three months, his stern refusal thus far to commit himself to any of the much advocated schemes of compromise, his refusal to have concessions extorted from him under the terror instituted by thievish conspirators and traitors, the cool and circumspect character of his replies to the various speeches, some delicate, appropriate, and sensible, and some rudely curious and prying, made to him during his circuitous route to Washington, the modesty with which he has pushed aside the various compliments bestowed upon him, all prove that he has not won deceitfully the title of Honest Old Abe. True, indeed, he has made no immoderate promises to the cause of freedom. His party has made none. But what were small in Chicago, will be found large at Washington, and what were moderate in the canvass, have become much augmented by the frowning difficulties since flung in the way of their accomplishment by the movement for disunion. It was a small thing six months ago to say, as the Republican party did say, that the Union shall be preserved, but events have now transpired, which make this a very solemn matter to reduce to practice. Most things are easier said than done, and this thing belongs to the general rule. That declaration in the Chicago platform implied that those who uttered it, believed that this Government possesses ample power for its own preservation, and that those powers should be in their hands, faithfully wielded for that purpose. This, then, is the first question: Will Mr. Lincoln boldly grapple with the monster of Disunion, and bring down his proud looks?

Will he call upon the haughty slave masters, who have risen in arms, to break up the Government, to lay down those arms, and return to loyalty, or meet the doom of traitors and rebels? He must do this, or do worse.—He must do this, or consent to be the despised representative of a defied and humbled Government. He must do this, or own that party platforms are the merest devices of scheming politicians to cheat the people, and to enable them to crawl up to place and power. He must do this, or compromise the fundamental principle upon which he was elected, to wit, the right and duty of Congress to prohibit the farther extension of Slavery. Will he compromise? Time and events will soon answer this question. For the present, there is much reason to believe that he will not consent to any compromise which will violate the principle upon which he was elected; and since none which does not utterly trample upon that principle can be accepted by the South, we have a double assurance that there will be no compromise, and that the contest must now be decided, and decided forever, which of the two, Freedom or Slavery, shall give law to this Republic. Let the conflict come, and

God speed the Right, must be the wish of every true-hearted American, as well as of that of an onlooking world.

[Source: *Douglass' Monthly,* March 1861.]

## *[What Should Be Done with Emancipated Slaves?]*

Having raised the question of what should be done with slaves if they are emancipated, Douglass takes this much discussed issue and dismisses it as an impertinence. Blacks would determine their own lives and freely endure the trials of liberation.

It is curious to observe, at this juncture, when the existence of slavery is threatened by an aroused nation, when national necessity is combining with an enlightened sense of justice to put away the huge abomination forever, that the enemies of human liberty are resorting to all the old and ten thousand times refuted objections to emancipation with which they confronted the abolition movement twenty-five years ago. Like the one stated above, these pro-slavery objections have their power mainly in the slavery-engendered prejudice, which every where pervades the country. Like all other great transgressions of the law of eternal rectitude, slavery thus produces an element in the popular and depraved moral sentiment favorable to its own existence. These objections are often urged with a show of sincere solicitude for the welfare of the slaves themselves. It is said, what will you do with them? they can't take care of themselves; they would all come to the North; they would not work; they would become a burden upon the State, and a blot upon society; they'd cut their masters' throats; they would cheapen labor, and crowd out the poor white laborer from employment; their former masters would not employ them, and they would necessarily become vagrants, paupers and criminals, over-running all our alms houses, jails and prisons. The laboring classes among the whites would come in bitter conflict with them in all the avenues of labor, and regarding them as occupying places and filling positions which should be occupied and filled by white men; a fierce war of races would be the inevitable consequence, and the black race would, of course, (being the weaker,) be exterminated. In view of this frightful, though happily somewhat contradictory picture, the question is asked, and pressed with a great show of earnestness at this momentous crisis of our nation's history, What shall be done with the four million slaves if they are emancipated?

This question has been answered, and can be answered in many ways. Primarily, it is a question less for man than for God—less for human intellect than for the laws of nature to solve. It assumes that nature has erred; that the law of liberty is a mistake; that freedom, though a natural want of the human soul, can only be enjoyed at the expense of human welfare, and that men are better off in slavery than they would or could be in freedom; that slavery is the natural order of human relations, and that liberty is an experiment. What shall be done with them?

Our answer is, do nothing with them; mind your business, and let them mind theirs. Your *doing* with them is their greatest misfortune. They have been undone by your doings, and all they now ask, and really have need of at your hands, is just to let them alone. They suffer by every interference, and succeed best by being let alone. The negro should have been let alone in Africa—let alone when the pirates and robbers offered him for sale in our Christian slave markets—(more cruel and inhuman than the Mohammedan slave markets)—let alone by courts, judges, politicians, legislators and slave-drivers—let alone altogether, and assured that they were thus to be let alone forever, and that they must now make their own way in the world, just the same as any and every other variety of the human family. As colored men, we only ask to be allowed to *do* with ourselves, subject only to the same great laws for the welfare of human society which apply to other men, Jews, Gentiles, Barbarian, Sythian. Let us stand upon our own legs, work with our own hands, and eat bread in the sweat of our own brows. When you, our white fellow-countrymen, have attempted to do anything for us, it has generally been to deprive us of some right, power or privilege which you yourself would die before you would submit to have taken from you. When the planters of the West Indies used to attempt to puzzle the pure-minded Wilberforce with the question, How shall we get rid of slavery? his simple answer was, "quit stealing." In like manner, we answer those who are perpetually puzzling their brains with questions as to what shall be done with the negro, "let him alone and mind your own business." If you see him plowing in the open field, leveling the forest, at work with a spade, a rake, a hoe, a pick-axe, or a bill—let him alone; he has a right to work. If you see him on his way to school, with spelling book, geography and arithmetic in his hands—let him alone. Don't shut the door in his face, nor bolt your gates against him; he has a right to learn—let him alone. Don't pass laws to degrade him. If he has a ballot in his hand, and is on his way to the ballot-box to deposit his vote for the man whom he thinks will most justly and wisely administer the Government which has the power of life and death over him, as well as others—let him *alone;* his right of choice as much deserves respect and protection as your own. If you see him on his way to the church, exercising religious liberty in accordance with this or that religious persuasion—let him alone.—Don't meddle with him, nor trouble yourselves with any questions as to what shall be done with him.

The great majority of human duties are of this negative character. If men were born in need of crutches, instead of having legs, the fact would be otherwise. We should then be in need of help, and would require outside aid; but according to the wiser and better arrangement of nature, our duty is done better by not hindering than by helping our fellow-men; or, in other words, the best way to help them is just to let them help themselves.

We would not for one moment check the outgrowth of any benevolent concern for the future welfare of the colored race in America or elsewhere; but in the name of reason and religion, we earnestly plead for justice before all else. Benevolence with justice is harmonious and beautiful; but benevolence without justice is a mockery. Let the American people, who have thus far only kept the colored race staggering between partial philanthropy and cruel force, be induced to try what virtue there is in justice. First pure, then peaceable—first just, then generous.—The sum of the black man's misfortunes and calamities are just here: He is everywhere treated as an exception to all the general rules which should operate in the relations of other men. He is literally scourged beyond the beneficent range of truth and justice.—With all the purifying and liberalizing power of the Christian religion, teaching, as it does, meekness, gentleness, brotherly kindness, those who profess it have not yet even approached the position of treating the black man as an equal man and a brother. The few who have thus far risen to this requirement, both of reason and religion, are stigmatized as fanatics and enthusiasts.

What shall be done with the negro if emancipated?

Deal justly with him. He is a human being, capable of judging between good and evil, right and wrong, liberty and slavery, and is as much a subject of law as any other man; therefore, deal justly with him. He is, like other men, sensible of the motives of reward and punishment. Give him wages for his work, and let hunger pinch him if he don't work. He knows the difference between fullness and famine, plenty and scarcity. "But will he work?" Why should he not? He is used to it. His hands are already hardened by toil, and he has no dreams of ever getting a living by any other means than by hard work. But would you turn them all loose? Certainly! We are no better than our Creator. He has turned them loose, and why should not we?

But would you let them all stay here?—Why not? What better is *here* than *there?* Will they occupy more room as freemen than as slaves? Is the presence of a black freeman less agreeable than that of a black slave? Is an object of our injustice and cruelty a more ungrateful sight than one of your justice and benevolence? You have borne the one more than two hundred years—can't you bear the other long enough to try the experiment? "But would it be safe?" No good reason can be given why it would not be. There is much more reason for aprehension from slavery than from freedom. Slavery provokes and justifies incendiarism, murder, robbery, assassination, and all manner of violence. —But why not let them go off by themselves? That is a matter we would leave exclusively to themselves. Besides, when you, the American people, shall once do justice to the enslaved colored people, you will not want to get rid of them. Take away the motive which slavery supplies for getting rid of the free black people of the South, and there is not a single State, from Maryland to Texas, which would desire to be rid of its black people. Even with the obvious disadvantage to slavery, which such contact is, there is scarcely a slave State which could be carried for the unqualified expulsion of the free colored people. Efforts at such expulsion have been made in Maryland, Virginia and South Carolina, and all have failed, just because the black man as a freeman is a useful member of society. To drive him away, and thus deprive the South of his labor, would be as absurd and monstrous as for a man to cut off his right arm, the better to enable himself to work.

There is one cheering aspect of this revival of the old and threadbare objections to emancipation—it implies at least the presence of danger to the slave system. When slavery was assailed twenty-five years ago, the whole land took the alarm, and every species of argument and subterfuge was resorted to by the defenders of slavery. The mental activity was amazing; all sorts of excuses, political, economical, social, theological and ethnological, were coined into barricades against the advancing march of anti-slavery sentiment. The same activity now shows itself, but has added nothing new to the argument for slavery or against emancipation.—When the accursed slave system shall once be abolished, and the negro, long cast out from the human family, and governed like a beast of burden, shall be gathered under the divine government of justice, liberty and humanity, men will be ashamed to remember that they were ever deluded by the flimsy nonsense which they have allowed themselves to urge against the freedom of the long enslaved millions of our land. That day is not far off.

*"O hasten it in mercy, gracious Heaven!"*

[Source: *Douglass' Monthly,* Januarv 1862.]

## *[The Progress of Blacks Twenty Years after Emancipation]*

Surveying the progress made by blacks since emancipation, Douglass describes advances in education, morality, religion, and physical well-being. For his *Harper's* readers, "a generation to whom slavery is little more than a name, and who have no adequate idea of what that name covered," Douglass places this progress in the context of the oppression blacks suffered before and after emancipation. Characteristically, he seeks to educate his readers about the actual conditions of blacks in America.

Whether the lately emancipated slaves in the Southern States have made any sensible degree of progress since they obtained their freedom is a question often put to me in a tone of doubt and denial. Another question, equally pertinent, and even more momentous . . . is this: Have the recent slave-holders made any sensible degree of progress in civilization since the emancipation of their slaves? Are they more industrious, honest, and humane than when they bought, sold, and flogged their fellowmen to toil for them without wages? These two questions, like the two sides of a horse, should go together, since they are largely dependent upon each other. Plainly enough the recent bondsmen can make little progress without the consent and co-operation of the ruling class among whom they live, and who own the land upon which they live. Nobody seems to doubt the progress of the masters, but everybody is curious to know how the freedmen are getting along.

Well, it is not for me to speak for the late slave-holders. They have never been in want of defenders. It is mine, by your leave and magnanimity, to speak for the class less favored. The answer to the question now put to them is of vital importance. If it shall be found that the freedmen are progressive and improving, that they only need time, patience, and a fair chance in the race of life to become useful citizens, making the nation prosperous in peace and powerful in war, there is, I believe, justice and generosity enough in the American people to supply the needed conditions of success. If, on the other hand, they are found to be non-progressive, worse masters to themselves than their old masters were to them, that liberty neither improves their character nor condition, they are sure to be treated in the end as cumberers of the ground, and will in due season perish from the earth. Civilization is all love and tenderness toward whatever accords and co-operates with it, but implacable, cruel, and remorseless to all obstacles. It spares neither forest, mountain, nor ocean, and it will not spare Indian, Mongolian, or Ethiopian. All must go along with it, or be crushed beneath its swift-flying wheels.

Before answering *pro* or *con* concerning the progress of the freedmen, candid men will see the justice of another inquiry, namely, what these people were before they were emancipated, under what conditions they were emancipated, and what have been the means of improvement within their reach since they were emancipated? All will admit that it would be manifestly and grossly unfair to judge the freedmen without taking their antecedents into account. They should be measured, not from the height yet to be attained, but from the depths from which they have come.

My relation to these people does not make me close my eyes against facts favorable or unfavorable to them. I know no race in my regard but the human race. The same feeling that led me to risk my life to save that of a white boy in my boyhood made me espouse the cause of the slave as soon as I was able to think.

The question asked at the beginning of this article includes mental, moral, and material improvement. What the American people want to know, and have a right to know, is whether the lately enslaved lead better lives and have made for themselves more comfortable conditions of existence than slavery—whether during these twenty years they have advanced, stood still, or retrograded.

Let us first compare their mental condition of twenty years ago with what it is at present. Prior to emancipation the colored intellect of the South made no visible sign—and could make no sign—of life or power. It was suppressed and shrouded in darkness. Letters were unknown. The law made fine and imprisonment the penalty for teaching one of these able children to read. So far down were they in the scale of intelligence that they were deemed by many incapable of mastering the rudiments of an English education. Even in religion nothing more than oral instruction was allowed them. "Servants, obey your masters, and be contented with your lot," was the most they got of this, but of this they got abundance, both by arguments from the pulpit on Sunday and by the rhetoric of the lash in the field on Monday. In those days a colored man who could read was a curiosity, and was generally set down in the estimation of the white people as a dangerous character. It would be easy to enlarge upon this mental midnight darkness, but I will leave something to the reflection of the intelligent reader.

I affirm that in nothing have these illiterate and

benighted people made more progress than in the acquisition of knowledge. There are now in the Southern States, according to statistics in the Bureau of Education at Washington, between two and three hundred thousand colored children attending schools during some portion of the year. Of course this is but a small proportion of the children there of school age, and for whom there is no provision. The amount of illiteracy is therefore still great and deplorable. The indisposition inherited from slavery to allow the States to be taxed for the education of the laboring classes is still strong, and the general government, which had no hesitation in crossing State lines to catch slaves, has thus far too much respect for the sovereign dignity of the States to cross their lines to secure civil rights or education to its citizens.

It may be adduced as a fair argument that the freed people have made some progress in the matter of education, that now nobody can be found to deny their capacity for education. If any such could be found, they would only need to visit the public schools here in Washington, and witness the qualifications of the colored teachers and the aptitude of the colored pupils to have their doubts and denials made ridiculous. Colored children, to the credit of the statesmen of twenty years ago, have commodious school-houses, competent teachers, and are pursuing the same course of study that white children pursue, and with almost equal success.

With respect to the moral progress of the lately enslaved class I am sorry to speak in a somewhat lower tone. But the same rule of judgment should be applied here as elsewhere. They are in this respect, as well as others, the legitimate results of their antecedents. The sense of right and the voice of conscience had little chance of cultivation in the relation of master and slave. Conduct in that relation was guided by force and fear.

Mutual interest and common welfare were excluded from that relation. Its corner-stone was composed of the blood-cemented fragments of the moral constitution of human nature. Each party to it found himself impelled to do that which was not to the advantage of the other. They were mutual enemies on the same territory, and in daily unfriendly contact. In his notes on Virginia Mr. Jefferson says, "The whole commerce between master and slave is a perpetual exercise of the most boisterous passions, the most unlimited despotism on the one part, and degrading submission on the other." In such a state of society the moral sense was blunted, and the voice of conscience suppressed. The attributes of a manly character such as liberty now demands had no chance of development. The master forced what he could and all he could from the slave, and the slave in turn stole all he could from the master, his only restraint being the fear of detection and punishment. He was born into a society organized to defraud him of the results of his labor, and he naturally enough thought it no robbery to obtain by stealth—the only way open to him—a part of what was forced from him under the hard conditions of the lash. I do not pretend to deny that there was ever a generous slave-holder or honest slave, for I know the contrary, but I equally know that the system made tyrants of one class and thieves of the other.

As to social relations, the system was even more destructive and deadly. Its victims were herded together like horses, sheep, and swine, without the restraints of moral instruction or decency. The master was made more important by every addition to his slaves. Marriage did not exist; the family was abolished. The young had no reputation to gain, and the old none to lose.

Let it be remembered in respect to the morals of these people that streams are not easily diverted from well-worn channels; that the moral character formed under the conditions thus feebly described is not easily or speedily reformed. There is not only much to learn, but much to unlearn. It is sad to think of the multitude who only dropped out of slavery to drop into prisons and chain-gangs, for the crimes for which they are punished seldom rise higher than the stealing of a pig or a pair of shoes; but it is consoling to think that the fact is not due to liberty, but to slavery, and that evil will disappear as these people recede from the system in which they were born.

From what has been now said it must not seem that I have conceded that there has been no improvement in the manners and morals of the freedmen since emancipation. I do not admit any such thing, for in morals, as in mental power, according to my knowledge, obtained from many sources of information, there is a visible and growing improvement both as to honesty and chastity. What was once done among these people not only with impunity, but with mirthful boasting, and without apparent sense of wrong or shame, does not now escape the rebuke and reprobation of a large and growing class of their own color. There is everywhere among them a dawning recognition of the new order of life and society into which freedom has brought them, and they are gradually adjusting themselves to the requirements of a higher civilization. Churches, preachers, teachers, Sunday-schools, night schools, day schools, singing schools, and other schools, societies for mutual aid, debating societies, libraries, and literary clubs, lawyers, doctors, editors, and newspapers, have sprung up and have multiplied with wonderful rapidity. These come not from immorality. Sin is death to such effort. They show an upward tendency which may well invite patient and benevolent effort in their behalf. . . .

It is noticeable, too, that the old camp-meeting emotional religion is subsiding among them, and that thought is taking the place of feeling. In the dark time of slavery, when this world held only toil, stripes, and pain for them, they were easily wrought into paroxysms of momentary joy by the painted and promised glories of another world. They are now beginning to see that something can be made of this world as well as of the other. Of course some of them are still wearing the old cast-off theological hats and coats of fifty years ago, but the young people who have learned to read and write have no further use for these old garments. They now demand an educated, chaste, and upright ministry. This spirit of improvement has cost the old-time preachers many sighs and groans. They see in it only decline of true religious feeling. However that may be, it is evident that morals and manners have gained by the change, and will continue to gain as the lamp of knowledge grows brighter among them. No doubt that even the wild incoherent Sambo sermons were a help in time of slavery. It was something to be told that their suffering time would soon be over, and that for stripes on earth they would have stars in heaven, even though it was clumsily and wildly told; but the rant of those days will not do for these. These old-fashioned preachers minister to passion, decry the intellect, and induce contentment in ignorance and stupidity, and are hence a hindrance to progress. The effect aimed at by their preaching is to excite feeling, and raise a shout—a thing which can be as well done by an eloquent stump-speaker as by any modern Whitefield.

Among the instrumentalities which have been most effective in lifting up these people to a higher plane of life none is more worthy of mention than the American Missionary Association. While it has taken the church among the freedmen, it has not forgotten to take the school-house. But nearly all denominations, Catholic as well as Protestant, have rushed into this vast field, each after its kind, to labor for the salvation of the late slaves. This is the more surprising in view of the long years during which our churches could more easily see the heathen thousands of miles over the wide waste of waters than at home. But let the dead past bury its dead.

I now come to the question as to what was the physical condition of these people before emancipation; and in referring to it I bear in mind that I am speaking to many of a generation to whom slavery is little more than a name, and who have no adequate idea of what that name covered. I have had this class of readers in mind in all I have said, and I deem it fortunate that you have allowed me to speak my word on this subject through your respected journal. With the exception of a few highly favored house servants, the physical condition of the slaves was indescribably wretched. A bushel of corn and eight pounds of salt pork per month were considered a large allowance for a full-grown man. The huts in which they lived left them largely exposed to the mercy of the elements. Their beds were boards, and their covering a miserable blanket, with which they were served not even once a year. Much of the time they were worked under the lash in all weathers. Want, exposure, and cruelty brought to them bodily ills and general physical deterioration often to the extent of repulsive deformity. That physical well-being is essential to physical perfection is easily demonstrated both in the case of man and beast. Men laugh at the irregular make-up of the negro, but forget that no people, white or black, could preserve the finer attributes of physical manhood subjected to two hundred and fifty years of slavery. The woes of the slave mother can be read in the faces of her children. Slavery has twisted their legs, flattened their feet, and imparted a depressed and cowardly aspect to their features. Let those who laugh rather be ashamed of the crime against human nature which has produced the deformity over which they make merry.

Looking at the freedmen to-day, in that class which remains on the old plantation, we see but little improvement in food or raiment, in form or feature. Twenty years are but a speck in the life of a race. Still, even here there is improvement. Many have managed to get a few acres and a little home of their own. In the State of Louisiana colored people pay taxes on more than twenty millions' worth of property, and in Georgia, according to the late Senator Hill, of that State, they paid taxes five years ago on six millions. I doubt not of a showing equally creditable in North Carolina, Virginia, and other of the old Slave States. The manner in which these people were set free should never be overlooked. No people were ever emancipated under conditions more unfavorable for good results. The Israelites had spoils of the Egyptians; the serfs of Russia had three acres of land given to each head of a family; the West India slave was permitted to remain upon the old plantation; but the American slave was turned loose to the open sky without money, land, or friends, and, worst of all, under the fierce resentment of those who owned the land from which he must obtain his bread. These in the heat of momentary wrath drove him away; and away he went, free, but free only to want, hunger, and pain; free to the chilling blasts of winter, free to starve. Off he went with his sick and well, young and old, and the infant in arms. Many died, and the mortality for a time caused the belief that the race would speedily die out. From the gallery of the United States Senate I heard an able Senator from the North answer Mr. Sumner's plea for suffrage with the remark that it was useless to legislate for these people, since they were sure to die out in a short time. But the old masters who thus resented emancipation relented, if they did not repent, and after a time called back the freedmen to their old fields and quarters. They saw that they had sent away the hands, but had left the mouths, and that they still needed the negro to work their fields—a fortunate discovery for both. Instead of dying out, as predicted, the census tells us these people have increased ten per cent faster than the native-born white people of the South.

In conclusion:

When I consider that these people have only been free during the last twenty years, and that this freedom has been more in name than in fact; when I consider the manner in which their emancipation was brought about, not with the consent, but against the consent, of the masters; when I consider the fact that it was born of blood boiling over on the battle-field, the wounded pride and sullen determination it left in the old master class smarting under defeat, and the many obstacles thrown in the way of the progress of these people—I am far from discouraged or dissatisfied. On the contrary, I see the colored people steadily rising, and I believe they will ultimately fully justify all the endeavors made in their behalf, and fulfill the highest hopes of their friends.

[Source: *Harper's Weekly*, 8 December 1883.]

## *[The Future of Blacks in the United States]*

Throughout his long career Douglass resisted emigration plans for blacks. He insisted that blacks were in America to stay and that their destiny was linked to the same social, economic, and political conditions as that of white Americans. He continued to believe that blacks would ultimately succeed in the United States through "self-assertion and eternal vigilance."

It would require the ken of a statesman and the vision of a prophet combined to tell with certainty what will be the ultimate future of the colored people of the United States, and to neither of these qualifications can I lay claim. We have known the colored man long as a slave, but we have not known him long as a freeman and as an American citizen. What he was as a slave we know; what he will be in his new relation to his fellow-men, time and events will make clear. One thing, however, may safely be laid down as probable, and that is, that the negro, in one form and complexion or another, may be counted upon as a permanent element of the population of the United States. He is now seven millions, has doubled his number in thirty years, and is increasing more rapidly than the more favored population of the South. The idea of his becoming extinct finds no support in this fact. But will he emigrate? No! Individuals may, but the massess will not. Dust will fly, but the earth will remain. The expense of removal to a foreign land, the difficulty of finding a country where the conditions of existence are more favorable than here, attachment to native land, gradual improvement in moral surroundings, increasing hope of a better future, improvement in character and value by education, impossibility of finding any part of the globe free from the presence of white men,—all conspire to keep the negro here, and compel him to adjust himself to American civilization.

In the face of history I do not deny that a darker future than I have indicated may await the black man. Contact of weak races with strong has not always been beneficent. The weak have been oppressed, persecuted, driven out, and destroyed. The Hebrews in Egypt, the Moors in Spain, the Caribs in the West Indies, the Picts in Scotland, the Indians and Chinese in our own country, show what may happen to the negro. But happily he has a moral and political hold upon this country, deep and firm, one which in some measure destroys the analogy between him and other weak peoples and classes. His religion and civilization are in harmony with those of the people among whom he lives. He worships with them in a common temple and at a common altar, and to drag him away is to destroy the temple and tear down the altar. Drive out the negro and you drive out Christ, the Bible, and American liberty with him. The thought of setting apart a State or Territory and confining the negro within its borders is a delusion. If the North and South could not live separately in peace, and without bloody and barbarous border wars, the white and black cannot. If the negro could be bottled up, who could or would bottle up the irrepressible white man? What barrier has been strong enough to confine him? Plainly enough, migration is no policy for the negro. He would invite the fate of the Indian, and be pushed away before the white man's bayonet.

Nor do I think the negro will become more distinct as

a class. Ignorant, degraded, and repulsive as he was during his two hundred years of slavery, he was sufficiently attractive to make possible an intermediate race of a million, more or less. If this has taken place in the face of those odious barriers, what is likely to occur when the colored man puts away his ignorance and degradation and becomes educated and prosperous? The tendency of the age is unification, not isolation; not to clans and classs, but to human brotherhood. It was once degradation intensified for a Norman to associate with a Saxon; but time and events have swept down the barriers between them, and Norman and Saxon have become Englishmen. The Jew was once despised and hated in Europe, and is so still in some parts of that continent; but he has risen, and is rising to higher consideration, and no man is now degraded by association with him anywhere. In like manner the negro will rise in social scale. For a time the social and political privileges of the colored people may decrease. This, however, will be apparent rather than real. An abnormal condition, born of war, carried him to an altitude unsuited to his attainments. He could not sustain himself there. He will now rise naturally and gradually, and hold on to what he gets, and will not drop from dizziness. He will gain both by concession and by self-assertion. Shrinking cowardice wins nothing from either meanness or magnanimity. Manly self-assertion and eternal vigilance are essential to negro liberty, not less than to that of the white man.

Frederick Douglass

[Source: *North American Review,* JULY 1884.]

HAWTHORNE, NATHANIEL: *The Scarlet Letter* (30921)
HEGEL, GEORG WILHELM FREIDRICH: *The Philosophy of Hegel* (30976)
HERODOTUS: *The Persian Wars* (30954)
IBSEN, HENRIK: *Eight Plays* (32865)
JAMES, HENRY: *The Bostonians* (30959)
JAMES, HENRY: *The Portrait of a Lady* (30947)
JOHNSON, JAMES WELDON, (Ed.): *Utopian Literature* (30996)
LOOMIS, ROGER SHERMAN AND LOOMIS, LAURA HIBBARD, (Ed.): *Medieval Romances* (30970)
MACHIAVELLI, NICCOLO: *The Prince and the Discourses* (30925)
MALRAUX, ANDRE: *Man's Fate* (30975)
MANN, THOMAS: *Death in Venice* (30999)
MANN, THOMAS: *The Magic Mountain* (30993)
MELVILLE, HERMAN: *Moby Dick* (30926)
MILTON, JOHN: *Paradise Lost* (30994)
OATES, WHITNEY J. AND O'NEILL, EUGENE, JR., (Ed.): *Seven Famous Greek Plays* (30930)
O'NEILL, EUGENE: *The Later Plays* (30991)
PLATO: *The Work of Plato* (30971)
POE, EDGAR ALLAN: *The Selected Poetry and Prose* (30958)
PROUST, MARCEL: *Swann's Way* (30967)
QUINTANA, RICARDO, (Ed.): *Eighteenth-Century Plays* (30980)
SHELLEY, PERCY BYSSHE: *Selected Poetry and Prose* (30950)
SOLOMON, ROBERT C., (Ed.): *Existentialism* (31704)
SWIFT, JONATHAN: *Gulliver's Travels and Other Writings* (30932)
TACITUS: *The Complete Works* (30953)
TENNYSON, ALFRED LORD: *Selected Poetry* (30960)
THOREAU, HENRY DAVID: *Walden and Other Writings* (32666)
THUCYDIDES: *The Peloponnesian War* (32978)
TOCQUEVILLE, ALEXIS DE: *Democracy in America* (32675)
TOLSTOY, LEO: *Anna Karenina* (30936)
TURGENEV, IVAN S.: *Fathers and Sons* (30938)
VOLTAIRE: *Candide and Other Writings* (30964)
WHITMAN, WALT: *Leaves of Grass and Selected Prose* (32661)
WINE, M. L., (Ed.): *Drama of The English Renaissance* (30866)
WORDSWORTH, WILLIAM: *Selected Poetry* (30941)